Lg roasting chicken

(2
(3

# Mable Hoffman's
# COMPLETE CROCKERY COOKERY

# Mable Hoffman's
# COMPLETE CROCKERY
# COOKERY

※

HPBOOKS

HPBooks
Published by The Berkley Publishing Group
A division of Penguin Putnam Inc.
375 Hudson Street
New York, New York 10014

This book includes recipes from *Mable Hoffman's Crockery Cookery* and *Healthy Crockery Cookery.*

*Mable Hoffman's Crockery Cookery* copyright © 1975, 1983, 1985 by Price Stern Sloan, Inc.; revised edition
copyright © 1995 by HPBooks. *Mable Hoffman's Crockery Cookery* recipe development and testing: Mable
Hoffman, Jan Robertson. *Mable Hoffman's Crockery Cookery* coauthors: Bill Fisher, Helen Fisher, Howard
Fisher, Karen Fisher

*Health Crockery Cookery* copyright © 1998 by Mable Hoffman
*Healthy Crockery Cookery* food stylist: David Pogul

Cover photograph by George Kerrigan
Cover design by Dawn Velez-Le'Bron
Interior photography by Glenn Corimer/Corimer Photography

First edition: June 2000

The Penguin Putnam Inc. World Wide Web site address is
http://www.penguinputnam.com

Library of Congress Cataloging-in-Publication Data

Hoffman, Mable, 1922–
    Mable Hoffman's complete crockery cookery / Mable Hoffman
        p. cm.
    Includes index.
    Includes recipes from Mable Hoffman's crockery cookery and Healthy crockery cookery.
    ISBN 1-55788-349-1
        1. Electric cookery, Slow. 2. Casserole cookery. I. Hoffman, Mable, 1922– Mable Hoffman's crockery cookery.
    II. Hoffman, Mable, 1922– Healthy crockery cookery. III. Title.

TX827.H58 2000
641.5'884—dc21
                                                                                        00-025623

Printed in the United States of America

10   9   8   7   6   5   4   3   2   1

# ACKNOWLEDGMENTS

Special thanks to Jan Robertson for her invaluable assistance. Thanks to Grace Wheeler for recipe testing and to Mike Robertson for word processing.

# CONTENTS

# INTRODUCTION

$W$elcome to *Mable Hoffman's Complete Crockery Cookery.* With over five million copies in print, the original *Crockery Cookery* became the bestselling recipe book for slow cookers and one of the biggest-selling cookbooks of all time.

Since its introduction in 1975, *Crockery Cookery* has heralded the delicious, slow-cooking method. Cooks everywhere clamored for that book about the joys of slow cooking. As a result it became the #1 *New York Times* bestseller for thirteen weeks and was on best-selling lists for more than a year.

Cooking styles and eating habits are constantly changing. Today, people are spending more time working and thus have less time to spend in the kitchen. Again the slow cooker comes to the rescue. Mable Hoffman brings you this new edition that includes all the recipes from her *Crockery Cookery* and her *Healthy Crockery Cookery.* This volume reflects the way we eat today. You'll find new flavor combinations, more herbs and spices, and less salt and fat.

You'll enjoy great new recipes such as Thai Chicken, Creole-Asian Strips, Red Beans & Rice, Lentil Casserole, Persimmon Pudding and more! Of course many traditional favorites have been kept, including Green Beans Portuguese Style, Cranberry-Honey Pork Roast, Soy-Glazed Spareribs and Apple Peanut Crumble.

Slow cooking is the secret of good cooks the world over. With a slow cooker you can enjoy the delicious simmered-in flavors of some of the world's best dishes without the time-consuming necessity of constant attention.

Whether you're cooking for one or two, or for many more, you can go to work or spend a day at leisure while your slow cooker gently mingles flavors and spices. Then you can return home to a piping-hot dinner that's ready to serve. It doesn't matter even if you're an hour or two late. It won't burn or taste overcooked. Dinner is ready when you are!

Superb and truly nourishing meals can be prepared with less expensive meats because slow cooking tenderizes in a special way that broiling or frying just can't duplicate. Meats are juicy and never cooked dry because slow cooking seals in the moisture. Farm-kitchen favorites such as stews and hearty soups simmer to perfection.

Slow cookers are also popular because they save time, money and energy. On a LOW setting, you'll be cooking with less energy than a 100-watt bulb. You can cook all day for only a few pennies—far less than the cost of cooking the same meal on your kitchen stove. You will also find that the slow cooker does not make your kitchen hot in the summertime.

Slow cooking is different and requires special recipes. The recipes in this book were developed specifically for slow cookers. Every recipe has been tested and retested to ensure your success with each meal you prepare. Within each chapter you will find a tantalizing variety of recipes so you can plan and serve meals to fit your tastes and preferences.

Welcome to the new world of slow cooking!

## Healthful Cooking in the Slow Cooker

Foods prepared in slow cookers yield healthful yet hearty meals. This is because of the slow, moist cooking method and starting with the right ingredients. By using a slow cooker, the natural juices from meats and vegetables are retained in the pot rather than boiled away, resulting in flavorful, juicy and nutritious dishes.

In this book, we have emphasized the healthy advantages of slow cooking for family meals without imposing drastic dietary limitations. We have included foods that children and teenagers enjoy and that families like to eat together, while maintaining a healthy balance with limited fat.

Because the slow cooker does not need fat for cooking there is little added fat except in the case of some desserts. Fat content of the recipes is controlled by choosing lean meats and trimming off the fat before cooking and by removing excess fat, and often the skin, from poultry.

Here are a few of the guidelines we followed in developing many of the recipes for this book.

- When purchasing meat, look for the leaner cuts.

- For cuts of meat with visible strips of fat around the edges, carefully trim off and discard the fat before placing the meat in the slow cooker.

- Although a small amount of marbling is flavorful in a pot roast, you can reduce the fat content by first browning both sides of the roast in a regular skillet. Then add the browned pot roast to the slow cooker with the seasonings and vegetables.

- Slightly reduce the size of meat servings. Currently the recommended amount per serving is about 3 ounces of cooked meat.

- Increase the proportion of vegetables in any slow cooker recipe that includes meats and vegetables.

- To extend meat or chicken flavor in soups or stews without excess fat or calories, add a can of beef broth or fat-free chicken broth.

- If the cut of meat has more fat than you would like, make your slow cooker dish the day before you plan to use it. Transfer the dish to a bowl, refrigerate it overnight and skim off the hard fat on the surface before reheating the dish. This technique works particularly well with soups and stews.

- Cook any large cut of meat on a rack in the slow cooker. Discard cooking juices, skim off surface fat, or only use a small amount of the fat-laden juices to cut the calories and fat content.

## Nutritional Analysis

To help those of you who are trying to eat more healthily, we have analyzed many of the recipes using a nutritional database. If the recipe lists a range for ingredients or number of servings, the smaller amount is used. Optional ingredients are not included in the analysis.

## *Percentage of Fat in the Diet*

The recommended percentage of calories from fat is 30 percent as the average for the total diet. Some foods and even some meals in a healthy diet may exceed this amount without causing concern. What is important is that the average diet is around the recommended level of fat. As you plan meals, balance higher-fat foods with low-fat or nonfat choices.

For instance, someone eating 2,000 calories a day should consume about 65 grams total of fat. Only about 10 percent or less of the total fat should be from saturated fat.

## *Reducing Sodium*

To further reduce the amounts of sodium used in these recipes, substitute reduced- or low-sodium products for the regular bouillon granules, broths, soy sauce, and canned items. For example, reduced-sodium bouillon granules have one-third less sodium than the regular granules. Draining and rinsing canned dried beans will reduce their sodium content.

If you need to reduce sodium intake for health reasons, always read the nutritional labels to determine the sodium content before purchasing items such as canned goods, prepared sauces and ready-to-eat foods.

# USE & CARE

## Slow Cooking

Low temperature is the success factor in slow cooking. Low heat and long cooking times help simmer flavor into food. It is best to use recipe times suggested in this book; however, if you cook longer, don't worry. Your food will not burn because it does not overheat.

## Leave It Alone

The advantage of slow cooking is that you can set it and forget it because there is no need to watch the pot. Don't hesitate to leave your house to do what you want.

## Stirring

Stirring is not required for recipes in this book or for slow cooking in general. Basting and brushing are needed for some recipes.

## Keep It Covered

Leave the lid on. There is no need to keep looking at food as it simmers in a slow cooker. Steam and nutrients are trapped on the lid, condensed and returned to the cooking pot. This keeps food moist and nutritious even after cooking many hours. The steam atmosphere above the food helps cook from the top. Every time you take the lid off, the slow cooker loses steam. After you put the lid back on, it takes 15 to 20 minutes to regain the lost steam and temperature. Thus taking the lid off means longer cooking times. *Never remove the lid during the first 2 hours when baking breads or cakes.*

## Cooking Times

Until you become familiar with your slow cooker, follow the suggested recipe times. If you prefer softer vegetables or more well-done meat, cook longer than the indicated times.

Generally 1 hour on HIGH is equal to 2 hours on LOW.

## Temperatures

Recipes in this book refer to two temperature settings, LOW and HIGH. LOW is 200F (93C) and HIGH is 300F (149C). Food in the slow cooker seldom gets hotter than 212F (100C).

## High-Altitude Cooking

At high altitudes (over 4,000 feet), allow more time than given in the recipe. Whether you are using a slow cooker, stove or oven, food takes longer to cook at high altitudes.

At high altitudes, beans take about double the time given in the recipes. To reduce cooking time for beans, cover with water, bring to a boil in a pan on the stove, and simmer for 2 minutes. Let cool 1 hour. Or soak overnight. Return beans to slow cooker and proceed with the recipe.

Baking also requires longer cooking times at high altitudes.

## Temperature Switches

Slow cookers generally have a three-position switch, OFF-LOW-HIGH. The switch snaps into the desired position as you turn it. You must snap this switch to LOW or HIGH to cook, not in between.

## Spices

Because little evaporation takes place when cooking with your slow cooker, there are more juices when you finish than you would have with other cooking methods. For this reason you may want to increase the amount of spices you use in the recipes so they will suit your taste.

## Frozen Foods

Frozen foods should be thawed before placing them in your slow cooker. Otherwise several extra hours must be added to the cooking time to compensate for the time required for the food to thaw before cooking actually begins.

## Meat Rack

A metal meat rack or trivet will keep a roast out of juices and fats in the bottom of the cook pot and prevent the meat from sticking to the bottom. Use a meat rack only when the recipes say to; it is not necessary or useful for all meats.

## Baking

Baking requires a separate pan inside your slow cooker. The Puddings, Cakes & Breads chapter suggests ways to use molds, coffee cans and other containers.

## Before You Start Cooking

Wash the inside of your new slow cooker with soapy water. Do not immerse the slow cooker in water. Crockery, stoneware, Corning Ware, glass and nonstick surfaces may have a manufacturer's finished coating you can't see and don't want in your food. Washing removes it.

## Cleaning Your Slow Cooker

Preventive maintenance and care will keep your slow cooker looking new. Don't allow food stains to burn into the finish. Soak the inside of the slow cooker with warm soapy water to loosen food, then scrub lightly with a plastic or nylon pad. Rinse well and dry. Slow cookers are now made of many different materials. Refer to manufacturer's instructions for cleaning.

# APPETIZERS & BEVERAGES

$T$hink of your slow cooker as an extra helper when entertaining. Avoid the last-minute rushing about by starting several hours before a party. Combine the ingredients for one of the hot drinks, turn the control on the slow cooker to LOW, and the drink will be ready to serve when your guests arrive. What's more, it can be kept hot in a slow cooker without fear of scorching, boiling over or sticking to the pan. Perhaps you can borrow an extra slow cooker and have several silent helpers.

Cooking in a slow cooker is an especially good way to plan a get-together after the theater or ball game. You can plug in the slow cooker with ingredients for All-American Snack, then leave for the show. When you return with your friends, you can immediately offer them a hot snack and drink, or people can serve themselves whenever they are ready for refreshments.

For most of the beverage recipes, exact times are relatively unimportant. After several hours, the various fruit juices blend together for a smooth taste. However, if left on too many hours over the suggested time, they may become slightly bitter.

Relax and enjoy the festivities at your next party by letting your slow cooker keep your favorite appetizer hot. There is no reason for you to rush back and forth to the range or oven to serve hot snacks. Just heat them in a slow cooker. Have a group of small bowls and cups so guests can help themselves whenever they are ready for another serving. When you make Short-Cut Chili con Queso or Refried Bean Dip in a slow cooker, they will be the right consistency and temperature for all to enjoy.

For watching a game or viewing a special TV program, have spicy finger foods like Curried Almonds, Chili Nuts or East Indian Snack. Choose a fruity beverage like Spiced Apricot Punch or Tropical Tea. Holiday gatherings are the perfect occasions for Hot Spiced Burgundy or Bishop's Wine, and children too can join in sipping Hot Mint Malt or Padre Punch.

# Mediterranean Caponata

*A* variation of a traditional Sicilian recipe that may be served as a salad on lettuce-lined plates or spread on crackers for an appetizer. ▪ MAKES 6 TO 8 SERVINGS

1 large eggplant, peeled and chopped
1 onion, chopped
2 plum tomatoes, peeled and
   chopped
1 tablespoon capers, drained
1/2 cup chopped celery
1/2 cup pimiento-stuffed green olives,
   chopped
1 clove garlic, crushed

2 tablespoons olive oil
1 tablespoon lemon juice
1/2 teaspoon salt
1/8 teaspoon pepper
6 to 8 anchovies, finely chopped
   (optional)
1/2 cup toasted pine nuts (see Note,
   below)

Combine eggplant, onion, tomatoes, capers, celery, olives, garlic, oil, lemon juice, salt and pepper in a slow cooker. Cover and cook on LOW 5 to 6 hours. Stir in anchovies, if using. Refrigerate 2 or 3 hours or until cool. Sprinkle with pine nuts.

NOTE: To toast nuts, heat in a 350F (175C) oven about 10 minutes or until golden brown.

# Chicken & Leek Terrine

*W*hen slicing a leek, use all the white part, plus the tender light-green section; discard the tough deep-green leaves. ■ MAKES 16 TO 20 APPETIZERS OR 6 TO 8 MAIN-DISH SERVINGS

| | |
|---|---|
| 1 lb. lean ground chicken or turkey | 1/8 teaspoon pepper |
| 12 oz. bulk hot pork sausage | 1/4 cup dry white wine |
| 2 eggs, slightly beaten | 1 tablespoon margarine or butter |
| 1/4 teaspoon dried marjoram | 1 small leek, thinly sliced |
| 1/4 teaspoon dried thyme | 2 cups hot water |
| 1/4 teaspoon dried tarragon | Crackers or toast rounds |
| 1/2 teaspoon salt | |

In a large bowl, combine chicken, sausage, eggs, marjoram, thyme, tarragon, salt, pepper and wine. Set aside.

In a medium skillet, melt margarine or butter. Add sliced leek and sauté over medium heat until leek is limp. Place leek on bottom of a 6-cup mold or baking dish that fits into your slow cooker. Carefully spoon chicken mixture over leeks. Press lightly with the back of a spoon. Cover with foil.

Place a small metal rack in the bottom of the slow cooker; pour in hot water. Set filled mold or baking dish on rack. Cover and cook on HIGH about 3 hours. Remove mold from pot. Leaving meat in the mold, cover and refrigerate several hours or overnight. Cut into wedges or thin slices. Serve with crackers or toast rounds.

# Party-Style Ratatouille

✕✕✕✕✕✕✕✕✕✕✕✕✕✕✕✕✕✕✕✕✕✕✕✕✕✕✕✕✕✕✕

**K**eep this warm in the slow cooker and let guests help themselves. ■ MAKES ABOUT 4 CUPS

1 medium eggplant, peeled and finely chopped
1 zucchini, chopped
¼ cup sun-dried tomatoes in oil, drained and chopped
1 yellow bell pepper, finely chopped
1 medium red onion, finely chopped
1 clove garlic, crushed

¼ cup chopped fresh cilantro
3 tablespoons chopped fresh basil
2 tablespoons olive or vegetable oil
2 tablespoons white wine vinegar
½ teaspoon salt
¼ teaspoon pepper
Pita or sourdough rolls, cut into small wedges

Combine all ingredients except bread in a slow cooker. Cover and cook on LOW 6 to 7 hours or until vegetables are tender. Spoon on pita or sourdough wedges.

# Curried Cauliflower Appetizer

✕◈✕◈✕◈✕◈✕◈✕◈✕◈✕◈✕◈✕◈✕◈✕◈✕◈✕◈✕◈✕◈✕◈✕◈✕◈✕◈✕◈✕

*C*hoose a firm, compact, creamy white head of cauliflower for an attractive presentation.

■ MAKES 12 TO 16 SERVINGS

| | |
|---|---|
| 1 large (about 2½-lb.) head cauliflower | ¼ teaspoon salt |
| ½ cup water | ¼ teaspoon ground white pepper |
| 1 tablespoon fresh lemon juice | 1 teaspoon curry powder |
| ½ cup light mayonnaise | Fresh sprigs of parsley, for garnish |
| ½ cup nonfat plain yogurt | Paprika, for garnish (optional) |
| ¼ teaspoon ground ginger | Wheat crackers (optional) |

Remove and discard outer leaves of cauliflower. Cut out core, about 1½ inches deep. Place cauliflower, stem side down, in a 3½-quart slow cooker. Combine water and lemon juice. Pour over cauliflower. Cover and cook on LOW 4 to 6 hours or until very tender. Meanwhile, in a small bowl, mix mayonnaise, yogurt, ginger, salt, pepper and curry powder. Cover and refrigerate at least 1 hour for flavors to blend. Arrange cauliflower on a serving plate. Spread mayonnaise mixture evenly over cooked cauliflower. Surround with sprigs of fresh parsley. Dust the top lightly with paprika and serve with crackers, if desired.

Per serving: Cal 46 · Carb 7 gm · Prot 3 gm · Total fat 2 gm · Sat fat 0 gm · Cal from fat 18 · Chol 2 mg · Sodium 106 mg

# Short-Cut Chili con Queso

※※※※※※※※※※※※※※※※※※※※※※※※※※※※※※※※※※※※※※※

*A* hearty, easy dip that's always a hit at potlucks or family get-togethers.  ■ MAKES ABOUT 4 CUPS

    1 lb. pasteurized processed cheese spread, cubed
    1 (1-lb.) can chili without beans
    4 green onions, finely chopped
    1 (4-oz.) can diced green chiles, drained
    Corn or tortilla chips

Combine cheese spread, chili, green onions and chiles in a slow cooker. Cover and heat on LOW 2 to 3 hours. Serve as a dip for corn or tortilla chips.

# Refried Bean Dip

※※※※※※※※※※※※※※※※※※※※※※※※※※※※※※※※※※※※※※※

*A*n easy dip that requires just a few minutes preparation time—keep the slow cooker plugged in for a warm, self-serve appetizer.  ■ MAKES ABOUT 3 CUPS

    1 (16-oz.) can refried beans
    1 cup shredded Cheddar cheese
    ½ cup chopped green onions
    2 tablespoons taco sauce
    Tortilla or corn chips

In a slow cooker, combine beans, cheese, onions and taco sauce. Cover and heat on LOW 2 to 2½ hours. Use as a dip for tortilla or corn chips.

# Eggplant & Squash Veggie Dip

*T*his dip is somewhat chunky; if you prefer a smoother texture, slightly mash cooked mixture with a fork. ■ MAKES 3½ TO 4 CUPS

1 medium eggplant, peeled and cut into ½-inch cubes
1 medium butternut squash, peeled, seeded, and cut into ½-inch cubes
1 onion, chopped
1 mild green chile, seeded and diced
1 clove garlic, crushed
1 tablespoon vegetable oil

1 tablespoon red wine vinegar
1 teaspoon honey
½ teaspoon salt
2 tablespoons chopped fresh cilantro
1 teaspoon chopped fresh basil
Pita bread, cut into wedges, or corn chips

Combine eggplant, butternut squash, onion, chile, garlic, oil, vinegar, honey and salt in a 3½-quart slow cooker. Cover and cook on LOW about 7 hours or until vegetables are tender.

Stir in cilantro and basil. Transfer to a serving bowl, cover and refrigerate until chilled. Serve as a dip with pita bread or corn chips.

Per ¼ cup: Cal 29 · Carb 5 gm · Prot 0 gm · Total fat 1 gm · Sat fat 0 gm · Cal from fat 9 · Chol 0 mg · Sodium 77 mg

# All-American Snack

*F*eel free to mix and match other cereals in the same amounts.  ■ MAKES ABOUT 3 QUARTS

3 cups thin pretzel sticks
4 cups Wheat Chex cereal
4 cups Cheerios cereal
1 (13-oz.) can salted peanuts
1 teaspoon garlic salt

1 teaspoon celery salt
½ teaspoon seasoned salt
2 tablespoons grated Parmesan cheese
¼ cup margarine or butter, melted

In slow cooker, mix together pretzels, cereals and peanuts. Sprinkle with garlic salt, celery salt, seasoned salt and cheese. Drizzle mixture with the margarine or butter and toss until well mixed. Cover and cook on LOW 3 to 4 hours. Uncover the last 30 to 40 minutes. Serve as an appetizer or snack.

# East Indian Snack

*E*njoy a snack that's just a little different; adjust the amount of curry powder to suit your taste.  ■ MAKES ABOUT 6 CUPS

1 (5-oz.) can crisp Chinese noodles
1½ cups (about 6 oz.) salted cashew
nuts
2 cups Rice Chex cereal
½ cup flaked coconut

1 teaspoon curry powder
¼ teaspoon ground ginger
¼ cup margarine or butter, melted
1 tablespoon soy sauce

In slow cooker, mix together noodles, cashews, cereal and coconut. Sprinkle with curry and ginger. Add margarine or butter and soy sauce. Toss until well mixed. Cover and cook on LOW 3 to 4 hours. Uncover the last 30 to 40 minutes. Serve as appetizer or snack.

# Chili Nuts

*T*his spicy snack is just the thing for the next time you sit down to watch a television event. Have lots of cold drinks available, too. ■ MAKES ABOUT 5 CUPS

2 (12-oz.) cans cocktail peanuts
¼ cup margarine or butter, melted
1 (1⅝-oz.) package chili seasoning mix

Add nuts to a slow cooker. Pour margarine or butter over nuts and sprinkle with dry chili mix. Toss until well mixed. Cover and heat on LOW 2 to 2½ hours. Turn control to HIGH, remove top and cook on HIGH 10 or 15 minutes. Serve warm or cool in small nut dishes.

# Curried Almonds

*E*ach brand of curry powder is different. Try several and select your favorite blend.
■ MAKES ABOUT 3 CUPS

2 tablespoons margarine or butter, melted
1 tablespoon curry powder
½ teaspoon seasoned salt
1 lb. blanched almonds

Combine margarine or butter with curry powder and seasoned salt in a medium bowl. Stir in almonds. Add to a slow cooker. Cover and cook on LOW 2 to 3 hours. Turn to HIGH, uncover and cook on HIGH 1 to 1½ hours. Serve hot or cold, as a snack.

# Spiced Apricot Punch

※※※※※※※※※※※※※※※※※※※※※※※※※※※※※※※※※※

*A* harmonious blend of flavors, this beverage can be served from the pot.  ▪ MAKES 12 SERVINGS

    1 (46-oz.) can apricot nectar
    3 cups orange juice
    1/4 cup packed brown sugar
    2 tablespoons fresh lemon juice
    3 cinnamon sticks
    1/2 teaspoon whole cloves

In a slow cooker, combine apricot nectar, orange juice, brown sugar and lemon juice. Tie cinnamon and cloves in a small cheesecloth bag; add to juices. Cover and heat on LOW 2 to 5 hours. Remove cheesecloth bag. Serve hot.

# Cranberry Wine Punch

※※※※※※※※※※※※※※※※※※※※※※※※※※※※※※※※※※

*T*his deep crimson punch will add sparkle to any holiday occasion.  ▪ MAKES 6 TO 8 SERVINGS

    2 cups cranberry-raspberry juice
    1 cup water
    3/4 cup sugar
    1 (750-ml) bottle Burgundy wine
    1 lemon (unpeeled), thinly sliced
    2 cinnamon sticks
    6 whole cloves

Combine juice, water, sugar, wine and lemon in a slow cooker. Tie cinnamon and cloves in a small cheesecloth bag; add to cooker. Cover and heat on LOW 1 to 2 hours. Remove cheesecloth bag. Punch may be kept hot and served from slow cooker on the lowest setting.

# Padre Punch

*A* great flavor and golden amber color make this a very popular punch during the fall season. ■ MAKES 7 TO 10 SERVINGS

| | |
|---|---|
| 1 (6-oz.) can frozen orange juice, partially thawed | ¾ teaspoon ground ginger |
| 3 orange juice cans of water | 2 cinnamon sticks |
| 4 cups (1 qt.) apple cider | 5 whole cloves |
| 1 teaspoon freshly grated nutmeg | Orange slices |

In a slow cooker, combine orange juice, water, cider, nutmeg and ginger. Tie cinnamon and cloves in a small cheesecloth bag; add to cooker. Cover and heat on LOW 4 to 6 hours. Remove cheesecloth bag. Garnish with orange slices. Keep hot and serve punch from slow cooker.

VARIATION: Recipe may be doubled if your slow cooker is large enough.

# Hot Buttered Rum Punch

*A*dd more or less rum, depending on your taste. ■ MAKES 10 TO 12 SERVINGS

| | |
|---|---|
| ¾ cup packed brown sugar | ¾ teaspoon ground cloves |
| 4 cups water | 2 (1-lb.) cans jellied cranberry sauce |
| ¼ teaspoon salt | 4 cups (1 qt.) pineapple juice |
| ¼ teaspoon freshly grated nutmeg | 1 cup rum |
| ½ teaspoon ground cinnamon | Cinnamon sticks |
| ½ teaspoon ground allspice | Butter |

In a slow cooker, combine brown sugar, water, salt, nutmeg, cinnamon, allspice and cloves. Break up cranberry sauce with a fork. Add cranberry sauce, pineapple juice and rum to cooker. Cover and heat on LOW 3 to 4 hours. Serve hot in individual mugs with cinnamon sticks. Dot each mug with butter.

# Tropical Tea

*I*f your slow cooker is cold, warm it first with hot tap water so it won't crack when the boiling water is added. ■ MAKES 10 SERVINGS

| | |
|---|---|
| 6 tea bags | 1½ cups orange juice |
| 6 cups boiling water | 1½ cups pineapple juice |
| ⅓ cup sugar | 1 orange (unpeeled), sliced |
| 2 tablespoons honey | 2 cinnamon sticks |

Put tea bags into a slow cooker. Pour boiling water over tea bags; cover and let stand 5 minutes. Remove tea bags. Stir in sugar, honey, orange juice, pineapple juice, orange slices and cinnamon sticks. Cover and heat on LOW 2 to 3 hours. Serve from cooker.

# Mulled Cider

*A* slow cooker keeps hot cider at the ideal temperature until you are ready to serve it.
■ MAKES 10 TO 12 SERVINGS

| | |
|---|---|
| 2 quarts apple cider | 1 orange (unpeeled), sliced |
| ¼ cup packed brown sugar | 2 cinnamon sticks |
| ⅛ teaspoon ground ginger | 1 teaspoon whole cloves |

Combine cider, sugar, ginger and orange in a slow cooker. Tie cinnamon and cloves in a small cheesecloth bag; add to cooker. Cover and heat on LOW 2 to 5 hours. Remove cheesecloth bag. Serve from cooker.

# Hot Mint Malt

*I*t's easy to produce a favorite chocolate mint drink in your slow cooker. ■ MAKES 6 SERVINGS

3 to 4 chocolate-covered, cream-filled mint patties (1 1/2 inches in diameter)
5 cups milk
1/2 cup malted milk powder
1 teaspoon vanilla extract
Whipped cream

In a slow cooker, combine mint patties, milk, malted milk powder and vanilla. Cover and heat on LOW 2 hours. Beat with a rotary beater until frothy. Pour into cups; top with whipped cream.

# Spicy Tomato Juice Cocktail

*F*or additional spiciness, add a cup of salsa to this juice. ■ MAKES ABOUT 6 CUPS

4 lb. fresh tomatoes (12 to 14)
1/2 cup chopped celery
1/4 cup chopped onion
2 tablespoons fresh lemon juice
1 1/2 teaspoons sugar

1/2 teaspoon salt
1 teaspoon prepared horseradish
1 teaspoon Worcestershire sauce
1/8 teaspoon hot pepper sauce

Wash tomatoes; remove stem ends and cores. Remove seeds and chop tomatoes. In a slow cooker, combine tomatoes, celery and onion. Cover and cook on LOW 8 to 10 hours. Press through a food mill or sieve. Return juice to slow cooker. Cover and cook on HIGH 30 minutes. Add lemon juice, sugar, salt, horseradish, Worcestershire sauce and hot sauce. Cook on HIGH another 10 minutes. Cover and refrigerate until chilled.

# Mediterranean Coffee

❊❊❊❊❊❊❊❊❊❊❊❊❊❊❊❊❊❊❊❊❊❊❊❊❊❊❊❊❊❊❊❊❊

*T*his popular chocolate-coffee combination is further enhanced with spices and citrus flavors. ■ MAKES 12 SERVINGS

2 quarts strong hot coffee
¼ cup chocolate syrup
⅓ cup sugar
½ teaspoon anise flavoring (optional)
4 cinnamon sticks

1½ teaspoons whole cloves
Peel of 1 lemon, in strips for twists
Peel of 1 orange, in strips for twists
Whipped cream

Combine coffee, chocolate syrup, sugar and anise, if using, in a slow cooker. Tie cinnamon and cloves in a small cheesecloth bag; add to cooker. Cover and cook on LOW 2 to 3 hours. Remove cheesecloth bag. Ladle coffee into cups. Add a twist of lemon peel, a twist of orange peel and a dollop of whipped cream to each cup.

# Bishop's Wine

❊❊❊❊❊❊❊❊❊❊❊❊❊❊❊❊❊❊❊❊❊❊❊❊❊❊❊❊❊❊❊❊❊

*P*ut this together several hours ahead for flavors to blend together. ■ MAKES 10 SERVINGS

2 tablespoons whole cloves
3 oranges
2 (750-ml) bottles dry red or white wine
½ cup sugar
1 cinnamon stick

Stick whole cloves into peel of oranges. Prick skin several times with a fork. Place in bottom of a slow cooker. Add wine, sugar and cinnamon. Cover and cook on LOW 3 to 4 hours. Serve hot from the cooker. If desired, cut oranges into wedges as a garnish for each serving.

# Hot Spiced Burgundy

Combine ingredients in your slow cooker and let flavors blend while you prepare accompanying treats.  ■ MAKES 6 TO 8 SERVINGS

2 tablespoons sugar
2 tablespoons fresh lemon juice
1/2 teaspoon freshly ground cinnamon
1/4 teaspoon freshly grated nutmeg
1/2 cup hot water
1 (750-ml) bottle Burgundy wine

In a slow cooker, combine sugar, lemon juice, cinnamon, nutmeg and water. Stir until well blended. Pour in wine, cover and heat on LOW 2 to 2½ hours. Serve hot from the cooker.

# SOUPS & CHILI

*A*fter you have tried some of our new soup and chili recipes, you will be convinced that slow cookers were made just for this purpose. Zesty new flavor combinations and traditional favorites use a great variety of vegetables to make many of these hearty soups a true meal in a bowl.

What is more appetizing after a tough day at the office than the aromatic flavors of a pot of soup or chili greeting you when you open your front door? There's no worry about overcooking or burning if you are away from home slightly longer than expected.

Just put the ingredients into your slow cooker before you leave. When you get home, the soup will be ready to serve in large portions directly from the pot. To complete the meal, heat thick slices of buttered French bread. What could be easier?

Slow cookers seem to maximize flavors, using only a minimum amount of meat. In many recipes, we have extended meat or chicken flavors with the addition of broth or bouillon. We have found that fat-free homemade or canned chicken broth is especially handy for this purpose. Turkey sausage or small amounts of well-trimmed lean meats also provide meaty flavors with very little fat.

Notice how the cooking times vary for these soups. Some take all day, and others can be prepared in an afternoon. Georgia Peanut Soup and French Onion Soup are two faster recipes. Even so, at such low temperatures most soups are fine if they are cooked a little longer. At the minimum recommended cooking time, lift the lid and stick a fork into the meat and several of the larger vegetable pieces to test for doneness. Try not to keep the lid off any longer than necessary because steam and heat escape very fast. It takes a long time to replace the heat loss after you've re-covered the cooker.

# Fennel-Bean Soup

※※※※※※※※※※※※※※※※※※※※※※※※※※※※※※※※※※※※

*W*hen you trim the fennel, save a few small clusters of feathery leaves to sprinkle on each bowl of soup just before serving. ■ MAKES 6 TO 8 SERVINGS

| | |
|---|---|
| 2 carrots, peeled and sliced ⅛-inch thick | ½ teaspoon salt |
| 1 small fennel bulb, trimmed and sliced | ⅛ teaspoon pepper |
| 1 large onion, chopped | 1 (15-oz.) can cannellini beans (white kidney beans), undrained |
| 1 clove garlic, crushed | 2 cups coarsely shredded fresh spinach |
| 4 cups chicken broth | Fennel leaves |

In a slow cooker, combine carrots, fennel, onion, garlic, chicken broth, salt and pepper. Cover and cook on LOW 7 to 8 hours or until carrots are tender but not mushy. Turn control to HIGH. Add beans with liquid and shredded spinach. Cover and cook on HIGH 20 to 25 minutes. Spoon hot soup into large soup bowls. Top each with sprigs of fennel leaves.

# Fennel and Potato Soup

*F*ennel, called *finocchio* in some Italian markets, has a sweet, mild aniselike flavor.

■ MAKES 5 TO 6 SERVINGS

1 fennel bulb
2 (14½-oz.) cans fat-free chicken broth
3 medium potatoes, peeled and diced
½ cup chopped celery
1 small onion, chopped
½ teaspoon salt
⅛ teaspoon ground black pepper

Chop feathery fennel leaves and save for garnish. Trim fennel. Remove tough base and discard. Quarter bulb and chop into small strips. Combine fennel in a 3½-quart slow cooker with chicken broth, potatoes, celery, onion, salt and pepper. Cover and cook on LOW about 8 hours or until vegetables are tender.

Ladle into soup bowls. Sprinkle each serving with reserved fennel leaves.

Per serving: Cal 90 · Carb 19 gm · Prot 4 gm · Total fat 0 gm · Sat fat 0 gm · Cal from fat 0 · Chol 0 mg · Sodium 651 mg

# Curried Lentil Soup

*P*resoaking is not necessary with lentils; just combine ingredients and cook in a slow cooker. ■ MAKES 6 TO 7 SERVINGS

¾ cup dried lentils
1 (28-oz.) can crushed tomatoes
1 teaspoon curry powder
2 tablespoons chopped fresh basil
¼ teaspoon salt

⅛ teaspoon ground black pepper
1 leek, thinly sliced
2 (14½-oz.) cans fat-free chicken
  broth

Combine all ingredients in a 3½-quart slow cooker. Cover and cook on LOW 6½ to 7 hours or until lentils are tender.

Ladle into soup bowls.

Per serving: Cal 85 · Carb 19 gm · Prot 7 gm · Total fat 0.5 gm · Sat fat 0 gm · Cal from fat 5 · Chol 0 mg · Sodium 662 mg

# Herbed Spinach Soup

✕✕✕✕✕✕✕✕✕✕✕✕✕✕✕✕✕✕✕✕✕✕✕✕✕✕✕✕✕✕✕✕✕✕✕✕✕✕✕✕✕✕✕✕✕✕

*Y*ou don't have to be Popeye to appreciate this soup. Serve it with hot biscuits.　■ MAKES 8 SERVINGS

3 green onions, finely chopped
3 parsley sprigs
1/4 small head lettuce, sliced
1 bunch fresh spinach
2 tablespoons margarine or butter
1/2 teaspoon salt
1/8 teaspoon pepper

1 teaspoon dried tarragon
4 (10 1/2-oz.) cans condensed beef
　broth
1/2 cup half-and-half
1 hard-cooked egg, chopped
Pinch freshly grated nutmeg

In a slow cooker, combine onions, parsley, lettuce, spinach, margarine or butter, salt, pepper, tarragon and broth. Cover and cook on LOW 4 to 6 hours. Process in a blender or food processor in batches until vegetables are finely chopped. Turn control to HIGH. Pour blended mixture into the slow cooker. Stir in half-and-half. Cover and cook on HIGH 20 to 30 minutes. Serve hot, garnished with chopped hard-cooked egg and a pinch of nutmeg.

# Touch of Green Soup with Goat Cheese Topping

✕✕✕✕✕✕✕✕✕✕✕✕✕✕✕✕✕✕✕✕✕✕✕✕✕✕✕✕✕✕✕✕✕✕✕✕✕✕✕✕✕✕✕✕✕✕

*A* very special combination of flavors, designed to impress your guests.　■ MAKES ABOUT 6 SERVINGS

1 medium head cauliflower, cut into
　flowerets
1 celery stalk, coarsely chopped
1 small leek, thinly sliced
3 cups chicken broth
1/2 teaspoon salt

1/8 teaspoon white pepper
1/4 cup dry white wine
1/2 cup crumbled goat cheese (about
　2 1/2 oz.)
1/4 cup toasted chopped pine nuts or
　pistachios (see Note, page 3)

Combine cauliflower, celery, leek, broth, salt, pepper and wine in a slow cooker. Cover and cook on LOW 9 to 10 hours or until vegetables are tender. Process in a blender or food processor until pureed. Reheat soup until hot if needed. Pour into individual soup bowls. Top with goat cheese and chopped nuts.

# Georgia Peanut Soup

*E*mbellish each serving with about a tablespoon of chopped peanuts on the top, if desired.

■ MAKES 4 SERVINGS

| | |
|---|---|
| 3 cups chicken broth | ½ cup peanut butter |
| ¼ cup finely chopped celery | 1 cup milk or half-and-half |
| ¼ teaspoon salt | 2 tablespoons cornstarch dissolved in |
| 1 small onion, finely chopped | ¼ cup water |
| 2 tablespoons margarine or butter | |

Combine broth, celery, salt, onion, margarine or butter and peanut butter in a slow cooker. Cover and cook on HIGH 2 to 3 hours. Add milk or half-and-half and cornstarch mixture. Cover and cook on HIGH 15 to 20 minutes or until slightly thickened, stirring several times. Serve hot.

# Sweet-Hot Pumpkin Soup

*C*hoose either one or two jalapeño chiles, depending on how "hot" you enjoy your soup.

■ MAKES 5 TO 6 SERVINGS

1 (16-oz.) can pumpkin
4 cups chicken broth
2 carrots, peeled and chopped
1 onion, chopped
2 tablespoons chopped watercress
1 or 2 jalapeño chiles, seeded and
    chopped

3 tablespoons honey
½ teaspoon curry powder
½ teaspoon salt
¼ cup Sauterne wine
Watercress leaves, for garnish

Combine pumpkin, chicken broth, carrots, onion, watercress, chiles, honey, curry powder, salt and wine in a slow cooker. Cover and cook on LOW 9 to 9½ hours or until vegetables are very soft. Process in a blender or food processor until pureed. Reheat soup until hot if needed. Garnish with additional watercress leaves.

# Gold 'n' Green Squash Soup

*W*hen trimming leeks, remove and discard the roots and thick tough green leaves. Sand can accumulate between the layers, so rinse leeks under running water. ▪ MAKES 6 TO 8 SERVINGS

1½ lb. banana squash
1 leek
1 green apple, peeled, cored, and chopped
1 orange, peeled, seeded, and cut into chunks
2 (14½-oz.) cans fat-free chicken broth

¼ teaspoon salt
⅛ teaspoon ground black pepper
1 teaspoon chopped fresh thyme
Several drops of hot sauce (optional)
Chopped chives

Peel squash and cut into about 1-inch pieces. Trim leek, quarter lengthwise, and wash to remove dirt. Cut leek into ½-inch pieces. Combine squash, leek, apple, orange, broth, salt, pepper and thyme in a 3½-quart slow cooker. Cover and cook on LOW about 6 hours or until vegetables are tender.

Puree soup mixture, in batches, in a blender or food processor. Add hot sauce, if using. Ladle into soup bowls. Sprinkle each serving with chopped chives.

Per serving: Cal 86 · Carb 21 gm · Prot 2 gm · Total fat 0 gm · Sat fat 0 gm · Cal from fat 0 · Chol 0 mg · Sodium 267 mg

# Golden Squash Soup with Pesto Topping

*T*his mild-flavored soup comes alive with flavor when topped with zesty pesto.  ■ MAKES 6
TO 8 SERVINGS

| | |
|---|---|
| 2 lb. banana squash | 3 cups chicken broth or bouillon |
| 1 onion, finely chopped | 1/2 teaspoon salt |
| 1 celery stalk with leaves, sliced crosswise | 1/8 teaspoon pepper |
| 1 clove garlic, crushed | 1/2 cup light evaporated milk or half-and-half |

### JALAPEÑO PESTO

| | |
|---|---|
| 1 fresh jalapeño chile, seeded and finely chopped | 2 tablespoons sun-dried tomatoes in oil, drained and chopped |
| 1/4 cup coarsely chopped cilantro leaves | 2 tablespoons olive oil |
| 1 small yellow or red bell pepper, chopped | |

Peel squash; cut into 1-inch cubes. In a slow cooker, combine squash, onion, celery, garlic, broth, salt and pepper. Cover and cook on LOW 7 to 8 hours or until vegetables are soft. While soup cooks, prepare Jalapeño Pesto.

Process soup in a blender or food processor until pureed. Return to the slow cooker or to a saucepan. Add evaporated milk or half-and-half and heat to desired temperature. Pour into individual soup bowls. Top each serving with 1 1/2 to 2 tablespoons Jalapeño Pesto.

## Jalapeño Pesto

Combine ingredients in a small bowl.

# French Onion Soup

*S*erve with a sandwich for an easy supper.  ■ MAKES 4 SERVINGS

3 large onions, thinly sliced
¼ cup margarine or butter
4 cups beef broth
1 teaspoon Worcestershire sauce
¼ teaspoon salt
4 to 5 slices French bread, toasted
¼ cup grated Parmesan cheese

In a slow cooker, combine onions and margarine or butter, broth, Worcestershire sauce and salt. Cover and cook on HIGH 4 to 6 hours. Pour hot soup into individual bowls. Top each bowl with toasted French bread and sprinkle with cheese.

# Fragrant Brown Rice and Mushroom Soup

*A*n array of spices adds an exotic flavor to this soup—an ideal starter or an entree when served with a salad. ■ MAKES 8 TO 10 SERVINGS

¾ cup long-grain brown rice
6 ounces mushrooms, finely chopped (about 2 cups)
1 medium onion, finely chopped
1 large stalk celery, finely chopped
1 teaspoon ground mustard
1 teaspoon ground black pepper
½ teaspoon salt
¼ teaspoon ground coriander

⅛ teaspoon ground cardamom
⅛ teaspoon ground cinnamon
⅛ teaspoon ground cloves
6 cups beef bouillon or stock
⅓ cup chopped fresh cilantro leaves
¼ cup nonfat plain yogurt
3 tablespoons finely chopped green onions, including some tops

Combine all ingredients, except cilantro leaves, yogurt, and green onions in a 3½-quart slow cooker. Cover and cook on LOW 5 to 6 hours or until rice is tender. Stir in chopped cilantro. Ladle into soup bowls and garnish each serving with a dollop of yogurt and chopped green onion.

Per serving: Cal 92 · Carb 16 gm · Prot 5 gm · Total fat 1 gm · Sat fat 0 gm · Cal from fat 9 · Chol 0 mg · Sodium 733 mg

# Roasted Red Pepper and Eggplant Soup

*T*his peasant-type soup is delicious with either shredded Parmesan cheese or crumbled goat cheese. ■ MAKES 6 SERVINGS

1 medium eggplant, diced
1 medium onion, diced
1 (15-oz.) jar roasted red bell peppers, well drained and cut into small pieces
3 large cloves garlic, minced
2 (14½-oz.) cans fat-free chicken broth
½ cup vermouth or dry white wine
1 cup day-old French bread cubes

½ teaspoon dried oregano leaves, crushed
½ teaspoon dried thyme leaves, crushed
½ teaspoon salt
½ teaspoon ground black pepper
¼ cup minced fresh parsley
6 tablespoons crumbled goat cheese or shredded Parmesan cheese

Combine all ingredients, except parsley and cheese, in a 3½-quart slow cooker. Mix well. Cover and cook on LOW 7 to 8 hours or until eggplant is very tender. Just before serving, stir in parsley. Ladle into soup bowls and garnish each serving with 1 tablespoon of the cheese.

Per serving: Cal 134 · Carb 21 gm · Prot 4 gm · Total fat 2.5 gm · Sat fat 1 gm · Cal from fat 22 · Chol 8 mg · Sodium 658 mg

# Gingered Carrot Soup

𝕏𝕏𝕏𝕏𝕏𝕏𝕏𝕏𝕏𝕏𝕏𝕏𝕏𝕏𝕏𝕏𝕏𝕏𝕏𝕏𝕏𝕏𝕏𝕏𝕏𝕏𝕏𝕏𝕏𝕏𝕏𝕏𝕏𝕏𝕏𝕏𝕏𝕏

*I*f your food processor can't handle all the vegetables at one time, process half at a time.

■ MAKES 5 TO 6 SERVINGS

| | |
|---|---|
| 8 medium carrots, peeled and cut into 1-inch chunks | 1/2 teaspoon salt |
| 1 medium potato, peeled and cut into 1-inch chunks | 1/8 teaspoon ground black pepper |
| | 1 (14 1/2-oz.) can fat-free chicken broth |
| 1 small onion, coarsely chopped | 1/4 teaspoon grated lemon peel |
| 2 teaspoons grated gingerroot | 1 (5-oz.) can evaporated skim milk |
| 2 tablespoons light brown sugar | |

Combine carrots, potato, onion, ginger, brown sugar, salt, pepper and broth in a 3 1/2-quart slow cooker. Cover and cook on LOW about 10 hours or until vegetables are tender.

Process vegetables with a little broth in a food processor or blender until coarsely chopped; return to slow cooker. Turn control to HIGH. Stir in lemon peel and milk. Cover and heat until hot, about 30 minutes. Ladle into soup bowls.

Per serving: Cal 128 · Carb 27 gm · Prot 5 gm · Total fat 0 gm · Sat fat 0 gm · Cal from fat 0 · Chol 1 mg · Sodium 496 mg

# Tavern Soup

*Y*ears ago, a tavern was the place to go for a good home-cooked meal. ■ MAKES 6 TO 8
SERVINGS

1 celery stalk, thinly sliced
1 carrot, peeled and thinly sliced
¼ cup finely chopped green bell
   pepper
1 small onion, finely chopped
3 (14½-oz.) cans chicken broth
1 (12-oz.) can light beer, room
   temperature

½ teaspoon salt
¼ teaspoon pepper
5 tablespoons cornstarch
¼ cup water
1 cup (4 oz.) shredded sharp Cheddar
   cheese

Combine celery, carrot, bell pepper and onion in a slow cooker. Add broth, beer, salt and
pepper. Cover and cook on LOW 5 to 6 hours. Process vegetables in a blender or food
processor in batches until pureed and return to cooker with broth. Turn control to HIGH.
Dissolve cornstarch in water; stir into pureed mixture. Add cheese gradually, stirring until
blended. Cover and cook on HIGH 15 to 20 minutes. Serve hot.

# Killarney Chowder

*A* sprinkle of watercress tops off this soup with an Irish accent. Serve this wonderful dish on Saint Patrick's Day. ■ MAKES 4 TO 6 SERVINGS

| | |
|---|---|
| 2 leeks | 1/2 cup coarsely chopped watercress |
| 3 small potatoes, peeled and | leaves |
| chopped | 1/2 teaspoon seasoned salt |
| 3 1/2 cups chicken stock | 1/8 teaspoon pepper |
| 1 (10-oz.) package frozen green peas, | 1/2 cup sour cream |
| thawed | Watercress leaves, for garnish |

Trim and clean leeks; slice crosswise. In a slow cooker, combine leeks, potatoes, stock, peas, watercress, seasoned salt and pepper. Cover and cook on LOW 5 to 6 hours or until vegetables are tender. Process one-third of the mixture at a time in a blender or food processor until pureed. Return mixture to cooker. Turn control to HIGH. Stir in sour cream. Cook on HIGH 15 to 20 minutes or until hot. Spoon into bowls. Garnish with a few watercress leaves.

# Down East Corn Chowder

*Y*our friends will enjoy the wholesome flavor of this simple chowder. ■ MAKES 6 TO 8 SERVINGS

| | |
|---|---|
| 3 cups fresh corn kernels, cut from | 1/2 teaspoon seasoned salt |
| cob, or 2 (16-oz.) cans whole-kernel | 1/8 teaspoon pepper |
| corn, drained | 2 cups chicken broth |
| 2 medium potatoes, peeled and finely | 2 cups milk |
| chopped | 1/4 cup margarine or butter |
| 1 onion, finely chopped | Ground mace |

Combine corn, potatoes, onion, seasoned salt, pepper and broth in a slow cooker. Cover and cook on LOW 7 to 9 hours. Pour into a blender or food processor and puree until almost smooth. Cover and refrigerate overnight, if desired, or return to cooker. Stir in milk and margarine or butter. Cover and cook on HIGH 1 hour. Pour hot soup into bowls; sprinkle with mace.

# Hamburger Soup

𝒴ou can put together this hearty soup in the morning, then have it ready when everyone comes home for dinner. ■ MAKES 5 TO 6 SERVINGS

| | |
|---|---|
| 1 lb. lean ground beef | 1 (8-oz.) can tomato sauce |
| ¼ teaspoon pepper | 1 tablespoon soy sauce |
| ¼ teaspoon dried oregano | 1 cup sliced celery |
| ¼ teaspoon dried basil | 1 cup thinly sliced carrots |
| ¼ teaspoon seasoned salt | 1 cup macaroni, cooked and drained |
| 1 (about 1-oz.) envelope dry onion soup mix | ¼ cup grated Parmesan cheese |
| 3 cups boiling water | 2 tablespoons chopped fresh parsley |

Crumble beef into a slow cooker. Add pepper, oregano, basil, seasoned salt and dry soup mix. Stir in water, tomato sauce and soy sauce, then add celery and carrots. Cover and cook on LOW 6 to 8 hours. Turn control to HIGH. Add cooked macaroni and Parmesan cheese. Cover and cook on HIGH 10 to 15 minutes. Sprinkle with parsley just before serving. Serve hot.

# Minestrone Soup

*T*his traditional dish is served in many Italian restaurants. Cannellini beans are white kidney beans and are usually only available in cans.  ■ MAKES 8 TO 10 SERVINGS

1 lb. beef stew meat, cut into 1-inch
   cubes
6 cups beef broth
1 onion, chopped
1 teaspoon dried thyme
2 tablespoons minced fresh
   parsley
½ teaspoon salt
¼ teaspoon pepper

1 (16-oz.) can peeled diced tomatoes
   in juice
2 cups chopped cabbage
1 (15-oz.) can cannellini beans,
   drained
1 zucchini, thinly sliced
1 cup uncooked small elbow
   macaroni (about 4½ oz.)
¼ cup grated Parmesan cheese

In a slow cooker, combine beef, broth, onion, thyme, parsley, salt, pepper, tomatoes and cabbage. Cover and cook on LOW 9 to 10 hours or until meat is tender. Turn control to HIGH. Add drained beans, zucchini and macaroni. Cover and cook on HIGH 30 to 45 minutes or until zucchini and macaroni are tender. Spoon hot soup into bowls. Top with cheese.

# Garbanzo & Macaroni Stew

$S$erve with thick slices of French bread for a hearty lunch or dinner. ■ MAKES ABOUT 8 SERVINGS

½ lb. boneless beef chuck steak, cut into ½-inch cubes
1 medium onion, diced
1 (14½-oz.) can beef broth
1 (28-oz.) can tomatoes, chopped
1 tablespoon chopped fresh parsley
1 tablespoon chopped fresh basil
1 (16-oz.) can garbanzo beans, drained

¼ head cabbage, shredded (about 3 cups)
½ teaspoon salt
⅛ teaspoon ground black pepper
1 cup small elbow macaroni
2 tablespoons grated Romano or Parmesan cheese (optional)

Combine beef, onion, broth, tomatoes, parsley, basil, beans, cabbage, salt and pepper in a 3½-quart slow cooker. Cover and cook on LOW about 8 hours or until beef is tender. Cook macaroni according to package directions; drain and stir into contents of slow cooker. Spoon into soup bowls. Sprinkle with cheese, if desired.

Per serving: Cal 227 · Carb 25 gm · Prot 13 gm · Total fat 8 gm · Sat fat 0 gm · Cal from fat 72 · Chol 24 mg · Sodium 705 mg

# Hearty Alphabet Soup

*D*id you ever have fun trying to spell your name with the noodles in the soup? ■ MAKES 6 TO 7 SERVINGS

½ lb. beef stew meat or round steak
1 (1-lb.) can Italian-style diced tomatoes
1 (8-oz.) can tomato sauce
3 cups water

1 (about 1-oz.) envelope onion soup mix
½ cup uncooked alphabet noodles
1 (16-oz.) package frozen Italian-style vegetables, cooked

Cut beef into small cubes. In a slow cooker, combine meat, tomatoes, tomato sauce, water and dry soup mix. Cover and cook on LOW 6 to 8 hours or until meat is tender. Turn control to HIGH. Add noodles. Cover and cook on HIGH 15 to 20 minutes or until noodles are cooked. Stir in cooked, drained vegetables. Serve hot.

# Lentil Soup, Crescenti Style

*T*his is a large recipe—freeze half for a quick meal another day, if desired. This is a thick, hearty soup, similar to a stew. ■ MAKES 8 SERVINGS

1 to 2 lb. beef neck bone or beef shanks
3 carrots, peeled and chopped
3 medium potatoes, peeled and chopped
1 large onion, peeled and chopped
3 celery stalks with tops, chopped
3 tomatoes, chopped

⅛ teaspoon dried marjoram
5 cups water
5 beef bouillon cubes, crumbled
½ lb. lentils
1 teaspoon salt
¼ teaspoon pepper
2 zucchini, chopped
½ small head cabbage, shredded

In a 4-quart or larger slow cooker, combine beef, carrots, potatoes, onion, celery, tomatoes, marjoram, water, bouillon cubes, lentils, salt and pepper. Cover and cook on LOW 9 to 10 hours or until lentils are tender. Remove beef bones from cooker; cut off meat and discard bones. Return meat to cooker. Turn control to HIGH. Add zucchini and cabbage, cover, and cook on HIGH 30 to 45 minutes or until vegetables are tender. Serve hot.

# Oxtail Soup

*T*his richly flavored soup is a meal in itself. If leeks are not available, substitute one onion.
■ MAKES 6 TO 8 SERVINGS

| | |
|---|---|
| 1 lb. oxtails | ½ cup rosé wine |
| 1 tomato, chopped | 5 to 6 cups water |
| 1 carrot, peeled and chopped | ½ teaspoon dried dill weed |
| 1 turnip, peeled and sliced | ½ cup frozen green peas |
| 1 leek, halved and sliced | 1 tablespoon chopped fresh basil |
| 1 clove garlic, crushed | |

Combine oxtails, tomato, carrot, turnip, leek, garlic, wine, water, and dill in a slow cooker. Cover and cook on LOW 4 to 6 hours. Remove oxtails; chop meat and discard bones. Return meat to cooker. Cover and cook on LOW 2 to 3 hours. Add peas about 30 minutes before serving. Sprinkle with basil and serve hot.

# Congressional Bean Soup

*H*ere is our version of the famous bean soup prepared regularly for the U.S. Senate.
- MAKES 6 TO 8 SERVINGS

| | |
|---|---|
| 8 cups water | 2 tablespoons finely chopped fresh |
| 1 lb. dried small white beans | parsley |
| 1 meaty ham bone or 2 cups diced | 1 teaspoon salt |
| cooked ham | ¼ teaspoon pepper |
| 1 cup finely chopped celery | 1 bay leaf |
| 1 onion, finely chopped | |

In a large pan, bring water to a boil. Add beans and boil gently 2 minutes. Turn off heat and let stand 1 hour. Pour into a slow cooker. Add remaining ingredients. Cover and cook on LOW 12 to 14 hours or until beans are very soft. Remove bay leaf and ham bone. Cut meat off bone; return meat to beans. Discard bone and bay leaf. Serve soup hot.

VARIATION: The beans may be soaked overnight in the water if preferred.

# Black-Eyed Pea Soup

*A* green salad and a roll make this a satisfying meal. ■ MAKES 8 TO 9 SERVINGS

| | |
|---|---|
| 1 lb. dried black-eyed peas | 2 small bay leaves |
| ½ lb. 97% fat-free smoked ham, cut | 1½ tablespoons imitation bacon bits |
| into ½-inch cubes (2 cups) | ½ teaspoon dried thyme leaves, |
| 1 medium onion, diced | crushed |
| 4 small carrots, peeled and sliced into | ¼ teaspoon ground black pepper |
| ¼-inch-thick rounds | 10 cups hot water |
| 1½ cups sliced celery | 1 teaspoon salt or to taste |
| 2 dried red chiles | ⅓ cup minced fresh parsley |

Sort peas and rinse. Place peas in a 6-quart slow cooker. Add remaining ingredients, except salt and minced parsley. Cover and cook on LOW 10 to 12 hours or until peas are tender. Stir in salt and parsley. Ladle into soup bowls.

Per serving: Cal 248 · Carb 41 gm · Prot 19 gm · Total fat 2 gm · Sat fat 0 gm · Cal from fat 18 · Chol 18 mg · Sodium 676 mg

# Double-Corn Stew

*This* hearty stew is enhanced by the flavors of fresh corn and tomatoes.   ■ MAKES 4 TO 5 SERVINGS

2 ears of corn
1 (14- to 15-oz.) can golden hominy, drained
1 medium onion, finely chopped
2 medium tomatoes, chopped

1 (14½-oz.) can fat-free chicken broth
¼ teaspoon ground black pepper
4 to 5 ounces ham steak or baked ham, coarsely chopped
Chopped cilantro

Remove husks and silk from corn. Cut off kernels and add to a slow cooker. Stir in hominy, onion, tomatoes, broth, pepper and ham. Cover and cook on LOW 5 to 6 hours or until vegetables are tender.

Ladle into soup bowls. Sprinkle each serving with cilantro.

Per serving: Cal 156 · Carb 23 gm · Prot 11 gm · Total fat 3 gm · Sat fat 1 gm · Cal from fat 27 · Chol 15 mg · Sodium 752 mg

# Potato Soup, Florentine Style

*T*haw frozen spinach in a medium strainer over a large bowl, then press out excess water with the back of a large spoon. ■ MAKES ABOUT 6 SERVINGS

| | |
|---|---|
| 4 medium potatoes, peeled and diced | ½ teaspoon seasoned salt |
| 1 onion, chopped | ⅛ teaspoon pepper |
| 1 smoked ham hock (about 1 lb.) or 1 cup chopped ham | 1 (9-oz.) package frozen chopped spinach, thawed and well drained |
| 4 cups chicken broth | 1 cup (4 oz.) shredded Jarlsberg or |
| 1 teaspoon dry mustard | Swiss cheese |

In a slow cooker, combine potatoes, onion, ham hock or ham, broth, mustard, seasoned salt and pepper. Cover and cook on LOW 7 to 8 hours or until potatoes are soft. Remove ham hock; chop meat and discard fat and bone. Return meat to cooker. Turn control to HIGH. Add drained spinach. Cover and cook on HIGH 15 to 20 minutes. Spoon hot soup into soup bowls and sprinkle with cheese.

# Split-Pea Soup

*T*his style of pea soup is also known as "Dutch" pea soup. ■ MAKES 8 SERVINGS

1 (1-lb.) package split peas
1 ham bone (with some meat left on)
   or 2 ham hocks
1 carrot, peeled and diced
1 onion, diced
1 small potato, peeled and diced

1 small smoked sausage, sliced
1 celery stalk, diced
8 cups water
½ teaspoon salt
¼ teaspoon pepper

Combine peas, ham bone or hocks, carrot, onion, potato, sausage, celery, water, salt and pepper in a slow cooker. Cover and cook on LOW 8 to 10 hours. Remove ham bone; cut meat off bones, dice meat, and discard bones. Return meat to soup. Serve soup hot.

# Italian Sausage and Vegetable Chowder

*C*anned tomatoes usually add a richer flavor to your soup as the tomatoes are harvested and canned at their peak. ■ MAKES 7 TO 8 SERVINGS

½ lb. (3 links) hot Italian turkey sausage
1 (28-oz.) can ready-cut tomatoes
4 cups hot water
½ cup dry red wine
2 teaspoons instant beef bouillon granules
1 medium onion, chopped
1 large clove garlic, peeled
1 (15-oz.) can garbanzo beans with liquid
2 cups lightly packed chopped green cabbage

¼ pound fresh green beans, cut into 1-inch pieces (about 1 cup)
1 medium carrot, peeled and diced
1 teaspoon dry Italian seasoning, crushed
1 teaspoon salt
¼ teaspoon ground black pepper
1 large zucchini, cut into ½-inch cubes
1 cup small elbow macaroni
¼ cup grated Parmesan cheese (optional)
¼ cup minced fresh parsley (optional)

Remove casing from sausage links. Cut into 1-inch-thick slices; set aside. Combine tomatoes, hot water, wine, beef bouillon granules, onion, garlic, garbanzo beans, cabbage, green beans, carrot, Italian seasoning, salt and pepper in a 4-quart slow cooker. Gently stir in sausage slices. Cover and cook on LOW 8 to 9 hours or until vegetables are almost tender.

Turn control to HIGH; add zucchini and macaroni. Stir, re-cover, and cook on HIGH 30 to 45 minutes longer or until zucchini and macaroni are tender.

Ladle into soup bowls. Sprinkle each serving with Parmesan cheese and minced parsley, if desired.

Per serving: Cal 228 · Carb 33 gm · Prot 13 gm · Total fat 5 gm · Sat fat 1 gm · Cal from fat 45 · Chol 17 mg · Sodium 1100 mg

# Smoked Sausage Chowder

*A*dd the larger amount of red pepper flakes if you like spicy chowder. ■ MAKES 5 TO 6 SERVINGS

¼ lb. light Polish kielbasa, chopped
1 cup mild green chile picante
   sauce
1 clove garlic, finely chopped
1 (10-oz.) package frozen whole-
   kernel corn, thawed
1 medium tomato, chopped

1 (14½-oz.) can fat-free chicken
   broth
1 (15½-oz.) can garbanzo beans,
   drained
1 tablespoon chopped fresh cilantro
⅛ to ¼ teaspoon crushed dried red
   pepper flakes

Combine all ingredients in a 3½-quart slow cooker. Cover and cook on LOW 3 to 4 hours.

Ladle into soup bowls.

Per serving: Cal 185 · Carb 33 gm · Prot 11 gm · Total fat 2 gm · Sat fat 1 gm · Cal from fat 18 · Chol 10 mg · Sodium 1100 mg

# Swedish Cabbage Soup

*L*amb creates a very rich-flavored broth that is the perfect match for these winter vegetables. ▪ MAKES 8 SERVINGS

| | |
|---|---|
| 1 lamb shank | 1 carrot, peeled and diced |
| 1 beef bouillon cube | ¼ cup thinly sliced celery |
| ¼ teaspoon pepper | 1 medium potato, peeled and diced |
| ¼ teaspoon salt | 2 tablespoons minced fresh parsley |
| 1½ teaspoons whole allspice | 4 cups water |
| 1 leek, chopped | 4 cups shredded cabbage |
| 1 parsnip, peeled and diced | |

Place lamb shank in a slow cooker with bouillon cube, pepper and salt. Tie allspice in a cheesecloth bag. Add allspice, leek, parsnip, carrot, celery, potato, parsley and water to cooker. Cover and cook on LOW 7 to 9 hours or until meat is tender. Remove allspice and meat from cooker. Cut meat off bones, dice meat, and discard bones. Return meat to cooker. Skim off fat from top of soup. Turn control to HIGH. Add cabbage. Cover and cook on HIGH 25 to 30 minutes or until cabbage is done. Spoon hot soup into bowls.

# Tortilla Soup

✕◈✕◈✕◈✕◈✕◈✕◈✕◈✕◈✕◈✕◈✕◈✕◈✕◈✕◈✕◈✕◈✕◈✕◈✕◈✕◈✕◈✕◈✕◈✕◈

*T*opped with thin strips of tortillas, this soup has a slightly spicy flavor. ■ MAKES 5 TO 6 SERVINGS

| | |
|---|---|
| 2 chicken breast halves, boned, skinned and cubed | ⅛ teaspoon pepper |
| 1 onion, finely chopped | 1 mild green chile, seeded and chopped |
| 1 clove garlic, crushed | 2 tablespoons vegetable oil |
| 3 medium tomatoes, peeled, seeded and chopped | 4 corn tortillas, halved and cut into ¼-inch strips |
| 4 cups chicken broth | 2 tablespoons coarsely chopped fresh cilantro |
| ¼ teaspoon salt | |

Combine chicken, onion, garlic, tomatoes, broth, salt, pepper and green chile in a slow cooker. Cover and cook on LOW 7 to 8 hours. Process in a food processor or blender until pureed. Heat oil in a large skillet. Add tortilla strips. Cook, stirring, over medium heat until crisp; drain on paper towels. Reheat soup if needed and spoon into individual bowls. Top with crisp tortilla strips. Sprinkle with cilantro.

# Chicken 'n' Vegetable Soup with Fresh Salsa

*I*t is easy to double the recipe for a potluck supper.  ■ MAKES 4 TO 5 SERVINGS

2 chicken thighs
2 potatoes, peeled and
  diced
2 ears of corn

3 cups fat-free chicken broth or
  bouillon
4 to 5 fresh mushrooms, sliced
¼ teaspoon salt

### FRESH AVOCADO SALSA

1 small tomato, diced
1 jalapeño chile, chopped
1 green onion, chopped

½ small avocado, peeled, pitted and
  chopped

Remove and discard skin and bones from chicken; finely chop the meat. Combine chicken and potatoes in a 3½-quart slow cooker. Remove husks and silk from corn. Cut off kernels and add to slow cooker. Stir in broth, mushrooms, and salt. Cover and cook on LOW about 4 hours or until potatoes are tender. While soup cooks, prepare Fresh Salsa.

Spoon soup into individual bowls. Top each serving with Fresh Salsa.

## Fresh Avocado Salsa

Combine ingredients in a small bowl.

Per serving: Cal 201 · Carb 28 gm · Prot 13 gm · Total fat 6 gm · Sat fat 1 gm · Cal from fat 54 · Chol 28 mg · Sodium 598 mg

# Turkey Tortilla Soup

※※※※※※※※※※※※※※※※※※※※※※※※※※※※※※※※※※

*T*his substantial soup can be used as a hearty main dish for lunch or supper. ■ MAKES 8 SERVINGS

| | |
|---|---|
| 2 medium turkey thighs | 2 (14½-oz.) cans fat-free chicken |
| 1 (15- or 16-oz.) can diced tomatoes | broth |
| in juice | ½ teaspoon salt |
| 1 medium onion, diced | 4 corn tortillas, cut into ¼-inch strips |
| 1 clove garlic, crushed | Chopped cilantro |
| 1 to 2 jalapeño chiles, seeded and | |
| chopped | |

Remove and discard skin and fat from turkey. Combine turkey, tomatoes, onion, garlic, jalapeño chiles, broth and salt in a 3½-quart slow cooker. Cover and cook on LOW 7 to 8 hours or until turkey is tender. Meanwhile, preheat oven to 400F (205C). Arrange tortilla strips in a single layer on a 15 × 10-inch baking sheet. Toast tortillas in oven 6 to 8 minutes or until golden, stirring once; set aside.

Remove turkey from slow cooker and cool slightly. Remove bones from turkey. Chop turkey; divide among soup bowls. Process remaining soup mixture in a blender or food processor until pureed. Pour over turkey in soup bowls. Top each serving with tortilla strips and cilantro.

Per serving: Cal 77 · Carb 10 gm · Prot 6 gm · Total fat 1 gm · Sat fat 0 gm · Cal from fat 9 · Chol 11 mg · Sodium 518 mg

# Turkey Noodle Soup

*T*his is the perfect soup to make from your leftover Thanksgiving turkey.  ■ MAKES 8 SERVINGS

| | |
|---|---|
| 1 turkey carcass, broken into several pieces | 2 celery stalks, chopped |
| 2 quarts water | 1 carrot, peeled and chopped |
| 1 teaspoon salt | 2 tablespoons chopped fresh parsley |
| 1/4 teaspoon pepper | 1/2 teaspoon dried marjoram |
| 1 onion, chopped | 1 bay leaf |
| | 6 oz. noodles, cooked and drained |

Combine turkey carcass and water in a slow cooker. Add salt, pepper, onion, celery, carrot, parsley, marjoram and bay leaf. Cover and cook on LOW 5 to 6 hours. Remove carcass and bay leaf from cooker. Take meat off bones; return meat to broth. Discard bones. Add cooked noodles to cooker. Cover and cook on HIGH 20 to 30 minutes. Discard bay leaf. Serve soup hot.

VARIATION: This recipe is designed for a 4½-quart slow cooker. For a 3½-quart or smaller slow cooker, use chunks of turkey meat cut off the bones, or chicken parts.

Clockwise from top left: Padre Punch (page 12), Chicken & Leek Terrine (page 4), Cranberry Wine Punch (page 11), Mediterranean Caponata (page 3), and East Indian Snack (page 9)

Clockwise from top left: Golden Squash Soup with Pesto Topping (page 26), Tortilla Soup (page 45), and Fennel-Bean Soup (page 19)

Clockwise from top: Homestead Ham Loaf (page 143), Spicy Brisket over Noodles (page 95), and Swedish Cabbage Rolls (page 122)

Clockwise from top: Red & Gold Sweet-Sour Chicken (page 194), Southeast Asian–Style Meatballs (page 214), and Chinese Pepper Steak (page 103)

# Hearty Confetti Fish Chowder

*I*mitation bacon bits add a slight smoky flavor without adding extra fat.  ■ MAKES 6 TO 8 SERVINGS

| | |
|---|---|
| 2 medium potatoes, peeled and cut into ¼-inch cubes | ¼ teaspoon ground white pepper |
| 2 medium carrots, peeled and thinly sliced | ¼ teaspoon ground thyme |
| | 1 teaspoon Worcestershire sauce |
| 1 stalk celery, thinly sliced | ¼ to ½ teaspoon hot sauce |
| 1 small leek, trimmed and thinly sliced | ⅓ cup dry nonfat milk powder |
| 2 cloves garlic, minced | ¼ cup all-purpose flour |
| 3 cups water | ½ cup water |
| ½ cup dry white wine | ¾ lb. firm white fish, cut into ½-inch cubes |
| 2 tablespoons imitation bacon bits | 1 (2-oz.) jar chopped pimientos, drained |
| ¾ teaspoon salt | |

Combine potatoes, carrots, celery, leek, garlic, water, wine, imitation bacon bits, salt, pepper, thyme, Worcestershire sauce and hot sauce in a 3 ½-quart slow cooker. Cover and cook on LOW 7 to 8 hours or until potatoes are tender.

Turn control to HIGH. In a small bowl, combine dry milk powder and flour. Gradually whisk in water; stir into mixture in slow cooker. Add fish and pimientos. Cover and cook on HIGH 15 to 20 minutes or until fish flakes easily with a fork and chowder is slightly thickened.

Ladle into soup bowls.

Per serving: Cal 181 · Carb 23 gm · Prot 16 gm · Total fat 1 gm · Sat fat 0 gm · Cal from fat 9 · Chol 22 mg · Sodium 432 mg

# New England Clam Chowder

*T*here are two types of clam chowder: New England always contains milk or cream; Manhattan has tomatoes instead of the milk. ■ MAKES 6 TO 7 SERVINGS

2 oz. salt pork or bacon, cut in small cubes
1 onion, chopped
2 medium potatoes, peeled and diced
½ teaspoon salt
⅛ teaspoon pepper
1 (8-oz.) bottle clam juice

2 cups water
2 (7-oz.) cans minced clams, drained, or 1 pint shucked fresh clams, cut up
2 cups half-and-half or evaporated milk
Paprika

Cook salt pork with onion in a skillet over medium heat until onion is softened. Combine pork and onion with potatoes, salt, pepper, clam juice and water in a slow cooker. Cover and cook on LOW 5 to 7 hours. Turn control to HIGH. Add clams and half-and-half. Cover and cook on HIGH 15 minutes. Serve hot, sprinkled with paprika.

# Bouillabaisse

※※※※※※※※※※※※※※※※※※※※※※※※※※※※※※※※※※※※※※※※※※

*D*ip slices of bread into this version of the French classic, which contains mixed seafood and a flavorful broth.  ■ MAKES 6 TO 7 SERVINGS

1 carrot, peeled and chopped
1 onion, chopped
1 clove garlic, minced
1 (1-lb.) can tomatoes, cut up
3 cups water
2 bay leaves
2 cups beef broth
¼ cup chopped fresh parsley
½ teaspoon dried thyme, crushed
1 tablespoon salt

1 teaspoon fresh lemon juice
A pinch powdered saffron or 1
   teaspoon turmeric
¼ lb. large uncooked shrimp, shelled
½ lb. fresh or frozen fish fillets,
   thawed and cut into 2-inch chunks
1 uncooked lobster tail, cut into 2-
   inch chunks
French bread

In a 4-quart or larger slow cooker, combine carrot, onion, garlic, tomatoes, water, bay leaves, broth, parsley, thyme, salt, lemon juice and saffron or turmeric. Cover and cook on LOW 6 to 8 hours. Strain; return broth to cooker. Turn control to HIGH. Add shrimp, fish fillets and lobster. Cover cooker and cook on HIGH 20 to 30 minutes or until seafood is done. Serve hot in large bowls with French bread.

VARIATION: If using cooked lobster tails, add them 5 minutes before serving.

# Beef and Bulgur Chili Caliente

*B*ulgur wheat adds a chewy texture that tricks the palate into thinking the chili is rich with meat. ■ MAKES 7 TO 8 SERVINGS

| | |
|---|---|
| ½ lb. extra-lean ground beef | 1 medium onion, diced |
| ¼ cup bulgur wheat | ½ cup diced green bell pepper |
| 3 to 4 tablespoons chili powder | 1 to 2 tablespoons hot sauce |
| 1 tablespoon beef bouillon granules | 1 (28-oz.) can diced tomatoes with juice |
| 1 teaspoon ground cumin | 1 (27-oz.) can red kidney beans, undrained |
| 1 teaspoon dried oregano leaves, crushed | 1 (7-oz.) can whole green chiles, drained and cut into large chunks |
| ½ teaspoon salt | ¼ cup tequila (optional) |
| ¼ teaspoon ground black pepper | |
| 3 large cloves garlic, minced | |
| 2 large stalks celery, diced | |

Crumble meat into a slow cooker. Add bulgur wheat. Sprinkle with chili powder, bouillon granules, cumin, oregano, salt and black pepper; mix well. Add garlic, celery, onion, bell pepper, hot sauce, tomatoes and beans with liquid. Mix well. Cover and cook on LOW 8 to 10 hours or until meat is tender.

Stir in chiles and tequila, if using. Cover and cook 20 to 30 minutes for flavors to blend. Ladle into individual bowls.

Per serving: Cal 244 · Carb 33 gm · Prot 15 gm · Total fat 7 gm · Sat fat 2 gm · Cal from fat 63 · Chol 22 mg · Sodium 784 mg

# Corn 'n' Bean Chili

*A* hearty, filling main dish with less meat than traditional chilies.  ■ MAKES 6 SERVINGS

¾ lb. lean boneless beef chuck,
   chopped
1 medium onion, chopped
1 clove garlic, crushed
1 red bell pepper, chopped
1 (27-oz.) can red kidney beans,
   drained and rinsed
½ teaspoon chili powder

¼ teaspoon ground sage
¼ teaspoon ground cinnamon
1 (11-oz.) can whole-kernel corn,
   undrained
1 (4-oz.) can chopped green chiles,
   drained
¼ cup low-fat plain yogurt
Chopped cilantro

Crumble meat into a 3½-quart slow cooker. Add onion, garlic, bell pepper, beans, chili powder, sage, cinnamon, corn with liquid and chiles. Cover and cook on LOW 6½ to 7 hours or until meat is tender.

Ladle into individual bowls. Top each serving with yogurt, then with chopped cilantro.

Per serving: Cal 250 · Carb 26 gm · Prot 15 gm · Total fat 10 gm · Sat fat 4 gm · Cal from fat 90 · Chol 22 mg · Sodium 426 mg

# Chili con Carne

*E*njoy the flavors of a simple Mexican dish. Serve this colorful mixture of meat and vegetables with warm flour tortillas and salsa. ■ MAKES 5 TO 6 SERVINGS

1½ lb. beef stew meat
2 cloves garlic, crushed
½ teaspoon pepper
½ teaspoon salt
1 teaspoon chili powder
1 onion, chopped
1 teaspoon beef bouillon granules

1 (16-oz.) can sliced tomatoes with
    juice
1 (4-oz.) can green chiles, chopped
3 tablespoons chopped fresh cilantro
1 (16-oz.) can pinto beans, drained
Cooked rice

Sprinkle meat with garlic, pepper, salt and chili powder. Pat spices into meat. Cut meat into ½-inch cubes. Place meat in a slow cooker. Cover with onion, bouillon granules, tomatoes and chiles. Cover and cook on LOW 6 to 8 hours or until meat is tender. Turn control to HIGH. Add cilantro and beans. Cover and cook on HIGH 20 minutes. Serve on a bed of rice.

# Black Bean Chili with Pork

*T*his colorful, hearty main dish offers a cool contrast with its yogurt topping. ■ MAKES 6 TO 8 SERVINGS

1 lb. boneless pork, cut into ½-inch cubes
2 (16-oz.) cans black beans, drained
1 red or yellow bell pepper, chopped
1 medium tomato, peeled, seeded and chopped
1 small red onion, thinly sliced
1 clove garlic, crushed

½ teaspoon ground cumin
2 teaspoons chili powder
½ teaspoon salt
1 (8-oz.) can tomato sauce
½ cup plain low-fat yogurt or sour cream
2 tablespoons chopped cilantro leaves

In a slow cooker, stir together pork, beans, bell pepper, tomato, onion, garlic, cumin, chili powder, salt and tomato sauce. Cover and cook on LOW 8 to 9 hours. Spoon into individual bowls; top with yogurt and cilantro.

# Hominy and Beef Sausage Chili

*T*his is a shortcut variation of a favorite traditional family recipe.  ■ MAKES 8 TO 10 SERVINGS

½ lb. smoked beef sausage, coarsely
  chopped
1 medium onion, chopped
1 clove garlic, crushed
1 jalapeño chile, seeded and chopped

1 (15-oz.) can yellow hominy, drained
1 (15-oz.) can white hominy, drained
1 (15-oz.) can Louisiana-style red
  beans, undrained

Combine all ingredients in a 3½-quart slow cooker. Cover and cook on LOW about 7 hours or until onion is tender.

Ladle into individual bowls.

Per serving: Cal 136 · Carb 19 gm · Prot 10 gm · Total fat 1 gm · Sat fat 0.5 gm ·
Cal from fat 9 · Chol 13 mg · Sodium 609 mg

# Blond Chili

✕✕✕✕✕✕✕✕✕✕✕✕✕✕✕✕✕✕✕✕✕✕✕✕✕✕✕✕✕✕✕✕✕✕✕✕✕✕✕✕✕✕✕✕✕

*B*reak tradition with a chili featuring yellow tomatoes and trendy cannellini beans, accented with crunchy jícama. ■ MAKES 6 TO 7 SERVINGS

¾ lb. breakfast turkey sausage links, cut into thirds

12 dried yellow or red tomato halves, coarsely chopped

3 or 4 shallots, peeled and chopped

1 small jícama, peeled and julienned

1 (4-oz.) can chopped green chiles, drained

¼ teaspoon ground cumin

¼ teaspoon ground chili powder

¼ teaspoon dried oregano

¼ teaspoon salt

⅛ teaspoon ground black pepper

2 (15-oz.) cans cannellini beans, drained

1 (14½-oz.) can fat-free chicken broth

2 ounces reduced-fat mozzarella cheese, shredded (½ cup)

Combine all ingredients except cheese in a 3½-quart slow cooker. Cover and cook on LOW 4½ to 5 hours or until tomatoes are tender. Ladle into individual bowls and sprinkle each serving with mozzarella cheese.

Per serving: Cal 246 · Carb 26 gm · Prot 19 gm · Total fat 8 gm · Sat fat 1 gm · Cal from fat 72 · Chol 47 mg · Sodium 665 mg

# Turkey Sausage Chili with Beans

*T*urkey sausage provides an exciting flavor that is slightly different from that of traditional chili, as well as a lower fat content. ■ MAKES 6 SERVINGS

14 to 16 oz. turkey breakfast sausage, diced
1 (28-oz.) can cut tomatoes in juice
1 jalapeño chile, seeded and finely chopped
1 onion, chopped
1 clove garlic, crushed

2 teaspoons chili powder
1 teaspoon low-sodium beef bouillon granules
1 (27-oz.) can red kidney beans, drained
2 tablespoons low-fat yogurt
2 tablespoons chopped fresh cilantro

Thoroughly combine turkey sausage, tomatoes, jalapeño chile, onion, garlic, chili powder and beef bouillon granules in a 3½-quart slow cooker. Stir in beans. Cover and cook on LOW about 6 hours or until onion is tender.

Ladle into individual bowls. Top each serving with about 1 teaspoon of yogurt, then chopped cilantro.

Per serving: Cal 265 · Carb 33 gm · Prot 20 gm · Total fat 8 gm · Sat fat 0 gm · Cal from fat 72 · Chol 49 mg · Sodium 920 mg

# Lamb and Black Bean Chili

✳✳✳✳✳✳✳✳✳✳✳✳✳✳✳✳✳✳✳✳✳✳✳✳✳✳✳✳✳✳✳✳✳✳✳✳✳✳✳✳✳

*T*he well-seasoned combination of lamb and black beans makes this a chili worth trying.

■ MAKES 4 TO 6 SERVINGS

¾ lb. boneless lean lamb, cut into 1-inch cubes
1 clove garlic, finely chopped
1 medium onion, chopped
1 tablespoon chili powder
2 teaspoons chopped fresh oregano leaves

¼ teaspoon salt
1 tablespoon chopped fresh cilantro
2 (15-oz.) cans black beans, drained
2 (14½-oz.) cans stewed tomatoes with bell pepper and onion, undrained

Combine lamb, garlic, onion, chili powder, oregano, salt, and cilantro in a 3½-quart slow cooker. Stir in beans and tomatoes. Cover and cook on LOW about 7 hours or until lamb is tender.

Ladle into individual bowls.

Per serving: Cal 234 · Carb 25 gm · Prot 24 gm · Total fat 4 gm · Sat fat 1 gm · Cal from fat 36 · Chol 54 mg · Sodium 902 mg

# Shortcut Turkey Chili

*P*ackaged ground turkey often has the skin ground in as a filler. For a lower-fat chili, have your butcher skin and grind the meat for you.  ■ MAKES 6 TO 7 SERVINGS

1 lb. uncooked ground turkey
1 onion, finely chopped
½ teaspoon salt
2 teaspoons chili powder
1 tablespoon Worcestershire sauce
1 (15-oz.) can tomato sauce
2 (16-oz.) cans kidney beans, drained

Thoroughly combine all ingredients in a slow cooker. Cover and cook on HIGH 3 to 4 hours or until onion is tender.

# SANDWICHES & WRAPS

*S*low cookers work fine as serving pots for hot sandwiches. Sloppy Joes, Sloppy Jane Sandwiches and Chili Dogs will be the favorites for casual parties. You can combine the sandwich mixture in your slow cooker and leave it for several hours. Family members can serve themselves and make their own sandwiches or a group of friends can enjoy these hearty mixes after a game.

Your slow cooker is also an ideal way to cook a variety of the ingredients that are used for the popular "wraps" or "pita pockets." In these sandwiches the meat or poultry is combined with seasonings and vegetables to make a complete meal. With the slow cooker, you can cook all the ingredients together, then slice or chop the meat or poultry. Keep the mixture warm in the slow cooker until you are ready to stuff the pita pockets or fill the tortillas.

# Barbecue Beef Sandwiches

*L*eftover meat takes on a new role as a filling for a hot sandwich. Serve over warm cornbread for a real treat. ■ MAKES 4 TO 5 SERVINGS

2 cups thinly sliced cooked beef or
   pork
2 tablespoons instant minced onion
1 tablespoon brown sugar
1 teaspoon paprika
½ teaspoon dried oregano, crushed
1 teaspoon chili powder
½ teaspoon cracked pepper
¼ teaspoon salt

1 bay leaf
1 clove garlic, minced
1 cup ketchup
¼ cup water
1 tablespoon salad oil
¼ cup tarragon vinegar
2 tablespoons Worcestershire sauce
2 or 3 drops liquid smoke

Combine all ingredients in a slow cooker. Cover and cook on LOW 4 to 6 hours. Remove and discard bay leaf. Serve hot over French rolls or toast.

# Barbecued Beef 'n' Bean Burgers

*S*o good to eat but so messy to pick up—it's best to serve these sandwiches with a knife and fork. ■ MAKES 5 TO 6 SERVINGS

1 (15-oz.) can small white or red
   beans, drained
3 green onions, including tops,
   chopped
2 stalks celery, finely chopped
½ pound extra-lean ground beef,
   crumbled into small pieces

1 (8-oz.) can tomato sauce
¼ teaspoon liquid smoke
1 tablespoon honey
¼ teaspoon grated lemon peel
5 to 6 hamburger buns

Spoon drained beans into a 3½-quart slow cooker. Add green onions, celery, ground beef, tomato sauce, liquid smoke, honey and lemon peel. Stir until thoroughly combined. Cover and cook on LOW about 4 hours or until vegetables are tender.

Preheat broiler. Split buns and place, cut sides up, on a baking sheet. Toast under broiler until lightly browned, about 5 minutes. Serve bean mixture on toasted buns.

Per serving: Cal 356 · Carb 48 gm · Prot 19 gm · Total fat 10 gm · Sat fat 7 gm · Cal from fat 90 · Chol 31 mg · Sodium 558 mg

# Chili Dogs

◇◇◇◇◇◇◇◇◇◇◇◇◇◇◇◇◇◇◇◇◇◇◇◇◇◇◇◇◇◇◇◇◇◇◇◇◇◇◇◇◇◇

*F*or a larger group, double the recipe and keep hot in the slow cooker; let guests serve themselves. ■ MAKES 8 TO 10 SERVINGS

1 (15-oz.) can chili with beans
1 (6-oz.) can tomato paste
¼ cup minced green bell pepper
¼ cup minced onion
1 teaspoon prepared mustard
½ teaspoon salt
½ teaspoon chili powder
8 to 10 hot dogs and hot dog buns

In a slow cooker, combine chili with beans, tomato paste, bell pepper, onion, mustard, salt and chili powder. Cover and cook on LOW 3 to 4 hours. In a large saucepan, cook hot dogs in boiling water, or microwave. Toast buns. Serve a hot dog on each bun. Spoon chili mixture over hot dogs.

# Sloppy Jane Sandwiches

◇◇◇◇◇◇◇◇◇◇◇◇◇◇◇◇◇◇◇◇◇◇◇◇◇◇◇◇◇◇◇◇◇◇◇◇◇◇◇◇◇◇

*T*hese are a special favorite of the younger generation. ■ MAKES 5 TO 6 SERVINGS

1 package (about 10) hot dogs, sliced
1 (28-oz.) can baked beans
1 teaspoon prepared mustard

1 teaspoon instant minced onion
⅓ cup chili sauce
5 to 6 hot dog buns, toasted

In a slow cooker, combine hot dogs, beans, mustard, onion, and chili sauce. Cover and cook on LOW 2 to 3 hours. Spoon over toasted hot dog buns.

# Sloppy Joes

XXXXXXXXXXXXXXXXXXXXXXXXXXXXXXXXXXXXXXXXXXXXXXX

*A* great way to feed a hungry group of people. Let friends spoon up their own servings. A popular dish for teenagers.  ■ MAKES 6 TO 7 SERVINGS

1½ lb. extra-lean ground beef
1 small onion, minced
2 celery stalks, minced
1 (12-oz.) bottle chili sauce
1 tablespoon brown sugar
1 tablespoon Worcestershire sauce

½ teaspoon salt
2 tablespoons sweet pickle relish
⅛ teaspoon pepper
Hamburger buns or French rolls,
    toasted

In a slow cooker, combine meat, onion, celery, chili sauce, brown sugar, Worcestershire sauce, salt, relish and pepper. Cover and cook on LOW 3 to 4 hours. If possible, break up meat with a fork or spoon once during cooking, then re-cover to continue cooking. Spoon over toasted hamburger buns or French rolls.

VARIATION: Recipe may be doubled and mixture kept warm in slow cooker for an after-the-game party.

# Ham-Stuffed French Rolls

XXXXXXXXXXXXXXXXXXXXXXXXXXXXXXXXXXXXXXXXXXXXXXX

*F*oil wrapping keeps these piping hot until you're ready to serve.  ■ MAKES 6 TO 8 SERVINGS

2 cups finely chopped cooked ham
2 hard-cooked eggs, finely chopped
2 tablespoons minced green onion
2 tablespoons chopped ripe olives
    (optional)
1 teaspoon prepared mustard

1 teaspoon sweet pickle relish
½ cup small cubes Cheddar cheese
⅓ cup mayonnaise
6 large or 8 small French rolls
Foil squares

In a large bowl, combine ham, eggs, onion, olives, mustard, relish, cheese and mayonnaise. Cut off tops or one end of rolls; scoop out most of soft center. Fill with ham mixture. Replace top or end of roll. Wrap each roll in foil. Place filled rolls in a slow cooker. Cover and heat on LOW 2 to 3 hours. Rolls may be kept hot and served from the cooker.

# Pele's Hot Chicken Sandwich

*T*his colorful and tasty topping for an open-face hot sandwich borrows flavors from the South Pacific. ■ MAKES 4 TO 5 SERVINGS

1 lb. boneless, skinless chicken
    breasts, cut into 2 × ½-inch strips
1 red bell pepper, cut into julienne
    strips
1 zucchini, cut into julienne strips
6 mushrooms, sliced
¾ cup pineapple juice
2 tablespoons teriyaki sauce
1 tablespoon honey

½ teaspoon salt
⅛ to ¼ teaspoon dried red pepper
    flakes
2 tablespoons cornstarch
2 tablespoons cold water
4 to 5 sesame bagels
1 small jícama, peeled and coarsely
    shredded

Combine chicken, bell pepper, zucchini, mushrooms, juice, teriyaki sauce, honey, salt and pepper flakes in a 3½-quart slow cooker. Cover and cook on LOW about 4 hours or until chicken is tender.

Turn control to HIGH. In a small bowl, dissolve cornstarch in cold water. Stir into contents of slow cooker. Cover and cook 15 to 20 minutes or until thickened.

Meanwhile, preheat broiler. Split bagels and place, cut sides up, on a baking sheet. Toast under broiler until lightly browned, about 5 minutes. Serve chicken mixture on bagels. Top with jícama.

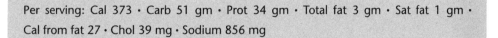

Per serving: Cal 373 • Carb 51 gm • Prot 34 gm • Total fat 3 gm • Sat fat 1 gm • Cal from fat 27 • Chol 39 mg • Sodium 856 mg

# Welsh Rarebit

**𝓘**n some parts of the country this is known as Welsh Rabbit. Whichever name you use, you know it means good eating. ▪ MAKES 4 TO 6 SERVINGS

1 (12-oz.) can beer
1 tablespoon dry mustard
1 teaspoon Worcestershire sauce
½ teaspoon salt
⅛ teaspoon pepper
1 lb. processed American cheese, cut into cubes

1 lb. sharp Cheddar cheese, cut into cubes
Bread slices or English muffins, toasted
Cooked bacon strips
Tomato slices

In a slow cooker, combine beer, mustard, Worcestershire sauce, salt and pepper. Cover and cook on HIGH 1 to 2 hours or until mixture boils. Add cheese a little at a time, stirring constantly, until all the cheese has melted. Heat on HIGH 20 to 30 minutes with lid off, stirring frequently. Serve hot over toasted bread or English muffins. Garnish with strips of crisp bacon and tomato slices.

# Home-Style Barbecue Beef Wraps

*A* flavorful tri-tip beef roast is a wonderful filling. ■ MAKES 7 WRAPS

1 (2-lb.) boneless beef loin tri-tip
  roast
¼ cup molasses
2 tablespoons prepared mustard
1 tablespoon vinegar
1 teaspoon chili powder
1 tablespoon Worcestershire sauce
½ cup ketchup

1 tablespoon minced green onion,
  including tops
7 (9-inch) chili-flavored or plain flour
  tortillas
1 (15-oz.) can chili beans, drained,
  not rinsed, and slightly mashed
1 (11-oz.) can whole-kernel corn,
  drained

Place beef in a 3½-quart slow cooker. Combine molasses, mustard, vinegar, chili powder, Worcestershire sauce, ketchup and green onion. Pour half of sauce over beef. Cover and refrigerate remaining sauce. Cover and cook on LOW about 7 hours or until beef is tender.

Preheat over to 350F (175C). Thinly slice beef across grain. Place about ½ cup beef on each tortilla. Top each with about 3 tablespoons beans, 3 tablespoons corn, and 1 tablespoon of the reserved sauce. Fold ends in and roll up. Wrap each in foil. Place in oven about 15 minutes or until heated through.

Per wrap: Cal 528 · Carb 53 gm · Prot 34 gm · Total fat 20 gm · Sat fat 6 gm · Cal from fat 180 · Chol 78 mg · Sodium 458 mg

# Teriyaki Beef Pitas

*S*erve with beans or rice for a more complete meal. ■ MAKES 5 TO 6 SERVINGS

¾ lb. lean beef round steak
½ cup teriyaki sauce
2 stalks celery, sliced
½ teaspoon dried thyme
1 medium onion, sliced
1 clove garlic, chopped

⅛ teaspoon ground black pepper
2 tablespoons cornstarch
2 tablespoons cold water
5 to 6 pita pocket rounds
Shredded lettuce

Cut round steak into about 2 × ¼-inch strips. Place in a 3½-quart slow cooker. Top with teriyaki sauce, celery, thyme, onion, garlic and pepper. Cover and cook on LOW 6 to 7 hours or until steak is tender. Turn control to HIGH. In a small bowl, dissolve cornstarch in cold water. Stir into contents of slow cooker. Cover and cook, stirring occasionally, 15 to 20 minutes or until thickened.

Slice about 1 inch off 1 side of each pita round. Spoon steak mixture into pita rounds; top with shredded lettuce.

Per serving: Cal 288 · Carb 30 gm · Prot 19 gm · Total fat 9 gm · Sat fat 2 gm · Cal from fat 81 · Chol 41 mg · Sodium 1367 mg

# Alsatian Pork Wraps

✻✻✻✻✻✻✻✻✻✻✻✻✻✻✻✻✻✻✻✻✻✻✻✻✻✻✻✻✻✻✻✻✻✻✻✻✻✻✻✻✻

*I*f you are a real mashed potato fan, use fresh potatoes.  ■ MAKES 6 WRAPS

½ small head cabbage, shredded
(about 4 cups)
2 medium apples, peeled, cored, and
cut into 8 wedges
1 (3-lb.) sirloin-cut pork roast with
bone
2 tablespoons sweet-hot mustard
¼ teaspoon ground cinnamon

1 teaspoon chili powder
1 tablespoon honey
½ teaspoon seasoned salt
⅛ teaspoon ground black pepper
3 (20 × 13-inch) sheets soft Armenian
cracker bread
¾ cup instant mashed potatoes
Hot pepper sauce (optional)

Place cabbage in bottom of a 3½-quart slow cooker; top with apples. Trim and discard any excess fat from pork. Add pork to slow cooker. In a small bowl, combine mustard, cinnamon, chili powder, honey, seasoned salt and pepper. Spoon over contents of slow cooker. Cover and cook on LOW 7½ to 8 hours or until pork is tender. Remove pork from slow cooker and cut into thin slices. Cut each cracker bread in half. Prepare potatoes according to package directions. Place about ⅔ cup pork on each bread half. Top with about ⅓ cup cabbage mixture and a scant ⅓ cup mashed potatoes, then 2 tablespoons of cooking juices. Fold in sides and roll up. Pass hot sauce, if desired.

Per wrap: Cal 520 · Carb 55 gm · Prot 36 gm · Total fat 17 gm · Sat fat 5 gm · Cal from fat 153 · Chol 78 mg · Sodium 548 mg

# Rangoon Chicken Wraps

*S*easoned with light coconut milk, chutney, gingerroot and lime peel, this richly flavored wrap includes fragrant jasmine rice.  ■ MAKES 8 WRAPS

1 (4-lb.) whole roasting chicken
2 carrots, peeled and julienned
1 green bell pepper, seeded and sliced
2 tablespoons fruit chutney
1/3 cup crunchy peanut butter
2 tablespoons soy sauce
1 tablespoon grated gingerroot
1/2 teaspoon grated lime peel

1/2 cup unsweetened reduced-fat
   coconut milk
1/2 cup chicken broth or bouillon
1 cup water
1/2 cup jasmine rice
8 (9-inch) sesame or spinach flour
   tortillas
8 to 10 snow peas

Remove excess fat from chicken. Remove giblets from chicken and refrigerate for another use. Rinse and drain chicken. Place carrots in a 4- or 5-quart slow cooker. Top with chicken, breast side down, then add bell pepper. Finely chop fruit pieces in chutney; combine in a small bowl with peanut butter, soy sauce, ginger and lime peel. Stir in coconut milk, then broth. Pour over chicken. Cover and cook on LOW about 5 hours or until chicken is tender.

In a small saucepan, bring water to a boil. Stir in rice. Reduce heat, cover, and cook over low heat about 15 minutes or until rice is tender.

Remove chicken from slow cooker. Remove and discard bones and skin and slice meat.

Fill tortillas with chicken, rice, bell pepper, and carrots. Spoon about 1½ tablespoons cooking juices over each. Cut snow peas into thin strips. Sprinkle on top of filling. Fold ends in and roll up.

Per wrap: Cal 630 · Carb 38 gm · Prot 52 gm · Total fat 30 gm · Sat fat 8 gm · Cal from fat 270 · Chol 113 mg · Sodium 590 mg

# Pesto- and Turkey-Stuffed Pita Pockets

*T*his is a half-size version of the popular wraps, featuring pita bread.  ▪ MAKES 7 TO 8 SERVINGS

2 uncooked turkey thighs
1 (8-oz.) can sliced water chestnuts,
    drained
2 cups broccoli flowerets
1 red bell pepper, sliced
½ teaspoon salt
⅛ teaspoon ground black pepper
2 teaspoons dry chicken bouillon
    granules
1 cup lightly packed fresh basil leaves

½ cup lightly packed fresh parsley
    leaves
1 clove garlic, peeled
2 teaspoons vegetable oil
8 ounces (about 1 cup) low-fat or
    nonfat ricotta cheese
7 to 8 (5- to 6-inch) pita bread
    rounds, halved crosswise

Remove and discard skin and excess fat from turkey thighs. Rinse turkey and pat dry with paper towels. Place turkey in a 3½-quart slow cooker. Add water chestnuts, broccoli and bell pepper. Sprinkle with salt, black pepper and bouillon granules. Cover and cook on LOW for 5 to 6 hours.

In a blender or food processor, combine basil, parsley, garlic, oil and ricotta cheese. Process until finely chopped.

Remove turkey meat from bones; cut meat into 1-inch strips. Spoon turkey, water chestnuts, broccoli, and green pepper into pita pockets. Top with basil mixture.

Per serving: Cal 233 • Carb 30 gm • Prot 15 gm • Total fat 6 gm • Sat fat 2 gm •
Cal from fat 54 • Chol 30 mg • Sodium 556 mg

# Taco-Seasoned Turkey Pitas

*T*his hearty and healthy dish is great for lunch or for impressing friends at a Sunday night supper. ■ MAKES ABOUT 8 SERVINGS

¾ lb. lean ground turkey
3 green onions, including tops, sliced
1 (1-oz.) package dry taco spices and seasonings
1 large bunch spinach, washed, stemmed, and cut into ¼-inch slices
2 carrots, peeled and shredded
8 pita bread rounds

Combine turkey, green onions, taco mix, spinach and carrots in a 3½-quart slow cooker. Stir to mix well. Cover and cook on LOW about 4 hours or until onions are tender.

Stir turkey mixture and let stand while heating pita rounds or for at least 5 minutes.

Preheat oven to 350F (175C). Halve pita rounds crosswise and place on a baking sheet. Heat pita rounds until warmed, about 10 minutes. Fill pita rounds with turkey mixture and serve.

Per serving: Cal 179 · Carb 23 gm · Prot 11 gm · Total fat 4 gm · Sat fat 1 gm · Cal from fat 36 · Chol 34 mg · Sodium 318 mg

# BEEF

✕✦✕✦✕✦✕✦✕✦✕✦✕✦✕✦✕✦✕✦✕✦✕✦✕✦✕✦✕✦✕✦✕

$S$low cooking makes beef so tender it nearly melts in your mouth! You'll love the rich and succulent flavors provided by simmering beef in the slow cooker.

You can enjoy a variety of internationally inspired recipes, including Slow-Cooker Fajitas and Swedish Cabbage Rolls. Creole-Asian Strips combines two distinct cuisines in a delightfully different mix of spices. Try newly available ingredients like dried shiitake mushrooms, featured in Black Forest Pot Roast.

Included are the best traditional favorites as well as new recipes. Beef provides main dishes for family meals and entertaining. By planning ahead, you can cook a dish now, freeze it, and serve it as a quick meal when needed. Try Flank Steak in Mushroom Wine Sauce for entertaining. Or, consider Beef Burgundy or California Tamale Pie for an especially satisfying family dinner.

It is not necessary to brown meat before you cook. Ordinarily, you can place most beef cuts directly in the bottom of the slow cooker with the seasonings and vegetables. When meat is fatty or when you don't want it to cook in the juices, put it on a rack, trivet or steamer basket placed on the bottom of the cooker. You can also create a vegetable rack by placing carrots, onions or potatoes in the cooker first, and then placing the meat on top of them.

You will notice a range of cooking times for all of the beef recipes. That's another advantage of slow cookers—you can leave in the morning, let the meat cook most of the day, and not worry about it sticking, burning or overcooking should you return later than expected. The low temperature is so low that an hour or two makes very little difference in slow-cooking recipes.

How do you decide when the beef is done? Cook until the minimum time suggested for the recipe. Then, just test it with a fork to see if it is as tender as you prefer. The thickness of the cut of beef, distribution of fat and amount of bone will change the cooking time, so always check before assuming the meat is ready to serve. Another way to test a roast or meat loaf for doneness is to use an instant-read thermometer. Ground beef should be cooked to an internal temperature of 160F (72C) and a roast should be cooked to between 145 and 170F (65 and 75C), depending on desired doneness.

Here is a secret for cooking vegetables with beef: Some vegetables take as long or longer to cook than beef. If you plan a beef dish with large chunks of carrots or celery, place these in the bottom or around the sides of the pot and cover them with liquid such as water, broth or tomato sauce. You may want to cut them slightly smaller than usual. Slow cookers are notoriously slow for cooking vegetables, and smaller pieces cook faster.

Another secret: The good juices of meat don't evaporate. As a result, you have more liquid with a rich, meaty flavor. Take advantage of these flavorful juices. At the end of cooking time remove the cooked beef from the slow cooker. Turn the control to HIGH and stir in cornstarch that is dissolved in cold water or bouillon. Cook 25 to 30 minutes; it will be transformed into a delicious sauce to spoon over the meat and vegetables.

# Black Forest Pot Roast

※◆※◆※◆※◆※◆※◆※◆※◆※◆※◆※◆※◆※◆※◆※◆※◆※◆※◆※◆※◆※◆※◆※◆※

*D*ried shiitakes are often labeled Black Forest mushrooms; they may be found in the produce section or in the Oriental food section of your market.  ■ MAKES 6 TO 7 SERVINGS

1 (3- to 3½-lb.) boneless beef chuck
   or round bone roast
1 onion, chopped
¼ cup water
4 dried shiitake mushrooms, stems
   removed, crumbled, and rinsed
¼ cup ketchup
¼ cup dry red wine

2 tablespoons Dijon-style mustard
1 tablespoon Worcestershire sauce
½ teaspoon salt
⅛ teaspoon pepper
1 clove garlic, crushed
2 tablespoons cornstarch
3 tablespoons water

Trim all visible fat from meat; place in a slow cooker. In a small bowl, combine onion, water, mushrooms, ketchup, wine, mustard, Worcestershire sauce, salt, pepper and garlic. Pour mixture over meat. Cover and cook on LOW about 8 hours. Remove meat and slice. Keep meat warm. Turn control to HIGH. Dissolve cornstarch in water; stir into cooker. Cover and cook on HIGH 15 to 20 minutes or until thickened. Serve sauce with meat.

# Beef Burritos

*S*hredded cheese and your favorite salsa may be added to this traditional combination.

■ MAKES 6 TO 8 SERVINGS

2 lb. boneless beef chuck or other pot roast
1 jalapeño chile, seeded and finely chopped
1 garlic clove, crushed
1 teaspoon beef bouillon granules or 1 beef bouillon cube
1 onion, chopped

½ teaspoon chili powder
½ teaspoon ground cumin
2 tablespoons chopped fresh cilantro
½ teaspoon salt
1 (16-oz.) can refried beans, heated
6 to 8 (12-inch) flour tortillas, warmed

Trim fat from beef and discard. In a slow cooker, combine meat, chile, garlic, bouillon granules or cube, onion, chili powder, cumin, cilantro and salt. Cover and cook on LOW 8 hours or until meat is very tender. Remove meat from slow cooker. With 2 forks, shred meat; combine with ¾ cup cooking juices. Spread warm tortillas with refried beans. Add shredded beef. Fold over tortilla sides, then roll up. Serve warm.

# Favorite Pot Roast

All the good traditional ingredients and flavors that we associate with pot roast are here.

■ MAKES 6 TO 7 SERVINGS

1 (3- to 3½-lb.) beef rump or chuck
   roast
½ teaspoon salt
½ teaspoon seasoned salt
¼ teaspoon seasoned pepper
¼ teaspoon paprika
1 onion, cut into 8 wedges

3 carrots, peeled and cut into 1-inch
   slices
4 potatoes, cut into eighths
1 celery stalk, coarsely chopped
1 cup beef broth
3 tablespoons cornstarch
¼ cup water

Trim visible fat from meat. Rub all sides of meat with salt, seasoned salt, seasoned pepper and paprika. Place vegetables in bottom of a slow cooker. Pour broth over vegetables. Place seasoned meat on top of vegetables. Cover and cook on LOW 8 to 9 hours or until meat and vegetables are tender. To thicken juices, remove meat and vegetables; keep warm. Turn control to HIGH. Dissolve cornstarch in water; stir into cooker. Cover and cook on HIGH 15 to 20 minutes or until slightly thickened. Serve with meat and vegetables.

# Pot Roast with Avocado-Chile Topping

*T*he topping adds a fresh flavor to a traditional pot roast.  ■ MAKES 8 TO 10 SERVINGS

1 (3- to 3½-lb.) boneless lean beef
   pot roast
¼ teaspoon salt
⅛ teaspoon ground black pepper
⅛ teaspoon garlic salt
1 large onion, sliced
1 small ripe avocado

2 tablespoons minced fresh cilantro
1 teaspoon fresh lemon juice
1 (4-oz.) can chopped green chiles,
   drained
1 teaspoon Worcestershire sauce
½ teaspoon prepared horseradish

Sprinkle roast with salt, pepper and garlic salt. Place in a 3½-quart slow cooker. Top with sliced onion. Cover and cook on LOW 8 to 9 hours or until roast is tender. While roast is cooking, peel, pit, and mash avocado. Combine avocado, cilantro, lemon juice, chiles, Worcestershire sauce and horseradish in a medium bowl. Cover and refrigerate.

Remove roast from slow cooker and slice. Arrange sliced roast on individual plates. Spoon onion and cooking juices over each serving and top with a dollop of avocado mixture.

Per serving: Cal 400 · Carb 5 gm · Prot 35 gm · Total fat 26 gm · Sat fat 9 gm · Cal from fat 234 · Chol 103 mg · Sodium 210 mg

# Old World Sauerbraten

*A* traditional main dish with enticing flavors and aromas. ■ MAKES 8 SERVINGS

1 (3½- to 4-lb.) beef rump or sirloin
   tip roast
1 cup water
1 cup vinegar
1 large onion, sliced
1 lemon (unpeeled), sliced

1 tablespoon salt
2 tablespoons sugar
10 whole cloves
4 bay leaves
6 whole peppercorns
12 gingersnaps, crumbled

Place meat in a deep ceramic or glass bowl. Combine water, vinegar, onion, lemon, salt and sugar. Tie cloves, bay leaves and peppercorns in a cheesecloth bag. Add to bowl. Pour marinade over meat. Cover and refrigerate 24 to 36 hours; turn meat several times during marinating.

Place beef in a slow cooker. Pour 1 cup of the marinade over meat, cover, and cook on LOW 6 to 8 hours. Place meat on a serving platter and keep warm. Strain meat juices and return to cooker. Turn control to HIGH. Remove cheesecloth bag. Stir in gingersnaps, cover, and cook on HIGH 15 to 20 minutes. Slice meat and serve with sauce.

# Moroccan-Style Pot Roast with Couscous

*T*he spices of this one-pot meal are reminiscent of those used in Morocco.  ■ MAKES 7 TO 8 SERVINGS

| | |
|---|---|
| 1 teaspoon ground ginger | 1 (3- to 4-lb.) boneless lean beef pot |
| ½ teaspoon turmeric | roast |
| ¼ teaspoon ground cumin | 1 medium onion |
| ½ teaspoon paprika | 7 or 8 parsnips |
| ½ teaspoon salt | 1 (10-oz.) package couscous |
| ¼ teaspoon ground black pepper | |

In a small bowl, combine ginger, turmeric, cumin, paprika, salt and pepper. Press into both sides of roast. Let stand while preparing vegetables. Slice onion; place on bottom of a 4- or 5-quart slow cooker. Peel parsnips and cut into 2-inch lengths. Place spiced beef on onion; top with parsnips. Cover and cook on LOW 7 to 8 hours or until roast is tender.

Prepare couscous according to package directions. Serve couscous with pot roast and vegetables.

Per serving: Cal 623 · Carb 48 gm · Prot 45 gm · Total fat 26 gm · Sat fat 10 gm · Cal from fat 237 · Chol 118 mg · Sodium 262 mg

# Shortcut Chuck Roast with Mushroom Sauce

*F*or even lower fat content, cook this recipe the day before you want to serve it. Refrigerate overnight; remove fat from surface and reheat the dish before serving.  ■ MAKES 6 TO 7 SERVINGS

1 (2- to 2½-lb.) boneless beef chuck roast
1 (1-oz.) envelope dry onion soup mix
1 (10¾-oz.) can reduced-fat condensed cream of mushroom soup
8 to 10 fresh mushrooms, sliced

Trim and discard visible fat from all sides of roast. Place roast in a 3½-quart slow cooker. In a small bowl, combine dry soup mix with condensed soup. Pour over roast. Add mushrooms. Cover and cook on LOW 6 to 8 hours or until roast is tender.

Remove roast from slow cooker and slice. Serve with cooking juices.

Per serving: Cal 466 · Carb 7 gm · Prot 30 gm · Total fat 33 gm · Sat fat 13 gm · Cal from fat 297 · Chol 103 mg · Sodium 925 mg

# Scandinavian Dilled Pot Roast

*This* hearty main dish is considered a symbol of hospitality in Scandinavia. If desired, place two or three baking potatoes on top of the roast and remove before making gravy.

■ MAKES 6 TO 8 SERVINGS

| | |
|---|---|
| 1 (3- to 3½-lb.) beef rump or chuck roast | ¼ cup water |
| ½ teaspoon salt | 1 tablespoon vinegar |
| ¼ teaspoon pepper | 4 teaspoons cornstarch |
| 2 teaspoons dried dill weed | 2 tablespoons water |
| | 1 cup sour cream |

Sprinkle all sides of meat with salt, pepper and 1 teaspoon of the dill. Place in a slow cooker. Add water and vinegar. Cover and cook on LOW 7 to 9 hours or until tender. Place meat on a platter and keep warm. Turn control to HIGH. Dissolve cornstarch in water; stir into meat drippings. Stir in remaining 1 teaspoon dill. Cook on HIGH about 10 to 15 minutes or until slightly thickened. Stir in sour cream. Slice meat; serve with sauce.

# Pot Roast with Basil, Sun-Dried Tomatoes and Pine Nuts

※※※※※※※※※※※※※※※※※※※※※※※※※※※※※※※※※※※※※※

*P*opular pesto ingredients are combined to produce a favorite pot roast. ▪ MAKES ABOUT 8 SERVINGS

⅓ cup dry-packed sun-dried tomatoes
½ cup boiling water
1 clove garlic, chopped
1 (2½- to 3-lb.) boneless beef round or pot roast

1 medium onion, sliced
2 tablespoons chopped fresh basil
¼ teaspoon salt
⅛ teaspoon ground black pepper
2 tablespoons toasted chopped pine nuts (see Note, page 3)

Combine tomatoes and boiling water in a medium bowl. Add garlic; let stand about 5 minutes.

Place roast in a 3½-quart slow cooker. Top with onion, basil, salt and pepper. Pour tomato mixture over all. Cover and cook on LOW about 8 hours or until roast is tender.

Remove roast to a serving dish. Sprinkle with pine nuts. Serve with tomato drippings, if desired.

Per serving: Cal 315 · Carb 3 gm · Prot 29 gm · Total fat 20 gm · Sat fat 7 gm · Cal from fat 180 · Chol 86 mg · Sodium 143 mg

# New England Chuck Roast

*A* classic recipe with a savory sauce—just the thing for a large family or for company.

■ MAKES 6 SERVINGS

| | |
|---|---|
| 1 (3-lb.) beef chuck roast | 1 tablespoon vinegar |
| 1 teaspoon salt | 2 cups water |
| ¼ teaspoon pepper | ½ small cabbage, cut into wedges |
| 1 onion, sliced | 3 tablespoons margarine or butter |
| 2 carrots, peeled and sliced | 1 tablespoon instant minced onion |
| 1 celery stalk, cut into 8 pieces | 2 tablespoons all-purpose flour |
| 1 bay leaf | 2 tablespoons prepared horseradish |

Sprinkle meat with ½ teaspoon of the salt and the pepper. Place onion, carrots and celery in a slow cooker. Top with meat. Add bay leaf, vinegar and water. Cover and cook on **LOW** 5 to 7 hours or until meat is tender. Remove meat. Turn control to **HIGH**. Add cabbage wedges. Cover and cook on **HIGH** 15 to 20 minutes or until cabbage is done.

Meanwhile melt margarine or butter in a saucepan. Stir in instant onion and flour. Remove 1½ cups beef broth from slow cooker. Pour broth, horseradish and the remaining ½ teaspoon salt into saucepan. Cook over low heat, stirring constantly, until thickened and smooth. Serve roast and vegetables with the sauce.

# Jícama-Cilantro Round Steak

*F*lavors will be more intense if you prepare the jícama mixture the day before and refrigerate it until serving time. ■ MAKES 5 TO 6 SERVINGS

| | |
|---|---|
| 1 to 1¼ lb. boneless beef round steak | 2 tablespoons chopped fresh cilantro |
| 1 tablespoon instant beef bouillon granules | 2 green onions, including some tops, chopped |
| ⅛ teaspoon ground black pepper | 1 teaspoon grated gingerroot |
| 1 large tomato, chopped | 1 small jalapeño chile, seeded and finely chopped |
| 1 small jícama, peeled and coarsely shredded | 1 teaspoon vegetable oil |

Trim and discard fat from steak; cut into 5 or 6 pieces. Place steak in a 3½-quart slow cooker. Sprinkle with bouillon granules and pepper. Top with tomato. Cover and cook on LOW 7 to 8 hours or until steak is tender.

While meat cooks, combine jícama, cilantro, green onions, ginger, jalapeño chile and oil in a small bowl and refrigerate.

Remove steak from slow cooker. Spoon jícama mixture over each serving.

Per serving: Cal 210 · Carb 3 gm · Prot 19 gm · Total fat 13 gm · Sat fat 5 gm · Cal from fat 117 · Chol 55 mg · Sodium 215 mg

# Swiss-Style Beef Birds

*T*he combination of allspice, caraway seeds and dill pickles creates a bold flavor. Carrot strips add a bright touch of color. ■ MAKES 5 TO 6 SERVINGS

1½ lb. beef round steak
1 teaspoon ground allspice
½ teaspoon caraway seeds
½ teaspoon salt
½ teaspoon pepper
2 medium carrots, peeled, halved and
   cut into strips

2 kosher dill pickles, cut into strips
¼ teaspoon garlic powder
1 (8-oz.) can tomato sauce
1 small onion, chopped
1 tablespoon all-purpose flour
3 tablespoons minced fresh parsley

With a mallet, pound beef to ¼-inch thickness. Sprinkle with allspice, caraway seeds, salt and pepper. Cut into 5 or 6 serving pieces. Place several carrot strips and 2 pickle strips on each piece of meat. Beginning at narrow end, roll up and secure with small skewers or wooden picks. Place meat in a slow cooker. In a small bowl, combine garlic powder, tomato sauce, onion and flour. Pour mixture over meat. Cover and cook on LOW 7 to 9 hours. Sprinkle with parsley before serving.

# Flank Steak in Mushroom Wine Sauce

*A* piquant wine sauce enhances the flavor of the steak; cut it into thin, diagonal strips before serving. ■ MAKES 4 TO 6 SERVINGS

| | |
|---|---|
| 1 (1- to 1½-lb.) beef flank steak | 1 tablespoon ketchup or tomato paste |
| ¼ cup Sauterne wine | 1 tablespoon prepared mustard |
| 1 tablespoon soy sauce | 1 small onion, finely chopped |
| 1 clove garlic, minced | 3 tablespoons cornstarch |
| 1 (10½-oz.) can condensed beef broth | ¼ cup water |
| | ¼ lb. fresh mushrooms, sliced |

Place steak in a slow cooker. In a small bowl, combine wine, soy sauce, garlic, broth, ketchup or tomato paste, mustard and onion; pour mixture over steak. Cover and cook on LOW 6 to 7 hours. Turn control to HIGH. Dissolve cornstarch in water in a small bowl; stir into sauce in cooker. Add mushrooms. Cover and cook on HIGH 20 to 30 minutes or until mushrooms are tender. Slice meat in thin strips and serve with sauce.

# Taste-of-Acapulco Flank Steak

*The* combination of tomatillos and baby corn gives the steak a distinctive yet pleasant flavor. ■ MAKES 6 TO 7 SERVINGS

1 (1½- to 2-lb.) beef flank steak
6 fresh tomatillos
1 (15-oz.) can whole baby corn-on-the-cob, drained
½ teaspoon salt

¼ teaspoon ground black pepper
¼ cup chopped fresh cilantro
1 small red onion, thinly sliced
¼ cup dry red wine

Trim all visible fat from steak. Place steak in a 3½-quart slow cooker. Remove and discard husk and stem from tomatillos; chop and add to steak. Top with baby corn, salt, pepper, cilantro and onion. Pour in wine. Cover and cook on LOW about 6 hours or until steak is tender.

Slice steak crosswise into strips; spoon vegetables and sauce over sliced steak.

Per serving: Cal 245 · Carb 14 gm · Prot 26 gm · Total fat 9 gm · Sat fat 4 gm · Cal from fat 81 · Chol 56 mg · Sodium 283 mg

# Three-Pepper Steak

*A* colorful array of peppers combined with onions and tomatoes yield an appetizing main dish. ■ MAKES 5 TO 6 SERVINGS

1 (1- to 1¼-lb.) beef flank steak
1 yellow bell pepper
1 green bell pepper
¼ teaspoon salt
½ teaspoon red pepper flakes

3 green onions, including some tops, chopped
2 tablespoons soy sauce
2 medium tomatoes, chopped

Trim all visible fat from steak. Place steak in a 3½-quart slow cooker. Remove stems and seeds from yellow and green peppers; cut into strips. Arrange bell peppers on steak. Sprinkle with salt. Top with red pepper flakes, green onions, soy sauce and tomatoes. Cover and cook on LOW 6 to 7 hours or until steak is tender.

Per serving: Cal 163 · Carb 5 gm · Prot 21 gm · Total fat 7 gm · Sat fat 3 gm · Cal from fat 63 · Chol 45 mg · Sodium 590 mg

# Stuffed Flank Steak with Currant Wine Sauce

*F*lank steak becomes more flexible when it is scored, making it possible to roll up like a jellyroll. ■ MAKES 4 TO 5 SERVINGS

1½ cups cubed bread stuffing
¾ cup sliced mushrooms (5 or 6 medium)
3 tablespoons water
2 tablespoons melted margarine or butter
2 tablespoons grated Parmesan cheese

1½ lb. beef flank steak, scored on both sides
2 green onions, thinly sliced
¼ cup dry red wine
½ cup beef broth
2 tablespoons cornstarch dissolved in 2 tablespoons water
⅓ cup currant or grape jelly

In a medium bowl, combine stuffing, mushrooms, water, margarine or butter and cheese. Spread stuffing over steak; starting from a short end, roll up meat jellyroll style. Fasten with skewers or string. Place in a slow cooker. Top with green onions. Pour wine and beef broth over steak. Cover and cook on LOW about 7 hours or until meat is tender. Remove meat; turn control to HIGH. Stir cornstarch mixture into drippings in cooker. Cover and cook on HIGH 10 to 15 minutes or until thickened. Stir in currant or grape jelly. Cut meat into crosswise slices. Serve with sauce.

# Barbecued Brisket 'n' Noodles

𝒦eep the calories as low as possible by selecting the leanest brisket and trimming off excess fat. ■ MAKES 8 TO 10 SERVINGS

1 (2- to 2½-lb.) flat-cut beef brisket
1 cup bottled hickory-smoke barbecue sauce
1 tablespoon prepared horseradish
1 teaspoon prepared mustard
¼ teaspoon salt
⅛ teaspoon ground black pepper
12 ounces wide noodles

Place brisket in a 3½-quart slow cooker. In a small bowl, combine barbecue sauce, horseradish, mustard, salt and pepper. Pour over brisket. Cover and cook on LOW 7 to 8 hours or until brisket is tender.

Cook noodles according to package directions; drain. Slice meat. Arrange sliced meat on noodles and top with sauce.

Per serving: Cal 514 · Carb 36 gm · Prot 26 gm · Total fat 28 gm · Sat fat 11 gm · Cal from fat 252 · Chol 80 mg · Sodium 410 mg

# Glazed Corned Beef

✕◈✕◈✕◈✕◈✕◈✕◈✕◈✕◈✕◈✕◈✕◈✕◈✕◈✕◈✕◈✕◈✕◈✕◈✕◈✕◈✕◈✕◈✕◈✕◈✕

*Z*esty seasonings create an appetizing finishing touch to cooked corned beef. ▪ MAKES 6 TO 8 SERVINGS

1 (3½- to 4-lb.) corned beef brisket
Water to cover
2 tablespoons prepared mustard
1½ teaspoons cream-style horseradish
2 tablespoons red wine vinegar
¼ cup molasses

In a slow cooker, cover corned beef with water. Cover and cook on LOW 10 to 12 hours or until tender. Drain corned beef; place on a broiler pan or ovenproof platter. Preheat oven to 400F (205C). In a small bowl, combine mustard, horseradish, vinegar and molasses. Brush on all sides of meat. Bake, brushing with sauce several times, about 20 minutes or until meat begins to brown. Cut into thin slices.

# Corned Beef

✕◈✕◈✕◈✕◈✕◈✕◈✕◈✕◈✕◈✕◈✕◈✕◈✕◈✕◈✕◈✕◈✕◈✕◈✕◈✕◈✕◈✕◈✕◈✕◈✕

*C*hoose your favorite mustard to accompany this dish: Dijon, coarse-grain or just plain old-fashioned yellow. Tender steamed cabbage is a traditional side dish. ▪ MAKES 6 TO 8 SERVINGS

1 (2½- to 3-lb.) corned beef brisket with pickling spices
1 medium onion, chopped
1 carrot, peeled and coarsely shredded
1 clove garlic, minced or pureed
Water to cover

Place corned beef in a slow cooker. Top with pickling spices, onion, carrot and garlic. Add enough water to cover meat. Cover and cook on LOW 8 to 9 hours or until meat is tender. Remove from cooker; slice and serve.

# Spicy Brisket over Noodles

*T*he intensity of "heat" varies with different picante sauces; choose the one that suits your taste. ■ MAKES 5 TO 6 SERVINGS

| | |
|---|---|
| 1 (2- to 2½-lb.) lean beef brisket | 1 cup picante sauce |
| ½ teaspoon salt | 1 (12-oz.) can beer |
| ¼ teaspoon pepper | 2 tablespoons cornstarch |
| 1 onion, sliced | 3 tablespoons water |
| 1 celery stalk, chopped | Cooked noodles |

Trim visible fat from brisket. Combine beef, salt, pepper, onion, celery, picante sauce and beer in a slow cooker. Cover and cook on LOW 7 to 9 hours or until meat is tender. Remove meat and vegetables from cooker. Skim off any excess fat. Turn control to HIGH. Dissolve cornstarch in water. Gradually add to liquid in cooker, stirring constantly. Cover and cook on HIGH, stirring every 10 minutes, about 20 minutes or until thickened. Cut meat into diagonal slices; arrange on noodles. Top with thickened sauce.

# Asparagus Cube Steak Roll-Ups

*A*n easy-to-put-together meal, the results are a meat and two vegetables from one pot.

- MAKES 5 TO 6 SERVINGS

8 to 10 small new potatoes
5 or 6 (5- to 7-oz.) cube steaks
10 to 12 asparagus spears, trimmed
1 (0.75-oz.) package dry garlic and herb salad mix

Place potatoes in a 3½-quart slow cooker. Top each cube steak with 2 asparagus spears. Roll up; secure with wooden picks if necessary. Place roll-ups, seam side down, over potatoes in slow cooker. Sprinkle dry salad mix over all. Cover and cook on LOW 5½ to 6 hours or until meat is tender.

Per serving: Cal 436 · Carb 35 gm · Prot 33 gm · Total fat 19 gm · Sat fat 7 gm · Cal from fat 171 · Chol 85 mg · Sodium 634 mg

# Flemish Carbonades

*B*eer acts as a tenderizer and adds its own unique flavor. ■ MAKES 5 TO 7 SERVINGS

2 to 3 lb. boneless beef chuck, cut
   into 1-inch cubes
1 onion, thinly sliced
1 teaspoon salt
⅛ teaspoon pepper
2 teaspoons brown sugar

1 clove garlic, minced
1 (12-oz.) can beer
2 bacon slices, cooked and crumbled
3 tablespoons cornstarch
¼ cup water
Cooked noodles

In a slow cooker, combine meat, onion, salt, pepper, brown sugar, garlic, beer and bacon. Cover and cook on LOW 5 to 7 hours or until meat is tender. Turn control to HIGH. Dissolve cornstarch in water. Stir into meat mixture. Cover and cook on HIGH 20 to 30 minutes or until slightly thickened. Serve over noodles.

# Slow-Cooker Fajitas

❋❋❋❋❋❋❋❋❋❋❋❋❋❋❋❋❋❋❋❋❋❋❋❋❋❋❋❋❋❋❋❋❋❋❋❋❋❋❋❋❋❋

*S*trips of beef or chicken absorb the flavors of the sauce during the slow-cooking process.

■ MAKES 8 TO 10 SERVINGS

1½ to 2 lb. flank or skirt steak, or
   boneless chicken
1 onion, thinly sliced
1 red or green bell pepper, sliced
1 clove garlic, crushed
1 jalapeño chile, seeded and finely
   chopped
2 teaspoons chili powder

½ teaspoon ground cumin
¼ teaspoon salt
¼ cup vegetable oil
1 tablespoon fresh lemon juice
8 to 10 warm flour tortillas
½ cup sour cream
1 avocado, peeled, pitted and thinly
   sliced

Cut meat across the grain into ½-inch diagonal strips. Place in a slow cooker. Top with onion and bell pepper. In a small bowl, combine garlic, chile, chili powder, cumin, salt, oil and lemon juice. Pour mixture over meat. Cover and cook on LOW 6 to 7 hours or until meat is tender. Spoon several slices of meat with sauce into center of each warm tortilla. Fold over. Top with sour cream and avocado.

# Creole Beef and Pepper Strips with Curly Noodles

*T*his is a popular and tasty way to make a small amount of meat serve more people.

■ MAKES 5 TO 6 SERVINGS

| | |
|---|---|
| ¾ lb. boneless beef round steak | 1 tablespoon chopped parsley |
| 1 green or red bell pepper, chopped | ½ teaspoon chopped fresh thyme |
| 1 medium onion, chopped | ½ teaspoon salt |
| 1 clove garlic, crushed | ⅛ teaspoon ground black pepper |
| 1 medium tomato, chopped | 2 tablespoons cornstarch |
| 1 beef bouillon cube | 2 tablespoons cold water |
| ½ cup boiling water | 6 ounces curly noodles |

Slice steak into diagonal strips about ¼ inch thick. Combine steak, bell pepper, onion, garlic and tomato in a 3½-quart slow cooker. Dissolve bouillon cube in boiling water. Add to slow cooker with parsley, thyme, salt and black pepper. Cover and cook on LOW about 7 hours or until steak is tender.

Turn control to HIGH. In a small bowl, dissolve cornstarch in cold water. Stir into slow cooker. Cover and cook on HIGH about 10 minutes or until slightly thickened.

Meanwhile, cook noodles according to package directions and drain. Spoon steak mixture over noodles.

Per serving: Cal 289 · Carb 31 gm · Prot 19 gm · Total fat 10 gm · Sat fat 4 gm · Cal from fat 90 · Chol 41 mg · Sodium 409 mg

# Beef Burgundy

*A* great classic made easy in your slow cooker.  ■ MAKES 6 SERVINGS

3 bacon slices, chopped
2 lb. beef sirloin tip or round steak,
  cut into 1-inch cubes
1/4 cup all-purpose flour
1/2 teaspoon salt
1/2 teaspoon seasoned salt
1/2 teaspoon dried marjoram
1/2 teaspoon dried thyme

1/2 teaspoon pepper
2 cloves garlic, minced
1 beef bouillon cube, crushed
1 cup Burgundy wine
1 cup sliced fresh mushrooms
2 tablespoons cornstarch dissolved in
  2 tablespoons water (optional)
Cooked wide noodles

In a large skillet, cook bacon several minutes. Remove bacon and set aside. Coat beef with flour and brown on all sides in bacon drippings. Combine beef, bacon drippings, cooked bacon, salt, seasoned salt, marjoram, thyme, pepper, garlic, bouillon and wine in a slow cooker. Cover and cook on LOW 6 to 8 hours or until beef is tender. Turn control to HIGH. Add mushrooms. Cover and cook on HIGH 15 minutes. To thicken sauce, if desired, add cornstarch mixture with mushrooms. Serve over noodles.

# Teriyaki Steak

*If* fresh ginger is not available, use ¼ teaspoon ground ginger. ■ MAKES 6 TO 8 SERVINGS

2 to 2½ lb. boneless chuck steak
¼ cup soy sauce
1 (20-oz.) can unsweetened pineapple chunks, drained, and ¼ cup juice reserved
1 teaspoon finely grated gingerroot

1 tablespoon sugar
2 tablespoons vegetable oil
2 cloves garlic, crushed
3 tablespoons cornstarch
3 tablespoons water
Cooked rice

Cut meat into ⅛-inch slices and place in a slow cooker. In a small bowl, combine soy sauce, reserved pineapple juice, gingerroot, sugar, oil and garlic. Pour sauce mixture over meat. Cover and cook on LOW 6 to 7 hours. Turn control to HIGH. Stir in pineapple. Combine cornstarch and water in a small bowl; add to cooker. Cook, stirring, until slightly thickened. Serve over rice.

# Hungarian Goulash

*Make* this dish a day before you need it. The flavors improve and reheating does not adversely affect it. ■ MAKES 4 TO 6 SERVINGS

1½ lb. beef stew meat, cut into 1-inch cubes
1 large onion, chopped
2 cloves garlic, crushed
½ teaspoon salt
½ teaspoon pepper
½ cup water
2 tablespoons tomato paste

1 to 2 tablespoons sweet Hungarian paprika
¼ cup all-purpose flour
½ cup water
¼ cup sour cream or plain yogurt
Cooked noodles or rice
2 teaspoons dried dill weed or poppy seeds

Place meat in a slow cooker; cover with onion and garlic. In a small bowl, combine salt, pepper, water, tomato paste and paprika. Pour over meat mixture. Cover and cook on LOW 8 to 9 hours. Turn control to HIGH. In a small bowl, combine flour, water and sour cream or yogurt. Stir into meat mixture. Cook uncovered on HIGH 10 to 15 minutes or until slightly thickened. Serve over cooked noodles or rice. Sprinkle with dill or poppy seeds.

# Baja Beef 'n' Beans

*T*he flavors of this dish are enhanced by salsa. ■ MAKES 5 TO 6 SERVINGS

| | |
|---|---|
| 1½ lb. boneless beef round steak | 1 onion, chopped |
| 1 clove garlic, minced | 1 teaspoon beef bouillon granules |
| ¼ teaspoon pepper | 1 cup fresh or bottled salsa |
| ¼ teaspoon salt | 1 (16-oz.) can red or kidney beans, |
| 1 teaspoon chili powder | drained |
| 1 tablespoon prepared mustard | |

Trim fat from meat. Combine garlic, pepper, salt, chili powder and mustard. Coat meat with mixture. Cut meat into ½-inch-wide strips. Place in a slow cooker. Stir in onion, bouillon granules and salsa. Cover and cook on LOW 7½ to 8 hours. Turn control to HIGH. Add beans. Cover and cook on HIGH 30 minutes.

# New-Style Beef Stroganoff

※※※※※※※※※※※※※※※※※※※※※※※※※※※※※※※※※※※※※※※

*R*educed-fat sour cream cuts the calories and fats, yet provides the traditional stroganoff flavor. ■ MAKES 6 TO 8 SERVINGS

| | |
|---|---|
| 1½ to 1¾ lb. boneless beef round steak | 1 (10½-oz.) can condensed beef broth |
| 1 onion, sliced | 2 tablespoons ketchup |
| 1 clove garlic, crushed | 1 tablespoon red wine |
| 1 tablespoon Worcestershire sauce | 3 tablespoons cornstarch |
| ¼ teaspoon ground black pepper | ¼ cup cold water |
| ¼ teaspoon salt | ¼ pound fresh mushrooms, sliced |
| ½ teaspoon paprika | ¾ cup reduced-fat sour cream |

Trim all visible fat from steak. Cut steak into ¼-inch-thick slices. Place steak in a 3½-quart slow cooker. Add onion, garlic, Worcestershire sauce, pepper, salt, paprika, broth, ketchup and wine. Cover and cook on LOW 6 to 8 hours or until steak is tender. Turn control to HIGH. Dissolve cornstarch in water. Add to slow cooker. Stir in mushrooms. Cover and cook 15 to 30 minutes or until bubbly. Stir in sour cream and serve.

Per serving: Cal 400 · Carb 21 gm · Prot 33 gm · Total fat 20 gm · Sat fat 6 gm · Cal from fat 180 · Chol 75 mg · Sodium 390 mg

# Chinese Pepper Steak

*E*veryone clamors for this very colorful dish with its exotic flavors.  ■ MAKES 4 TO 6 SERVINGS

1 to 1½ lb. boneless beef round steak
1 clove garlic, minced
½ teaspoon salt
¼ teaspoon pepper
¼ cup soy sauce
1 tablespoon hoisin sauce
1 teaspoon sugar
1 tomato, peeled, seeded and
  chopped

2 red or green bell peppers, cut into
  strips
3 tablespoons cornstarch
3 tablespoons water
1 cup fresh bean sprouts
4 green onions, finely chopped
Cooked rice

Trim fat from steak; slice into thin strips. Combine steak, garlic, salt, pepper, soy sauce, hoisin sauce and sugar in a slow cooker. Cover and cook on LOW about 4 hours. Turn control to HIGH. Add tomato and bell peppers. Dissolve cornstarch in water in a small bowl; stir into steak mixture. Cover and cook on HIGH 15 to 20 minutes or until thickened. Stir in bean sprouts. Sprinkle with onions. Serve with rice.

# Creole-Asian Strips

*T*wo great cuisines are blended in one outstanding dish. Serve with rice or over noodles.

■ MAKES 5 TO 6 SERVINGS

| | |
|---|---|
| ¼ teaspoon black pepper | 1½ lb. beef flank steak, cut into |
| ¼ teaspoon red (cayenne) pepper | ½-inch strips |
| ¼ teaspoon garlic powder | ½ green bell pepper, cut into strips |
| 1 teaspoon dried tarragon leaves | ¾ cup chicken broth |
| ½ teaspoon Chinese five-spice | 2 bay leaves |
| powder | 3 tablespoons cornstarch |
| ¼ teaspoon sugar | 3 tablespoons water |

In a small bowl, combine black pepper, cayenne pepper, garlic powder, tarragon, Chinese five-spice powder and sugar. Sprinkle spice mixture over meat strips, patting and turning strips to coat both sides. Place meat in a slow cooker. Add bell pepper strips, chicken broth and bay leaves. Cover and cook on LOW 6 to 8 hours; remove bay leaves and discard. Dissolve cornstarch in water; stir into cooker. Turn control to HIGH. Cover and cook on HIGH 20 to 25 minutes or until thickened.

# Gingery Beef Strips

✕✖✕✖✕✖✕✖✕✖✕✖✕✖✕✖✕✖✕✖✕✖✕✖✕✖✕✖✕✖✕✖✕✖✕✖✕✖✕✖✕✖✕✖

*A* pleasing one-dish meal with flavors from the Far East.  ■ MAKES 4 TO 5 SERVINGS

1 (1- to 1½-lb.) beef flank steak
1 (10½-oz.) can condensed beef
    broth
¼ cup soy sauce
1 teaspoon grated gingerroot
1 bunch green onions, sliced
    diagonally into 1-inch pieces

1 clove garlic, crushed
3 tablespoons cornstarch
2 tablespoons water
3 oz. Chinese pea pods
1½ cups fresh bean sprouts
Cooked rice

Thinly slice flank steak diagonally across the grain. In a slow cooker, combine steak, condensed broth, soy sauce, ginger, onions and garlic. Cover and cook on LOW 5 to 6 hours or until steak is tender. Turn control to HIGH. Dissolve cornstarch in water in a small bowl and stir into sauce in cooker. Cover and cook on HIGH 10 to 15 minutes or until thickened. During the last 5 minutes, drop in pea pods and bean sprouts. Serve over cooked rice.

# Old-Fashioned Beef Stew

*A* long cooking time makes this a wonderful hot meal to come home to after a cold workday. ■ MAKES 6 TO 8 SERVINGS

2 lb. beef stew meat, cut into ½-inch
  cubes
1 bay leaf
1 tablespoon Worcestershire sauce
4 cups beef broth
¼ teaspoon pepper
½ teaspoon salt
1 teaspoon sugar
5 carrots, peeled and sliced or
  quartered

2 celery stalks, thinly sliced
4 potatoes, peeled and cut into
  eighths
15 to 20 white pearl onions, peeled
2 medium turnips, peeled and cut
  into eighths
¼ cup cornstarch
¼ cup water
1 (10-oz.) package frozen green peas,
  thawed

In a slow cooker, combine beef, bay leaf, Worcestershire sauce, 1 cup of the broth, pepper, salt, sugar, carrots, celery, potatoes, pearl onions and turnips. Pour remaining broth over beef and vegetables. Cover and cook on LOW 8 to 10 hours. Turn control to HIGH. Dissolve cornstarch in water; stir into beef mixture in cooker. Remove bay leaf. Add peas. Cover and cook on HIGH 10 to 15 minutes or until slightly thickened.

# Navajo Beef and Chile Stew

※◇※◇※◇※◇※◇※◇※◇※◇※◇※◇※◇※◇※◇※◇※◇※◇※◇※◇※◇※◇※◇※

¶f you don't care for spicy food, reduce the amount of ground red pepper to ⅛ teaspoon.

■ MAKES ABOUT 4 SERVINGS

¾ lb. lean beef stew meat, cut into
  ¾-inch cubes
1 large onion, chopped
2 large cloves garlic, minced
1 (14½-oz.) can ready-cut tomatoes
  with juice
1 (7-oz.) can diced green chiles,
  drained

1 (8.5-oz.) can whole-kernel corn,
  undrained
1½ teaspoons dried oregano leaves,
  crushed
1 teaspoon ground cumin
½ teaspoon salt
¼ teaspoon ground red pepper
2 tablespoons yellow cornmeal

Combine all ingredients, except cornmeal, in a 3½-quart slow cooker, mixing well. Cover and cook on LOW 7 to 8 hours or until meat is tender.

Turn control to HIGH. Stir in cornmeal. Cover and cook on high 20 to 25 minutes.

Per serving: Cal 292 • Carb 27 gm • Prot 20 gm • Total fat 11 gm • Sat fat 4 gm • Cal from fat 99 • Chol 51 mg • Sodium 685 mg

# Farm-Style Stew

Zucchini and corn give this basic stew a different look.  ■ MAKES 5 TO 6 SERVINGS

1½ lb. beef stew meat, cut into
   1-inch cubes
½ teaspoon pepper
1 teaspoon paprika
1 teaspoon seasoned salt
4 medium zucchini, cut crosswise into
   1-inch-thick slices

1 cup hot water
2 tablespoons steak sauce
1 (17-oz.) can whole-kernel corn,
   drained
3 tablespoons cornstarch
3 tablespoons water

Sprinkle beef with pepper, paprika and seasoned salt. Place in a slow cooker with zucchini. Add hot water and steak sauce. Cover and cook on LOW 7 to 9 hours or until tender. Turn control to HIGH. Stir in corn. Dissolve cornstarch in water; add to meat mixture. Cover and cook on HIGH 15 to 20 minutes or until slightly thickened. Serve hot.

# Garden Vegetable–Beef Stew

*F*or the best flavor, use fresh herbs and vegetables. ■ MAKES ABOUT 6 SERVINGS

3 medium potatoes, peeled and cut into eighths
4 medium carrots, peeled and cut into 1-inch pieces
1 leek, cut into ½-inch pieces and rinsed
1 lb. lean beef stew meat, cut into 1-inch pieces
1 red or yellow bell pepper, cut into 1-inch pieces
2 cups fresh or frozen green beans
1 (14½-oz.) can beef broth
2 tablespoons chopped fresh parsley
1 teaspoon chopped fresh marjoram
1 teaspoon chopped fresh oregano
½ teaspoon salt
⅛ teaspoon ground black pepper
2 teaspoons Worcestershire sauce
3 tablespoons cornstarch
3 tablespoons cold water

Place potatoes, carrots and leek in a 3½-quart slow cooker. Top with beef, bell pepper and green beans. In a small bowl, combine beef broth with parsley, marjoram, oregano, salt, pepper and Worcestershire sauce. Pour broth mixture over beef and vegetables. Cover and cook on LOW 8 to 10 hours or until beef is tender. Turn control to HIGH. In a small bowl, dissolve cornstarch in cold water and add to stew mixture. Cover and cook on HIGH about 20 minutes, stirring occasionally, until thickened.

Per serving: Cal 268 · Carb 26 gm · Prot 19 gm · Total fat 10 gm · Sat fat 4 gm · Cal from fat 90 · Chol 45 mg · Sodium 482 mg

# Fiesta Tamale Pie

*C*hoose a mild or spicy salsa, depending on your family's preferences.  ■ MAKES ABOUT 6 SERVINGS

¾ cup yellow cornmeal
1 cup beef broth
1 lb. extra-lean ground beef
1 teaspoon chili powder
½ teaspoon ground cumin
1 (14- to 16-oz.) jar thick and chunky salsa

1 (16-oz.) can whole-kernel corn, drained
¼ cup sliced ripe olives
2 ounces reduced-fat Cheddar cheese, shredded (½ cup)

In a large bowl, mix cornmeal and broth; let stand 5 minutes. Stir in beef, chili powder, cumin, salsa, corn and olives. Pour into a 3½-quart slow cooker. Cover and cook on LOW 5 to 7 hours or until set.

Sprinkle cheese over top; cover and cook another 5 minutes or until cheese melts.

Per serving: Cal 350 · Carb 34 gm · Prot 21 gm · Total fat 16 gm · Sat fat 0 gm · Cal from fat 144 · Chol 57 mg · Sodium 935 mg

# Spaghetti Meat Sauce

*M*ake the sauce ahead of time and freeze it; thaw and heat just before serving. ■ MAKES 6
TO 8 SERVINGS

1 lb. lean ground beef
1 large onion, chopped
1 clove garlic, minced
2 (1-lb.) cans tomatoes, chopped
1 (8-oz.) can tomato sauce
1 (12-oz.) can tomato paste
1 cup beef broth
2 tablespoons minced fresh parsley

1 tablespoon brown sugar
1 teaspoon dried oregano leaves
1 teaspoon dried basil leaves
1 teaspoon salt
¼ teaspoon pepper
Cooked spaghetti, noodles, or other
    pasta

Break up pieces of meat with a fork. Combine meat in a slow cooker with remaining ingredients. Cover and cook on LOW 6 to 8 hours. Serve over hot spaghetti, noodles, or other pasta.

# Cabbage Burger Bake

*R*eminiscent of stuffed cabbage rolls, this dish is quicker to prepare when the cabbage is shredded and the spaghetti sauce is already prepared for you. ■ MAKES 6 SERVINGS

1 (1-lb.) package (about 6 cups) shredded cabbage and carrots
¾ lb. lean ground beef
½ teaspoon salt
¼ teaspoon ground black pepper
1 medium onion, finely chopped
1 cup long-grain rice

1 (26-oz.) can chunky low-fat spaghetti sauce
½ cup water
¼ teaspoon dried basil leaves, crushed
¼ teaspoon seasoned salt

Place half of the cabbage and carrots in a 3½-quart slow cooker. Crumble ground beef over top. Sprinkle with ¼ teaspoon of the salt and ⅛ teaspoon of the pepper. Evenly distribute onion, then rice over all. Top with remaining cabbage, salt and pepper. Combine spaghetti sauce, water, basil and seasoned salt; pour over cabbage. Cover and cook on LOW 5 to 6 hours or until rice is tender.

Per serving: Cal 358 • Carb 42 gm • Prot 16 gm • Total fat 14 gm • Sat fat 5 gm • Cal from fat 126 • Chol 42 mg • Sodium 985 mg

Corn-Stuffed Pork Chops (page 136), Stuffed Honeyed Sweet Potatoes (page 283) and steamed broccoli

Clockwise from top left: Calabacitas (page 276), Slow-Cooker Fajitas (page 97), Black Bean Chili with Pork (page 55), and Rio Grande Country Ribs (page 147)

Clockwise from top left: Acorn Squash, Indonesian (page 274), Confetti Bean Casserole (page 242), and Sweet-Sour Bean Trio (page 248)

Clockwise from top left: Carrot Coffee Cake (page 302), Stewed Pears with Ginger (page 319), and Apple-Cranberry Compote (page 327)

# Shell Casserole

*T*he children in our family request this over and over; see if yours like it as well. ■ MAKES
4 TO 5 SERVINGS

1 lb. lean ground beef
1 small onion, chopped
½ teaspoon salt
¼ teaspoon garlic powder
1 teaspoon Worcestershire sauce
¼ cup all-purpose flour
1¼ cups hot water

2 teaspoons beef bouillon granules
2 tablespoons red wine
6 oz. large shell-shaped pasta
1 (2-oz.) can sliced mushrooms,
   drained
1 cup sour cream

In a skillet, cook ground beef and onion until red color disappears. Drain beef; place in a
slow cooker. Stir in salt, garlic powder, Worcestershire sauce and flour. Add water, bouillon
and wine; mix well. Cover and cook on LOW 2 to 3 hours. Meanwhile, cook pasta according to package directions and drain. Add cooked pasta, mushrooms and sour cream to slow
cooker; stir to mix ingredients. Turn control to HIGH. Cover and cook on HIGH 10 to 15
minutes.

# Eight-Layer Casserole

⋇⋇⋇⋇⋇⋇⋇⋇⋇⋇⋇⋇⋇⋇⋇⋇⋇⋇⋇⋇⋇⋇⋇⋇⋇⋇⋇⋇⋇⋇⋇⋇⋇⋇⋇⋇⋇⋇⋇⋇⋇⋇⋇⋇⋇⋇

*T*his many-layered but quick-to-assemble, stick-to-the-ribs casserole is perfect for a family meal. ■ MAKES 4 TO 5 SERVINGS

½ lb. lean ground beef
2 tablespoons imitation bacon bits
1 small onion, chopped
1 (15-oz.) can tomato sauce
½ cup water
½ teaspoon chili powder

¼ teaspoon salt
¼ teaspoon ground black pepper
⅔ cup long-grain rice
1 (8¾-oz.) can whole-kernel corn, drained
½ cup chopped green bell pepper

Crumble ground beef evenly over bottom of a 3½-quart slow cooker. Sprinkle with bacon bits, then onion. In a medium bowl, combine tomato sauce, water, chili powder, salt and black pepper; pour half over beef and onion layers. Sprinkle rice evenly over top, then corn. Top with remaining tomato sauce mixture, then bell pepper. Cover and cook on LOW about 5 hours or until rice is tender.

Per serving: Cal 365 · Carb 47 gm · Prot 16 gm · Total fat 13 gm · Sat fat 5 gm · Cal from fat 117 · Chol 42 mg · Sodium 1071 mg

# Cheddar Cheese Meat Loaf

*C*heesecloth helps to hold meat together while lifting it into and out of the cooker.

■ MAKES 6 TO 7 SERVINGS

¾ cup crushed cheese crackers
1 small onion, finely chopped
2 tablespoons minced green bell
  pepper
¼ cup chili sauce
½ cup milk

2 eggs, beaten slightly
½ teaspoon salt
⅛ teaspoon pepper
1½ lb. lean ground beef
1 cup (4 oz.) shredded Cheddar
  cheese

In a large bowl, combine cracker crumbs, onion, bell pepper, chili sauce, milk, eggs, salt, pepper, ground beef and cheese. Form into a 6- or 7-inch round loaf. Place loaf on a 24 × 9-inch piece of cheesecloth. Place rack in a slow cooker. Gently lift loaf into cooker and place on rack. Loosely fold cheesecloth over top of meat. Cover and cook on LOW about 5 hours or until done. Holding ends of cheesecloth, lift cooked loaf from cooker. Remove cheesecloth; cut meat into 6 or 7 wedges.

# Sun-Dried Tomato Meat Loaf

*A*dding sun-dried tomatoes and couscous to traditional meat loaf results in an interesting flavor and texture variation. ■ MAKES 6 TO 7 SERVINGS

1 cup boiling water
¼ cup dry-packed sun-dried
   tomatoes
1¼ lb. lean ground beef
⅓ cup plain couscous
1 egg, slightly beaten
¼ cup milk

¼ cup chopped green bell pepper
2 green onions, including tops,
   chopped
¼ teaspoon salt
⅛ teaspoon ground black pepper
½ teaspoon chili powder

Pour boiling water over sun-dried tomatoes. Cover and let stand 2 or 3 minutes or until softened. Drain; finely chop.

In a medium bowl, combine tomatoes with ground beef, couscous, egg, milk, bell pepper, green onions, salt, black pepper and chili powder. Form into a 7 × 6-inch oval. Place on a trivet in a 3½-quart slow cooker. Cover and cook on LOW 5 to 6 hours or until done.

Per serving: Cal 314 · Carb 9 gm · Prot 20 gm · Total fat 21 gm · Sat fat 8 gm · Cal from fat 189 · Chol 108 mg · Sodium 177 mg

# Chile and Corn-Chip Meat Loaf

⬦⬦⬦⬦⬦⬦⬦⬦⬦⬦⬦⬦⬦⬦⬦⬦⬦⬦⬦⬦⬦⬦⬦⬦⬦⬦⬦⬦⬦⬦⬦⬦⬦⬦

Crushed corn chips provide an interesting texture with a south-of-the-border flavor.

■ MAKES 5 TO 6 SERVINGS

1 cup corn chips
1 small green chile, seeded and finely chopped
2 tablespoons finely chopped fresh cilantro
1 teaspoon chili powder

½ teaspoon ground cumin
¼ teaspoon salt
1 egg, slightly beaten
1 (8-oz.) can tomato sauce
1 lb. lean ground beef

Crush corn chips until they are coarse crumbs. In a large bowl, combine corn chips, green chile, cilantro, chili powder, cumin and salt. Stir in egg, half of the tomato sauce and the ground beef. Form mixture into an 8-inch round loaf. Place loaf on a trivet in a 3½-quart slow cooker. Spoon remaining tomato sauce over loaf. Cover and cook on LOW about 4 hours or until done.

Remove loaf and slice; spoon cooking juices over slices, if desired.

Per serving: Cal 300 · Carb 7 gm · Prot 18 gm · Total fat 21 gm · Sat fat 8 gm · Cal from fat 189 · Chol 110 mg · Sodium 477 mg

# Family Favorite Meat Loaf

*T*his is a time-honored dish that cooks while you're at work or play. ■ MAKES 6 SERVINGS

2 eggs, beaten
¾ cup milk
⅔ cup fine dry bread crumbs
2 tablespoons grated onion
½ teaspoon salt
½ teaspoon ground sage

1½ lb. lean ground beef
¼ cup ketchup
2 tablespoons brown sugar
1 teaspoon dry mustard
¼ teaspoon freshly grated nutmeg

In a large bowl, combine eggs, milk, bread crumbs, onion, salt, sage and meat. Mix well and shape into a 9 × 5-inch rectangle or oval, or about a 6-inch round. Carefully place in a slow cooker. Cover and cook on LOW 5 to 6 hours. Combine ketchup, brown sugar, mustard and nutmeg in a small bowl; pour mixture over meat. Turn control to HIGH. Cover and cook on HIGH 15 minutes. Slice and serve while hot or use cold slices for sandwiches.

# Confetti Meat Loaf

*T*his interesting flavor combination will encourage everyone to enjoy vegetables with his or her meat. ■ MAKES 6 SERVINGS

1 lb. lean ground beef
¼ lb. pork sausage
1 egg, slightly beaten
¼ cup finely chopped leek
⅓ cup fine dry bread crumbs
2 tablespoons taco sauce

½ teaspoon salt
⅛ teaspoon ground black pepper
2 teaspoons chopped fresh basil
1 medium to large zucchini, shredded
1 medium carrot, shredded

In a large bowl, combine beef, sausage, egg, leek, bread crumbs, taco sauce, salt, pepper, basil, zucchini and carrot. Form into a 5½-inch flattened round loaf. Place loaf on a trivet in a 3½-quart slow cooker. Cover and cook on LOW about 4 hours or until done.

Remove loaf and cut into 6 wedges; spoon cooking juices over each serving.

Per serving: Cal 285 · Carb 8 gm · Prot 18 gm · Total fat 20 gm · Sat fat 8 gm · Cal from fat 180 · Chol 100 mg · Sodium 431 mg

# Italian Meatball Stew

*Y*ou can vary this dish with your favorite combination of frozen or fresh vegetables.

■ MAKES 5 TO 6 SERVINGS

| | |
|---|---|
| 1½ lb. extra-lean ground beef | 1 clove garlic, crushed |
| ½ cup fine dry bread crumbs | 1 (6-oz.) can tomato paste |
| 2 eggs, slightly beaten | 2 cups beef broth |
| ¼ cup milk | ½ teaspoon seasoned salt |
| 2 tablespoons grated Parmesan cheese | ½ teaspoon dried oregano, crushed |
| | ½ teaspoon dried basil, crushed |
| ½ teaspoon salt | 1 (16-oz.) package frozen Italian-style |
| ¼ teaspoon pepper | vegetables, cooked and drained |

In a large bowl, combine beef with bread crumbs, eggs, milk, cheese, salt, pepper and garlic. Form into 2-inch balls. Place meatballs in bottom of slow cooker. Combine tomato paste, broth, seasoned salt, oregano and basil. Pour mixture over meat. Cover and cook on LOW 4½ to 5 hours. Stir in cooked vegetables. Cover and cook on HIGH 10 to 15 minutes or until mixture is hot.

# Porcupine Meatballs in Tomato Sauce

*K*ids will love these tasty morsels and adults will enjoy being kids again.  ■ MAKES 24 TO 26 MEATBALLS

2 (8-oz.) cans tomato sauce
1/4 teaspoon garlic powder
1/2 teaspoon ground thyme
1/2 cup water
1 1/4 lb. lean ground beef

1/2 cup long-grain rice
2 tablespoons minced onion
1/2 teaspoon salt
1/4 teaspoon ground black pepper

Combine tomato sauce, garlic powder, thyme and water in a 3 1/2-quart slow cooker.

In a medium bowl, combine beef, rice, onion, salt and pepper, mixing well. Shape into 24 to 26 balls about the size of golf balls. Place meatballs in tomato mixture in slow cooker. Cover and cook on LOW 7 to 8 hours or until rice is tender. Serve sauce over meatballs.

Per meatball: Cal 80 · Carb 4 gm · Prot 5 gm · Total fat 5 gm · Sat fat 2 gm · Cal from fat 45 · Chol 18 mg · Sodium 118 mg

# Meatballs in Sun-Dried Tomato Gravy

*T*hese meatballs are best when served over cooked noodles, fettuccine, or spaghetti.

■ MAKES 6 TO 7 SERVINGS

1 cup boiling water
¼ cup dry-packed sun-dried
   tomatoes
1 small onion, chopped
1 stalk celery, chopped
2 teaspoons chopped fresh basil
2 teaspoons chopped fresh oregano
1 tablespoon Worcestershire sauce
1 (10½-oz.) can condensed beef
   broth

¼ teaspoon salt
⅛ teaspoon ground black pepper
1 lb. extra-lean ground beef
½ lb. mild Italian turkey sausage
½ cup Italian-style dry bread crumbs
1 egg, slightly beaten
¼ cup milk
3 tablespoons cornstarch
¼ cup cold water

In a medium bowl, pour boiling water over tomatoes. Cover and let stand about 15 minutes or until softened. Drain; finely chop. Combine tomatoes, onion, celery, basil, oregano, Worcestershire sauce, beef broth, salt and pepper in a 3½-quart slow cooker.

In a medium bowl, combine beef, sausage, bread crumbs, egg and milk, mixing well. Form into 20 to 22 meatballs about the size of golf balls. Place meatballs in tomato mixture in slow cooker. Cover and cook on LOW 4 to 5 hours or until vegetables are tender.

Turn control to HIGH. In a small bowl, dissolve cornstarch in cold water. Stir into slow cooker. Cover and cook on HIGH 15 to 20 minutes. Serve sauce over meatballs.

Per serving: Cal 356 · Carb 20 gm · Prot 25 gm · Total fat 18 gm · Sat fat 1 gm · Cal from fat 162 · Chol 110 mg · Sodium 880 mg

# Swedish Cabbage Rolls

*A* handy dish to take to a potluck supper. Any leftovers freeze beautifully.  ■ MAKES 12 ROLLS

| | |
|---|---|
| 12 large cabbage leaves | 1 lb. lean ground beef |
| 1 egg, slightly beaten | 1/3 cup uncooked rice |
| 1/4 cup milk | 1 (8-oz.) can tomato sauce |
| 1/4 cup finely chopped onion | 1 tablespoon brown sugar |
| 1 teaspoon salt | 1 tablespoon fresh lemon juice |
| 1/4 teaspoon pepper | 1 teaspoon Worcestershire sauce |

Immerse cabbage leaves in a large pot of boiling water and cook about 3 minutes or until limp; drain. In a large bowl, combine egg, milk, onion, salt, pepper, beef and rice. Place about 3 tablespoons of meat mixture in center of each cabbage leaf. Fold in sides and roll ends over meat mixture. Place in a slow cooker. In a small bowl, combine tomato sauce, brown sugar, lemon juice and Worcestershire sauce. Pour sauce over cabbage rolls. Cover and cook on LOW 6 to 7 hours. Serve hot, topped with sauce.

# German Short Ribs

✕✕✕✕✕✕✕✕✕✕✕✕✕✕✕✕✕✕✕✕✕✕✕✕✕✕✕✕✕✕✕✕✕✕✕✕✕✕✕✕✕✕✕✕✕✕✕

*S*ucculent ribs with a tangy sauce. Select short ribs with the minimum amount of fat.

■ MAKES 5 TO 6 SERVINGS

| | |
|---|---|
| 3 to 3½ lb. beef short ribs | 3 tablespoons vinegar |
| ½ teaspoon salt | 1 tablespoon Worcestershire sauce |
| ⅛ teaspoon pepper | ½ teaspoon dry mustard |
| 2 medium onions, thinly sliced | ½ teaspoon chili powder |
| ½ cup dry red wine | 2 tablespoons cornstarch |
| ½ cup chili sauce | ¼ cup water |
| 3 tablespoons brown sugar | Cooked noodles |

In a slow cooker, combine ribs, salt, pepper, onions, wine, chili sauce, brown sugar, vinegar, Worcestershire sauce, mustard and chili powder. Cover and cook on LOW 6 to 8 hours. Turn control to HIGH. Dissolve cornstarch in water. Stir cornstarch mixture into rib mixture. Cover and cook on HIGH 10 to 15 minutes or until slightly thickened. Serve hot over cooked wide noodles.

# Home-Style Short Ribs

Here is an inexpensive cut of meat that becomes a satisfying meal. The hint of sweet and sour in the sauce gives added pleasure. ■ MAKES 4 TO 6 SERVINGS

2½ to 3 lb. lean beef short ribs
1 lb. red-skinned new potatoes,
  quartered
12 baby carrots, peeled and halved
1 onion, sliced
2 tablespoons cider or wine vinegar
2 tablespoons sugar

1 tablespoon cream-style horseradish
1 tablespoon prepared mustard
2 tablespoons ketchup
½ cup beef broth
¼ cup all-purpose flour
¼ cup water
Salt and pepper, to taste

Preheat broiler. Place ribs on broiler rack and brown under broiler on both sides. Discard drippings. Place potatoes, carrots and onion in a slow cooker. Arrange browned ribs over vegetables. In a small bowl, combine vinegar, sugar, horseradish, mustard, ketchup and beef broth. Pour mixture over meat. Cover and cook on LOW 7 to 8 hours. Remove ribs and vegetables, cover, and keep warm. Turn control to HIGH. Combine flour and water; stir into sauce. Cover and cook on HIGH 15 to 20 minutes or until slightly thickened. Season with salt and pepper. Serve hot.

# Marco Polo Short Ribs

※※※※※※※※※※※※※※※※※※※※※※※※※※※※※※※※※※※※※※

*A*n appetizing discovery for short rib fans who enjoy a sauce that's not too highly spiced.

■ MAKES 4 TO 6 SERVINGS

| | |
|---|---|
| 4 lb. lean beef short ribs | 1 teaspoon salt |
| 1 large tomato, chopped | ¼ teaspoon pepper |
| 1 cup beef broth | ½ teaspoon ground ginger |
| ¼ cup red wine | 3 tablespoons cornstarch |
| 1 small onion, sliced | 3 tablespoons water |
| 2 tablespoons prepared horseradish | |

In a slow cooker, combine ribs, tomato, broth, wine, onion, horseradish, salt, pepper and ginger. Cover and cook on LOW 6 to 7 hours. Remove meat from cooker, cover, and keep warm. Turn control to HIGH. Dissolve cornstarch in water in a small bowl. Stir cornstarch mixture into cooker. Cover and cook on HIGH 15 to 20 minutes or until sauce is thickened. Spoon sauce over meat.

# Sauerbraten-Style Short Ribs

*U*se lean short ribs if available and scoop off any excess fat from the top of the sauce before adding gingersnaps. ■ MAKES ABOUT 6 SERVINGS

2 to 2½ lb. beef short ribs
½ cup red wine
1 lemon, sliced
1 onion, sliced
5 peppercorns

10 whole cloves
1 tablespoon pickling spices
½ cup water
12 gingersnaps, crumbled

Place ribs in a large ceramic or glass bowl. In a small bowl, combine wine, lemon, onion, peppercorns, cloves, pickling spices and water. Pour over short ribs. Cover and refrigerate overnight, turning ribs at least once during marinating.

Place marinated ribs in a 3½-quart slow cooker. Pour marinade over ribs. Cover and cook on **LOW** about 8 hours or until ribs are tender. Remove ribs and keep warm. Strain juices and return to slow cooker. Turn control to **HIGH**. Stir in gingersnaps; cover and cook on **HIGH** about 15 minutes or until thickened. Spoon sauce over ribs.

Per serving: Cal 575 · Carb 12 gm · Prot 26 gm · Total fat 44 gm · Sat fat 17 gm · Cal from fat 396 · Chol 108 mg · Sodium 122 mg

# PORK & LAMB

*I*n the past, pork and lamb dishes were often heavily laden with calories and cholesterol. Today, we have the opportunity to purchase leaner cuts of these meats, because the animals are produced differently. Also, we have learned to trim and discard excess fat from roasts and chops before they are put into the slow cooker.

As a result, the cooked sauce in the slow cooker is a combination of natural meat juices and seasonings or your favorite vegetables. We have combined compatible flavors that enhance each specific kind of meat, such as a pork roast that is coated with lightly spiced cranberry sauce accented with candied ginger.

New recipes like Hawaiian Pork Chops, Indonesian Pork and Fruited Lamb Roll take advantage of the increasing popularity of these meats. When it comes to a choice of meats for your slow cooker, the sky is the limit. You can also use your slow cooker for variations of old favorites. This way you can add new variety to your menus with less effort.

Spareribs cook especially well in the slow cooker. They come out oh so tender. Some tempting sparerib recipes you'll love include Barbecued Spareribs, Chinese-Style Country Ribs and Buck County's Spareribs.

An easy way to test a roast or meat loaf for doneness is to use an instant-read thermometer. Ground pork and lamb should be cooked to an internal temperature of 160F (72C); a pork roast should be cooked to 160F (72C); and a lamb roast or chops to between 145 and 170F (65 and 75C), depending on desired doneness.

Some larger roasts will fit into only 4- or 5-quart and larger cookers. If yours is a 3½-

quart or smaller cooker, use a small-size roast and/or have the butcher remove any bones and tie the meat to make it more compact. Remember: Smaller roasts take slightly less cooking time.

You will have more meat juices when you finish than you would with other cooking methods. Make the most of the wonderful flavor these juices contain by spooning them over slices of the meat or by thickening them with flour or cornstarch dissolved in a little water. Pass the gravy to serve over pasta, rice or potatoes.

Pork—"To brown or not to brown?"—that is the question. It's a good idea to brown spareribs before cooking them in a slow cooker. Choose meaty ribs, lightly brown them in the oven or broiler and drain the excess fat before adding sauce and vegetables. If pork steaks and chops are fairly lean, either brown them or just trim the excess fat off the edges.

# Indonesian Pork

✦✦✦✦✦✦✦✦✦✦✦✦✦✦✦✦✦✦✦✦✦✦✦✦✦✦✦✦✦✦✦✦✦✦✦✦✦✦✦✦✦✦

*A* tangy sauce that's slightly sweet and spicy is sparked with a little heat from dried red pepper flakes.   ■ MAKES 5 TO 6 SERVINGS

*[handwritten: sprinkle dried ginger]*

*[handwritten: Excellent I used only 1/4 Cp butter High 6-7 hours]*

1 (4- to 5-lb.) pork roast
Salt and pepper, to taste
1/4 cup honey
1/4 cup soy sauce
1/2 teaspoon dried red pepper flakes

1/4 cup fresh lemon juice
1 tablespoon chopped crystallized ginger
3/4 cup crunchy peanut butter

Place a metal rack or trivet in the bottom of a slow cooker. Place meat on rack. Sprinkle with salt and pepper. In a small bowl, combine honey, soy sauce, pepper flakes and lemon juice. Pour mixture over meat. Sprinkle ginger over meat. Cover and cook on LOW 9 to 10 hours. Remove meat and keep warm. Skim off excess fat from juices. Turn control to HIGH. Stir in peanut butter and cook about 5 minutes. Slice meat and serve with sauce.

# Cranberry-Honey Pork Roast

✦✦✦✦✦✦✦✦✦✦✦✦✦✦✦✦✦✦✦✦✦✦✦✦✦✦✦✦✦✦✦✦✦✦✦✦✦✦✦✦✦✦

*T*art cranberries and honey accent the delicate flavor of pork roast.   ■ MAKES 6 TO 8 SERVINGS

1 (3- to 4-lb.) boneless or loin pork roast
Salt and pepper, to taste
1 cup ground or finely chopped cranberries

1/4 cup honey
1 teaspoon freshly grated orange peel
1/8 teaspoon ground cloves
1/8 teaspoon freshly grated nutmeg

Sprinkle roast with salt and pepper. Place in a slow cooker. In a small bowl, combine remaining ingredients; pour over roast. Cover and cook on LOW 8 to 10 hours or until roast is tender. Slice and serve hot.

# Pork and Apple Hot-Pot

*C*ut fairly thick slices of pork, then pass the sauce.  ■ MAKES ABOUT 8 SERVINGS

1 (3½- to 4-lb.) boneless pork
   shoulder roast
2 cooking apples, cored, peeled and
   quartered
1 onion, thinly sliced
1 cup apple cider or juice
1 teaspoon chopped fresh thyme

1 teaspoon chopped fresh parsley
½ teaspoon seasoned salt
⅛ teaspoon ground black pepper
1 tablespoon brown sugar
3 tablespoons cornstarch
¼ cup cold water

Place roast in a 4- to 6-quart slow cooker. Top with apples and onion; add cider or juice. Combine thyme, parsley, seasoned salt, pepper and brown sugar; sprinkle over all. Cover and cook on LOW about 9 hours or until meat is 170F (75C) on an instant-read thermometer.

Remove roast, apples and onion. Turn control to HIGH. In a small bowl, dissolve cornstarch in water. Add to juices in pot. Cover and cook, stirring occasionally, about 10 to 15 minutes or until slightly thickened. Slice roast; serve with sauce.

Per serving: Cal 543 · Carb 14 gm · Prot 35 gm · Total fat 37 gm · Sat fat 13 gm · Cal from fat 333 · Chol 145 mg · Sodium 221 mg

# Mustardy Orange-Flavored Pork Dinner

*A* complete dinner in the slow cooker saves energy. ▪ MAKES 8 SERVINGS

1 (6-oz.) can frozen orange juice concentrate, thawed
2 tablespoons Dijon mustard
1 teaspoon prepared horseradish
1 tablespoon honey
1 tablespoon grated onion
1/4 teaspoon salt

1/8 teaspoon ground black pepper
18 small white pearl onions, peeled
1 (4-lb.) lean pork butt roast with bone
3 medium sweet potatoes, peeled and quartered
1/4 cup cornstarch

Set aside about 6 tablespoons or half the orange juice concentrate. In a small bowl, combine remaining concentrate, mustard, horseradish, honey, grated onion, salt and pepper. Place pearl onions in bottom of a 4-quart slow cooker. Trim and discard visible fat from pork and add to slow cooker. Arrange sweet potatoes around roast. Brush everything with mustard mixture. Cover and cook on LOW 8 to 9 hours or until meat is 170F (75C) on an instant-read thermometer. Remove roast, onions and potatoes and cover with foil to keep warm. Dissolve cornstarch in reserved juice concentrate. Stir into cooking juices in slow cooker. Cover and cook on HIGH 15 to 20 minutes or until slightly thickened. Spoon over roast and vegetables.

Per serving: Cal 680 · Carb 29 gm · Prot 41 gm · Total fat 43 gm · Sat fat 14 gm · Cal from fat 387 · Chol 166 mg · Sodium 194 mg

*my pot took 4 hrs on low for boneless roast*

# Cranberry-Port Pork Roast

*T*his hearty yet elegant dish is one of our favorites.  ■ MAKES 6 TO 8 SERVINGS

1 (2½- to 3-lb.) lean boneless pork
   loin roast
1 (16-oz.) can whole-berry cranberry
   sauce
⅓ cup port or cranberry juice
¼ cup sugar
½ small lemon, thinly sliced
⅓ cup golden seedless raisins

1 large clove garlic, minced
2 tablespoons diced candied ginger
½ teaspoon dry mustard
½ teaspoon salt
¼ teaspoon ground black pepper
3 tablespoons cornstarch
2 tablespoons cold water
Cooked rice

Place pork roast in a 3½-quart slow cooker. In a medium bowl, combine cranberry sauce, port or juice and sugar. Stir in lemon, raisins, garlic, ginger, mustard, salt and pepper. Spoon over roast. Cover and cook on LOW 6 to 7 hours or until meat is 170F (75C) on an instant-read thermometer. Remove roast from slow cooker; cover with foil to keep it warm. Measure 3 cups of cooking juices and pour into a medium saucepan. Bring to a boil over medium-high heat. In a cup, dissolve cornstarch in cold water. Stir into saucepan. Cook, stirring, until thickened. Slice roast; serve with sauce and rice.

Per serving: Cal 514 · Carb 48 gm · Prot 35 gm · Total fat 18 gm · Sat fat 6 gm · Cal from fat 162 · Chol 98 mg · Sodium 275 mg

# Cantonese-Style Slow-Cooked Pork

*T*he results will be just as delicious if you wish to substitute skinned turkey or chicken for the pork. ■ MAKES ABOUT 4 SERVINGS

¾ lb. boneless lean pork, cut into strips
2 carrots, peeled and coarsely shredded
1 onion, chopped
1 red bell pepper, cut into ½-inch squares

2 cups small broccoli flowerets
2 tablespoons soy sauce
1 clove garlic, crushed
2 teaspoons grated gingerroot
1 tablespoon light brown sugar
¼ teaspoon ground black pepper
Cooked rice

Combine pork, carrots, onion, bell pepper and broccoli in a 3½-quart slow cooker. In a small bowl, combine soy sauce, garlic, ginger, brown sugar and pepper. Pour over pork and vegetables. Cover and cook on LOW 6 to 7 hours or until pork is tender. Serve over cooked rice.

Per serving without rice: Cal 175 · Carb 13 gm · Prot 20 gm · Total fat 5 gm · Sat fat 2 gm · Cal from fat 45 · Chol 56 mg · Sodium 582 mg

# Aloha Pork 'n' Rice

*P*eanut butter and chile add flavor keynotes to traditional Hawaiian pork.  ■ MAKES 4 SERVINGS

¾ lb. boneless lean pork
1 red bell pepper, cut into small strips
¼ cup crunchy-style peanut butter
1 tablespoon honey
1 tablespoon finely chopped candied ginger

1 small jalapeño chile, seeded and minced
2 tablespoons teriyaki sauce
½ cup basmati rice
2 tablespoons toasted coconut (see Note, below)

Cut pork into 1 × ¼-inch strips. Place pork and bell pepper in a 3½-quart slow cooker. In a small bowl, combine peanut butter, honey, ginger and jalapeño chile. Stir in teriyaki sauce. Spoon over pork. Cover and cook on LOW 4 or 5 hours or until pork is tender. Stir thoroughly before serving. Meanwhile, cook rice according to package directions. Spoon pork mixture over rice. Sprinkle with toasted coconut.

Per serving: Cal 325 · Carb 28 gm · Prot 24 gm · Total fat 14 gm · Sat fat 4 gm · Cal from fat 126 · Chol 56 mg · Sodium 423 mg

NOTE: To toast coconut, spread coconut in a 9-inch pie or cake pan. Heat in a 350F (175C) oven about 5 minutes or until golden.

# Rathskeller Pork

*I*nspired by an old German family recipe, this is an autumn favorite at our house. Remove cooked pork and cabbage with a slotted spoon, leaving liquid in the cooker. ▪ MAKES 5 SERVINGS

5 pork steaks or chops, about ¾ inch
 thick
2 cups shredded red cabbage
2 green onions, chopped
2 apples, peeled, cored and sliced

3 tablespoons apple jelly
2 tablespoons white wine vinegar
1 teaspoon seasoned salt
¼ teaspoon seasoned pepper
½ teaspoon caraway seeds

Trim all visible fat from pork. In a large bowl, combine cabbage, onions, apples, apple jelly, vinegar, seasoned salt, seasoned pepper and caraway seeds. Place cabbage mixture in a slow cooker; top with pork. Cover and cook on LOW 4½ to 5 hours or until pork is tender.

# Harvest Pork Chops

*W*hat could be more welcoming than coming home after an afternoon of shopping or errands to the delicious aroma of the spices in this dish! ▪ MAKES 5 SERVINGS

5 boneless pork chops or cutlets
 (about 1 lb.)
⅛ teaspoon ground red pepper
½ teaspoon garlic salt
1 (1- to 1¼-lb.) butternut or delicata
 squash

2 medium oranges, peeled and sliced
¼ teaspoon ground cinnamon
¼ teaspoon ground cloves
¼ teaspoon ground ginger

Sprinkle pork cutlets with red pepper and garlic salt. Place pork in a 4- or 5-quart slow cooker. Halve squash lengthwise; remove and discard seeds. Peel and cut crosswise into

½-inch-thick slices; add to slow cooker. Top with sliced oranges, then a combination of cinnamon, cloves and ginger. Cover and cook on LOW about 4 hours or until pork is tender.

Per serving: Cal 245 · Carb 15 gm · Prot 22 gm · Total fat 11 gm · Sat fat 4 gm · Cal from fat 99 · Chol 59 mg · Sodium 252 mg

# Corn-Stuffed Pork Chops

Green peppers and sun-dried tomatoes make a colorful stuffing for these pork chops, which are especially good with fruit salad and lemon-buttered broccoli.  ■ MAKES 5 TO 6 SERVINGS

5 or 6 pork chops, 1½ to 2 inches thick
1 (8-oz.) can whole-kernel corn, drained, liquid reserved
1 cup seasoned bread stuffing mix
2 tablespoons finely chopped onion
2 tablespoons minced green bell pepper

½ teaspoon salt
¼ cup chopped sun-dried tomatoes in oil, drained
2 tablespoons chopped fresh basil
4 teaspoons cornstarch
1 tablespoon water

Have the butcher cut a pocket in each pork chop, or use a sharp knife to cut a horizontal slit in the side of each chop, forming a pocket for stuffing. In a medium bowl, mix corn, 3 tablespoons reserved liquid from corn, stuffing mix, onion, bell pepper, salt, sun-dried tomatoes and basil. Stir until liquid is absorbed. Spoon corn mixture into pockets in chops. Close with wooden picks or small skewers. Place a metal rack or trivet in a slow cooker. Place chops on rack. Cover and cook on LOW 6 to 7 hours or until pork chops are tender. Turn slow cooker to HIGH. Remove chops and rack. Dissolve cornstarch in water. Stir into cooking juices. Cover and cook about 15 minutes, stirring at least once. Spoon sauce over chops.

# Hawaiian Pork Chops

✕✕✕✕✕✕✕✕✕✕✕✕✕✕✕✕✕✕✕✕✕✕✕✕✕✕✕✕✕✕✕✕✕✕✕✕✕✕✕✕

*Y*ou will think you are in the South Seas when you taste this tropical combination of fruit and nuts. ■ MAKES 6 SERVINGS

6 lean boneless pork chops or
   cutlets
1 tablespoon prepared mustard
2 tablespoons white wine vinegar
1 tablespoon hoisin sauce
½ teaspoon salt
⅛ teaspoon pepper

1 (8-oz.) can pineapple chunks in
   juice
2 tablespoons cornstarch
2 tablespoons water
1 papaya, peeled, seeded and sliced
Toasted coconut (see Note, page 134)
   and/or chopped macadamia nuts

Place chops in a slow cooker. In a small bowl, combine mustard, vinegar, hoisin sauce, salt and pepper. Drain juice from pineapple and add juice to mustard mixture; reserve pineapple chunks. Pour sauce over chops in cooker. Cover and cook on LOW 5 to 6 hours or until meat is tender. Remove chops and keep warm. Turn control to HIGH. Dissolve cornstarch in water in a small bowl; stir cornstarch mixture into juices in cooker. Cover and cook on HIGH 10 to 15 minutes. Stir in pineapple chunks and papaya. Serve chops accompanied by sauce and let each diner add coconut or macadamias as desired.

# Pork Chops with Minted Herb Relish

*A* refreshing, yet spicy combination of seasonings enhances the flavor of the pork chops.

■ MAKES 5 TO 6 SERVINGS

2 medium tomatoes, chopped
1 tablespoon chopped fresh basil
1 tablespoon chopped fresh mint
1 small jalapeño chile, seeded and
    finely chopped
2 teaspoons chopped fresh chives

2 teaspoons Dijon mustard
1 teaspoon prepared horseradish
¼ teaspoon salt
⅛ teaspoon ground black pepper
5 to 6 pork chops or cutlets

In a small bowl, combine tomatoes, basil, mint, jalapeño chile and chives. Cover and refrigerate.

In a small bowl, combine mustard, horseradish, salt and pepper. Spread on one side of each pork chop. Place chops in a 3½-quart slow cooker. Cover and cook on LOW about 4 hours or until meat is tender. Serve with chilled relish.

Per serving: Cal 200 · Carb 2 gm · Prot 21 gm · Total fat 11 gm · Sat fat 4 gm · Cal from fat 99 · Chol 59 mg · Sodium 172 mg

# Plantation Pork Chops

*I*t is important to purchase extra-thick pork chops so you have an adequate pocket for stuffing. ■ MAKES 4 SERVINGS

4 loin pork chops, about 1½ inches thick
1½ cups dry cornbread stuffing
2 tablespoons margarine or butter, melted
⅓ cup orange juice
1 tablespoon finely chopped pecans

¼ cup light corn syrup
½ teaspoon freshly grated orange peel
¼ teaspoon salt
⅛ teaspoon pepper
1 tablespoon cornstarch
1 tablespoon water

Have the butcher cut a pocket in each pork chop, or use a sharp knife to cut a horizontal slit in the side of each chop, forming a pocket for stuffing. Combine stuffing, margarine or butter, orange juice and pecans. Fill pockets with stuffing. Place a metal rack in a slow cooker. Place chops on rack. In a small bowl, combine corn syrup, orange peel, salt and pepper. Brush mixture over pork chops. Cover and cook on LOW about 6 hours.

Turn control to HIGH. Remove chops and rack from cooker and keep chops warm. Dissolve cornstarch in water in a small bowl; stir into liquid in cooker. Cover and cook on HIGH 15 to 20 minutes. Spoon sauce over cooked chops.

# Pork with Sweet Potatoes, Apples and Sauerkraut

※※※※※※※※※※※※※※※※※※※※※※※※※※※※※※※※※※※※※※※

*W*hen arranging vegetables in the pot, save the sauerkraut for the top, to provide some flavorful moisture for the ingredients in the bottom. ■ MAKES 5 SERVINGS

| | |
|---|---|
| 2 medium sweet potatoes | 1/4 teaspoon salt |
| 1 medium onion, sliced | 1/8 teaspoon ground black pepper |
| 2 apples, cored and sliced | 5 boneless pork chops or pork steaks |
| 1 tablespoon brown sugar | 1 (15- or 16-oz.) can sauerkraut, |
| 1/4 teaspoon ground cinnamon or | drained |
| nutmeg | |

Peel and cut sweet potatoes into slices about 1/2 inch thick. Arrange over bottom of a 3 1/2-quart slow cooker. Cover with onion, then apples. Sprinkle with brown sugar, cinnamon or nutmeg, salt and pepper. Top with pork chops, then sauerkraut. Cover and cook on LOW about 5 hours or until chops are tender.

Per serving: Cal 300 · Carb 27 gm · Prot 23 gm · Total fat 11 gm · Sat fat 4 gm · Cal from fat 99 · Chol 59 mg · Sodium 718 mg

# Vietnamese Pork in Savoy Cabbage

*T*hese miniature bundles of pork-filled cabbage leaves are as appetizing as they look. If you can't find savoy cabbage, use small green cabbage or lettuce leaves. ■ MAKES 20 SMALL CABBAGE ROLLS

20 leaves Savoy cabbage
1 lb. lean ground pork
1/4 cup chopped water chestnuts
1 large clove garlic, minced
3 tablespoons minced green onions, including tops

2 tablespoons minced fresh mint leaves
1 1/2 teaspoons minced gingerroot
1 1/2 teaspoons fresh lemon juice
1/4 teaspoon Chinese hot chili oil
1/4 teaspoon sugar
1/8 teaspoon salt

### VIETNAMESE SAUCE

1/3 cup soy sauce
3 tablespoons fresh lemon juice
1 1/2 teaspoons sugar
1 1/2 teaspoons minced gingerroot
1/4 teaspoon Chinese hot chili oil

1 medium clove garlic, minced
1 1/2 teaspoons minced fresh cilantro
1 1/2 teaspoons minced fresh mint leaves

Drop cabbage leaves into boiling water and cook 1 or 2 minutes or until pliable. Immediately plunge into cold water to stop cooking; drain well.

Use a trivet or crumble a large sheet of foil into bottom of slow cooker to keep rolls out of liquid. Cut a "V" from stem end of cabbage leaf; remove tough portion.

In a medium bowl, combine pork, water chestnuts, garlic, green onions, mint, ginger, lemon juice, chili oil, sugar and salt. Place about 1 1/2 tablespoons pork mixture in center of each cabbage leaf. Roll to enclose mixture. Place on trivet or foil, seam side down, stacking if necessary. Cover and cook on LOW 5 to 6 hours. While pork is cooking, prepare Vietnamese Sauce.

Remove cabbage rolls to a serving dish. Pour Vietnamese Sauce over rolls.

# Vietnamese Sauce

Bring ingredients to a boil in a small saucepan over medium heat, stirring constantly. Reduce heat and simmer 2 to 3 minutes

> Per cabbage roll: Cal 103 · Carb 5 gm · Prot 6 gm · Total fat 7 gm · Sat fat 1 gm · Cal from fat 63 · Chol 15 mg · Sodium 306 mg

# Crockery Ham

𝒜dd a festive touch to ham with this spicy currant sauce.  ■ MAKES 8 TO 10 SERVINGS

1 (5- to 7-lb.) cooked ham (with or without bone, butt or shank half)
Whole cloves
½ cup currant jelly
1 tablespoon vinegar
½ teaspoon dry mustard
¼ teaspoon ground cinnamon

Place a metal rack or trivet in a 4-quart or larger slow cooker. Place ham on rack. Cover and cook on LOW 5 to 6 hours. Remove ham. Pour off juices; remove skin and fat. Score ham; stud with whole cloves. In a small saucepan, melt jelly with vinegar, mustard and cinnamon. Remove metal rack or trivet. Return ham to slow cooker. Spoon sauce over ham. Cover and cook on HIGH 20 to 30 minutes, brushing with sauce at least once (several times if possible). Slice and serve hot or cold.

# Homestead Ham Loaf

*A* loaf that slices beautifully and makes a wonderful sandwich filling.  ■ MAKES 6 TO 8 SERVINGS

| | |
|---|---|
| 3 cups ground cooked ham | ¼ cup chopped fresh parsley |
| 8 oz. bulk pork sausage | 1 egg, slightly beaten |
| 3 green onions, chopped | ½ cup milk |
| 1 cup rolled oats | 2 tablespoons Dijon mustard |
| 1 celery stalk, chopped | 1 teaspoon prepared horseradish |

In a large bowl, combine ham, sausage, green onions, oats, celery, parsley, egg and milk. Form into a 6-inch round loaf or a 9 × 5-inch oval. Place in a slow cooker. Cover and cook on LOW 6 to 7 hours. Combine mustard and horseradish and spread over ham loaf. Slice loaf and serve.

NOTE: Ham can be cut into chunks and ground in a food processor or meat grinder.

# Chinese-Style Country Ribs

*S*oy sauce and orange marmalade are combined to give these ribs a different flavor.
■ MAKES 4 TO 6 SERVINGS

¼ cup soy sauce
¼ cup orange marmalade
2 tablespoons ketchup
1 clove garlic, crushed
3 to 4 lb. country-style or regular pork spareribs, cut into 2-rib pieces

In a small bowl, combine soy sauce, marmalade, ketchup and garlic. Brush both sides of ribs with mixture. Place in a slow cooker. Pour remaining sauce over ribs. Cover and cook on LOW 8 to 10 hours or until ribs are tender. Serve hot.

# Buck County's Spareribs

✳✳✳✳✳✳✳✳✳✳✳✳✳✳✳✳✳✳✳✳✳✳✳✳✳✳✳✳✳✳✳✳✳✳✳✳✳✳✳✳

*B*rown spareribs in the oven; then discard drippings before combining with other ingredients in slow cooker. ■ MAKES 4 TO 5 SERVINGS

2½ to 3 lb. spareribs
1 teaspoon salt
¼ teaspoon pepper
1 (1-lb.) can sauerkraut, drained
1 apple, cored and diced
1 tablespoon sugar

Preheat oven to 400F (205C). Cut spareribs into serving-size pieces. Sprinkle with salt and pepper. Place on a rack in a baking pan. Brown in oven 15 minutes; turn and brown other side about 10 to 15 minutes. Pour off fat. Spoon sauerkraut into bottom of a slow cooker. Top with apple; sprinkle sugar over apple. Place ribs on top. Cover and cook on LOW 5½ to 6 hours or until ribs are tender. Serve hot.

# Soy-Glazed Spareribs

✳✳✳✳✳✳✳✳✳✳✳✳✳✳✳✳✳✳✳✳✳✳✳✳✳✳✳✳✳✳✳✳✳✳✳✳✳✳✳✳

*H*oney, soy sauce and pineapple juice are blended into a delightful glaze. Finger licking is permitted when eating these morsels. ■ MAKES 5 TO 6 SERVINGS

4 to 5 lb. spareribs, cut into 2-rib
  pieces
Salt and pepper, to taste
½ cup pineapple juice
2 tablespoons garlic-flavored wine
  vinegar

¼ cup dry white wine
2 tablespoons soy sauce
2 tablespoons honey
½ cup chicken broth
2 tablespoons cornstarch
3 tablespoons water

Preheat oven to 400F (205C). Place spareribs on a rack in a shallow baking pan. Brown in oven 15 minutes; turn and brown on other side 10 to 15 minutes. Drain fat. Sprinkle ribs with salt and pepper. Place ribs in a slow cooker. In a small bowl, combine pineapple juice, vinegar, wine, soy sauce, honey and broth; pour mixture over ribs. Cover and cook on LOW 7 to 9 hours. Turn control to HIGH. In a small bowl, dissolve cornstarch in water; stir into rib mixture. Cover and cook on HIGH 10 to 15 minutes or until slightly thickened. Serve hot.

# Country-Style Ribs with Ginger-Nectarine Chutney

*B*e sure to use large country-style ribs with lots of meat attached to the bones, or substitute lean pork chops or cutlets. ■ MAKES 6 SERVINGS

| | |
|---|---|
| ½ teaspoon curry powder | ¼ teaspoon salt |
| ¼ teaspoon ground cumin | 6 country-style pork ribs |

### GINGER-NECTARINE CHUTNEY

| | |
|---|---|
| 2 nectarines, pitted and chopped | 2 tablespoons brown sugar |
| ¼ cup chopped golden raisins | 2 teaspoons fresh lemon juice |
| 2 tablespoons chopped pecans | ⅛ teaspoon hot pepper sauce |
| 1 teaspoon grated gingerroot | |

Combine curry, cumin and salt in a small bowl. Sprinkle on ribs. Place ribs in a 3½-quart slow cooker. Cover and cook on LOW 4 to 5 hours or until ribs are tender. While ribs cook, prepare Ginger-Nectarine Chutney.

Spoon Ginger-Nectarine Chutney over cooked, drained ribs.

# Ginger-Nectarine Chutney

Combine ingredients in a small bowl.

Per serving: Cal 277 · Carb 15 gm · Prot 15 gm · Total fat 17 gm · Sat fat 5 gm · Cal from fat 153 · Chol 59 mg · Sodium 140 mg

# Barbecued Spareribs

*T*his is a very popular barbecue sauce for traditional spareribs. ■ MAKES 5 TO 7 SERVINGS

4 to 5 lb. spareribs, cut into 2-rib
 pieces
1 cup ketchup
2 to 3 drops hot pepper sauce
¼ cup vinegar

¼ cup packed brown sugar
½ teaspoon salt
1 teaspoon celery seeds
1 small onion, finely chopped

Preheat oven to 400F (205C). Place spareribs on a rack in a shallow baking pan. Brown in oven 15 minutes; turn and brown on other side 10 to 15 minutes. Drain fat. Place ribs in a slow cooker. In a small bowl, combine ketchup, pepper sauce, vinegar, brown sugar, salt, celery seeds and onion. Pour mixture over ribs; turn ribs until evenly coated. Cover and cook on LOW about 6 hours or until ribs are tender. Serve hot.

# Rio Grande Country Ribs

*W*arm flour tortillas make a perfect accompaniment to this hearty dish. ■ MAKES 5 TO 6 SERVINGS

| | |
|---|---|
| 2½ to 3 lb. country-style pork ribs | 1 teaspoon prepared mustard |
| 1 onion, thinly sliced | ½ teaspoon chili powder |
| 1 (7-oz.) can green chile salsa | 2 tablespoons cornstarch |
| ¼ cup dry white wine | 3 tablespoons water |
| 3 tablespoons brown sugar | ⅓ cup sour cream |
| 1 tablespoon Worcestershire sauce | 1 tablespoon chopped fresh cilantro |

Combine ribs and onion in a slow cooker. In a medium bowl, combine salsa, wine, brown sugar, Worcestershire sauce, mustard and chili powder. Pour mixture over meat. Cover and cook on LOW 6 to 7 hours or until ribs are tender. Remove ribs from cooker and keep warm. Turn control to HIGH. In a small bowl, dissolve cornstarch in water; stir into drippings in cooker. Cover and cook on HIGH 15 to 20 minutes or until slightly thickened. Spoon sauce over ribs. Top each serving with a dollop of sour cream and sprinkle with cilantro.

# Knockwurst with Hot German Potato Salad

*P*otatoes are paired with bacon and sausage and topped with a pleasing sauce. ■ MAKES 4 SERVINGS

| | |
|---|---|
| 4 large potatoes | 1/4 teaspoon pepper |
| 1 onion, sliced | 1/3 cup vinegar |
| Water | 2/3 cup water |
| 4 bacon slices, diced | 1/2 teaspoon celery seeds |
| 2 tablespoons all-purpose flour | 4 knockwurst links |
| 2 tablespoons sugar | 1 tablespoon finely chopped fresh |
| 1 teaspoon dry mustard | parsley |
| 1/2 teaspoon salt | |

Peel and slice potatoes. Combine potatoes with onion in a slow cooker. Cover with water. Cover and cook on LOW 5 to 6 hours or on HIGH 2 to 3 hours. Remove from cooker; drain thoroughly and return to cooker. Meanwhile, cook bacon in a skillet over medium heat. Stir in flour, sugar, mustard, salt and pepper; mix well. Add vinegar, 2/3 cup water and celery seeds. Cook several minutes or until thickened. Pour over drained potatoes in slow cooker. Top with knockwurst. Turn control to HIGH. Cover and cook on HIGH 30 to 40 minutes or until mixture is hot. Sprinkle with parsley.

# Kielbasa & Napa Cabbage

*The* shape of Napa or Chinese cabbage is similar to that of romaine lettuce, but it is off-white or a very pale green color. If not available, use regular cabbage. ▪ MAKES 6 SERVINGS

    1 lb. kielbasa (Polish sausage)
    1 onion, thinly sliced
    1 small head Napa cabbage, coarsely shredded
    2 apples, peeled, cored and sliced
    1/2 teaspoon salt
    1 teaspoon caraway seeds
    2 cups chicken broth

Cut kielbasa into 2-inch chunks. In a slow cooker, arrange alternate layers of sausage with onion, cabbage and apples. Sprinkle with salt and caraway seeds. Add broth. Cover and cook on LOW 5 to 6 hours or until cabbage is tender. Serve with a slotted spoon to drain off liquid.

# Fruited Lamb Roll

*A*pricots and cranberries plump up in this moist, flavorful roast. Let the meat rest, covered, 10 to 15 minutes before serving. ▪ MAKES 6 TO 8 SERVINGS

    1 (3- to 4-lb.) rolled boneless lamb roast
    3 cloves garlic, crushed
    1/4 cup minced gingerroot
    1/2 cup dried cranberries
    6 oz. dried apricots
    2 tablespoons chopped fresh mint leaves

Open rolled roast. Sprinkle with garlic, ginger and cranberries. Arrange apricots in a single layer over roast. Sprinkle mint over apricots. Roll roast tightly and secure with string or skewers. Place roast on a rack in a slow cooker. Cover and cook on LOW 8 to 10 hours or until lamb is tender. Slice and serve hot.

# Marinated Leg of Lamb

*T*his size roast will not fit into a small slow cooker; it must be boned or cooked in a 5-quart cooker. ■ MAKES 8 TO 10 SERVINGS

1 (5- to 6-lb.) leg of lamb
2 cloves garlic
¼ cup kosher or coarse salt
2 tablespoons peppercorns, cracked
¼ cup cognac or brandy
2 cups dry red wine

Trim excess fat from lamb. Cut each garlic clove into 4 to 6 slices. Using a paring knife, make small slits in various places in the meat and insert the garlic slivers. Sprinkle salt and pepper over all sides of the lamb. Place meat in a large bowl; pour cognac or brandy over it. Refrigerate several hours or overnight, brushing with cognac or brandy and turning several times.

Drain meat; place in a slow cooker with wine. Cover and cook on LOW 9 to 10 hours or until meat is done. If possible turn roast once during cooking. Cut into thin slices.

# Garlic Lamb Dijon

*S*erve these flavor-filled lamb chops with cooked green peas or steamed green beans to round out the meal. ■ MAKES 4 SERVINGS

½ cup Dijon mustard
2 large cloves garlic, minced
1½ tablespoons mustard seeds
1 tablespoon minced fresh rosemary
¼ teaspoon ground black pepper

4 well-trimmed lean shoulder lamb
  chops
½ teaspoon paprika
Hot cooked rice
Fresh rosemary sprigs, for garnish

Combine mustard, garlic, mustard seeds, minced rosemary and black pepper in a small bowl. Spread mixture (about 1 tablespoon per side) evenly over both sides of lamb chops. Sprinkle top side of each chop with ⅛ teaspoon paprika. Arrange in a 3½-quart slow cooker, overlapping if necessary. Cover and cook on LOW 5 hours or until lamb is tender.

Serve chops with hot cooked rice and the cooking juices. Garnish with rosemary sprigs.

Per serving without rice: Cal 140 · Carb 1 gm · Prot 16 gm · Total fat 8 gm · Sat fat 3 gm · Cal from fat 72 · Chol 52 mg · Sodium 123 mg

# Greek Lamb, Vegetables and Feta Cheese

*P*ackets of tasty morsels are presented on individual dinner plates. Diners slit and pull back the foil to reveal the treasure inside. ■ MAKES 4 SERVINGS

Nonstick olive oil spray
1 lb. lean lamb, cut into bite-size pieces
4 small yellow crookneck squash, cut into 1/4-inch-thick slices
1/4 cup thinly sliced green onions, including tops
1 small red bell pepper, cut into 1-inch cubes

2 ounces feta cheese, diced
1 teaspoon dried oregano leaves
1/2 teaspoon garlic powder
1 teaspoon salt (optional)
1/4 teaspoon ground black pepper
4 teaspoons fresh lemon juice
1/4 cup water
4 lemon wedges

Cut 4 sheets of foil, about 18 × 11 inches each. Place foil, shiny side down, on work surface. Spray an area about the size of a salad plate in center of each piece with nonstick olive oil spray. Top each foil piece with one-quarter of the lamb, then with one-quarter of the squash, then one-quarter of the green onions, bell pepper and feta cheese. Sprinkle each portion with one-quarter of the oregano leaves, garlic powder, salt and black pepper. Drizzle each with 1 teaspoon lemon juice. Bring short sides of foil together; fold over twice. Fold sides up twice to seal. Place in a 4-quart slow cooker with folded side up. Pour water around packets. Cover and cook on LOW 6 to 7 hours or until lamb is tender.

To serve, place each sealed packet on a dinner plate. Garnish each with a wedge of lemon.

Per serving: Cal 206 · Carb 6 gm · Prot 26 gm · Total fat 8 gm · Sat fat 4 gm · Cal from fat 72 · Chol 84 mg · Sodium 229 mg

# Irish Lamb Stew

*T*he rich flavor of lamb is enhanced with herbs and vegetables. ■ MAKES 5 TO 6 SERVINGS

1½ lb. lamb stew meat, cut into
   1-inch cubes
1 onion, chopped
1 cup beef broth
3 medium potatoes, peeled and
   chopped
1 celery stalk, chopped
½ teaspoon salt

¼ teaspoon pepper
½ teaspoon dried marjoram
¼ teaspoon dried thyme leaves
1 (10-oz.) package frozen green peas,
   thawed
3 tablespoons cornstarch
¼ cup water
2 tablespoons chopped fresh parsley

Combine meat, onion, beef broth, potatoes, celery, salt, pepper, marjoram and thyme in a slow cooker. Cover and cook on LOW 8 to 10 hours or until meat and potatoes are tender. Turn control to HIGH. Add peas. In a small bowl, dissolve cornstarch in water; stir into stew. Cover and cook 15 to 20 minutes or until slightly thickened. Stir in parsley.

# Algerian Lamb Shanks

*F*ruits and meat are often combined in North African dishes. Serve this lamb mixture over couscous. ■ MAKES 5 TO 6 SERVINGS

| | |
|---|---|
| 4 lamb shanks | ½ cup orange juice |
| 1 teaspoon salt | 2 tablespoons vinegar |
| ¼ teaspoon pepper | 1 teaspoon ground allspice |
| 1 cup dried apricots | 1 teaspoon ground cinnamon |
| ½ cup pitted prunes | ½ teaspoon ground cloves |
| ½ cup slivered almonds | Cooked couscous or rice |
| ½ cup water | |

Coat lamb shanks with salt and pepper. Place in a slow cooker with meaty ends down. Add apricots, prunes and almonds. In a small bowl, combine water, orange juice, vinegar, allspice, cinnamon and cloves. Pour over meat and fruits. Cover and cook on LOW 7 to 9 hours or until meat is very tender. Remove meat from bones and return meat to cooker to reheat. Serve meat on a bed of couscous or rice.

# Greek Herbed Lamb with Rice

*T*raditional Greek flavors, including mint, oregano, and garlic, highlight this ethnic treat. ■ MAKES 4 TO 6 SERVINGS

| | |
|---|---|
| 4 lamb shanks | 1 teaspoon green peppercorns, crushed |
| 1 cup white wine | ¼ teaspoon salt |
| 1 tablespoon dried oregano, crushed | 2 cloves garlic, minced |
| 1 tablespoon dried mint, crushed | 1 cup uncooked rice |

Place lamb shanks in a slow cooker with meaty ends down. In a small bowl, combine wine, oregano, mint, peppercorns, salt and garlic. Pour mixture over lamb. Cover and cook on LOW 7 to 9 hours or until meat is tender. Remove meat from bones; discard bones. Return meat to cooker. Turn control to HIGH. Add rice; cover and cook 1 hour.

## Lamb Shanks with Sweet Potatoes and Dried Fruit

*I*n addition to convenience, a slow cooker also ensures flavorful results. ■ MAKES ABOUT 6 SERVINGS

| | |
|---|---|
| 2 medium sweet potatoes, peeled and cut crosswise into thick slices | ½ teaspoon ground cinnamon |
| | ¼ teaspoon ground nutmeg |
| 1 (8-oz.) package mixed dried fruit | 1 clove garlic, crushed |
| 3 or 4 (1- to 1½-lb.) lamb shanks | ¼ teaspoon salt |
| ½ cup orange juice | ⅛ teaspoon ground black pepper |

Place sweet potatoes on bottom of a 5-quart slow cooker. Top with dried fruit and lamb shanks. In a small bowl, combine orange juice, cinnamon, nutmeg, garlic, salt and pepper. Pour over lamb. Cover and cook on LOW 8 to 10 hours or until lamb is tender.

Per serving: Cal 285 · Carb 36 gm · Prot 25 gm · Total fat 5 gm · Sat fat 2 gm · Cal from fat 45 · Chol 72 mg · Sodium 181 mg

# Mexican Lamb with Red Wine

*A*uthentic Mexican flavor is easy with readily available chili powder and a few herbs.

■ MAKES 6 SERVINGS

4 lamb shanks
1 cup red wine
¼ cup chili powder
½ teaspoon ground ginger
1 teaspoon ground cumin

1 teaspoon dried oregano
2 cloves garlic, minced
¼ teaspoon salt
Rice or tortillas
Salsa

Place lamb in a slow cooker with meaty ends down. In a small bowl, combine wine, chili powder, ginger, cumin, oregano, garlic and salt. Pour mixture over lamb shanks. Cover and cook on LOW 7 to 9 hours or until meat is very tender. Remove meat from bones; discard bones. Return meat to liquid. Serve over rice or wrap in warm tortillas with salsa.

# Grace's Special Dolmas

*T*his popular Middle Eastern dish is an ideal addition to your buffet table. The dolmas (stuffed grape leaves) are delicious served warm or at room temperature. ■ MAKES 30 TO 33 DOLMAS

1 large onion, finely chopped
½ lb. lean ground lamb
2 tablespoons extra-virgin olive oil
½ cup long-grain white rice
1 medium tomato, peeled, seeded, and finely chopped
¼ teaspoon ground allspice
¾ teaspoon salt
½ teaspoon ground black pepper
½ cup water

2 tablespoons minced fresh parsley
2 tablespoons minced fresh mint leaves
1 (8-oz.) jar grape leaves in brine
2 cloves garlic, slivered
1 cup fat-free chicken broth or water
6 tablespoons fresh lemon juice
1 medium lemon, cut into wedges (optional)

In a heavy skillet over medium heat, sauté onion and lamb in 1 tablespoon olive oil for 3 minutes, stirring to break up lamb. Add rice and cook, stirring, about 5 minutes. Stir in tomato, allspice, salt, pepper and water. Cover and simmer 8 to 10 minutes or until the liquid is completely absorbed. Remove from heat. Stir in parsley and mint; set aside to cool.

Rinse and carefully separate grape leaves in a bowl of cold water. Remove stems, if necessary. Cover the bottom of slow cooker with 4 or 5 grape leaves, using any torn ones. Set aside four or five more.

On a work surface, lay remaining grape leaves out flat, rough or vein side up. Place a rounded tablespoon of rice mixture on center of each grape leaf. Fold stem end up over filling, then both sides to middle. Roll up, rather tight, like a small cylinder.

Place dolmas, seam side down, in a 3½-quart slow cooker, layering if necessary. Insert slivers of garlic between rolls. Combine chicken broth or water, remaining 1 tablespoon olive oil, and 3 tablespoons of the lemon juice; pour over rolls. Add a layer of reserved grape leaves. Top with an inverted plate. Cover and cook on LOW 4 to 5 hours or until leaves are tender.

Remove plate and arrange rolls on a serving plate. Drizzle with remaining 3 tablespoons lemon juice and garnish with lemon wedges, if using. Serve warm or at room temperature.

Per dolma: Cal 33 · Carb 3 gm · Prot 2 gm · Total fat 1 gm · Sat fat 0 gm · Cal from fat 9 · Chol 5 mg · Sodium 95 mg

# POULTRY

In many countries around the world, chicken is one of the most popular main dishes. Here at home, it has been one of our staples for entertaining as well as for family meals. The slow cooker makes it even more popular. Working parents like the idea of nourishing and satisfying food that's ready when the family returns home from school or work.

Favorites range from traditional chicken that's stuffed with mashed potatoes and celery to one with a slight Asian accent that's filled with a water chestnut mixture and brushed with soy sauce. For those with fond memories of grandma's kitchen, there's Old-Fashioned Chicken 'n' Noodles.

New recipes featuring some of the latest flavor combinations are also included in this chapter. For a California taste try Mission Chicken with grapes, orange juice, cinnamon, cloves and lemon pepper. Or how about Curried Island Chicken, Thai Chicken, Arroz con Pollo or Southeast Asian–Style Meatballs? If you like your food very spicy, there's the popular Caribbean "Jerked" Chicken. Many of the recipes take advantage of chicken's mild flavor, adding sun-dried tomatoes, mushrooms, more spices and herbs, even wine.

Remember that whole birds take longer to cook than do parts. An easy way to test poultry for doneness is to use an instant-read thermometer. Ground chicken or turkey should be cooked to an internal temperature of 165F (75C) and a whole chicken or turkey, or chicken or turkey part, should be cooked to 180F (80C). Stuffing should be cooked to 165F (75C).

Carrots, eggplant, celery and potatoes can take longer to cook than chicken. Be sure the vegetables are covered with liquid such as water, bouillon or tomato sauce. Also, you may want to place the vegetables on the bottom of the pot with the chicken on top. This way, the vegetables cook more evenly and should be done about the same time as the chicken.

During the past few years, turkey parts have become very popular in our supermarkets. They are handy for small families or for those who don't want to worry about what to do with the remains of a huge Thanksgiving turkey.

Remember to buy turkey parts that will fit into your slow cooker. If the turkey bones make the cut too large, buy boneless parts or have the bones removed. Turkey legs, thighs and wings lend themselves especially well to this cooking method. They are tender, juicy and very flavorful.

Rounding out the poultry section are recipes for turkey sausage, Cornish hens, and duckling.

# Chinese Roast Chicken

*T*astes as good cold as it does hot—try it in a chicken salad.  ■ MAKES 4 TO 6 SERVINGS

6 to 8 fresh parsley sprigs
1 celery stalk
2 (2-inch) pieces gingerroot, peeled
2 green onions
1 (4- to 5-lb.) roasting chicken
1 tablespoon soy sauce
2 teaspoons Chinese five-spice powder

Place a trivet or steamer basket in a slow cooker. Place parsley, celery, ginger and green onions inside roasting chicken. Tie chicken legs together with string. In a cup, mix soy sauce and Chinese five-spice powder to make a paste. Spread mixture over chicken; place chicken, neck down, on trivet. Cover and cook on LOW 5 to 6 hours. Discard vegetables from inside chicken. Slice chicken to serve.

# Roasted Chicken with Rosemary and Garlic

*F*resh rosemary and garlic add great flavor to the chicken.  ■ MAKES ABOUT 6 SERVINGS

1 (4- to 5-lb.) whole roasting chicken
5 cloves garlic, halved
10 small sprigs of fresh rosemary

Remove excess fat from chicken. Remove giblets from chicken and refrigerate for another use. Rinse and drain chicken. Starting at neck cavity, carefully loosen skin from breast with your fingers or a knife by gently pushing between the skin and meat. Insert 2 garlic pieces and 2 rosemary sprigs under breast skin at edge of wings. Continue pulling skin and insert

2 rosemary sprigs and 2 garlic pieces under drumstick skin. Make a small slit in skin on each wing. Insert a garlic piece and a rosemary sprig into each. Insert 2 garlic pieces and 2 rosemary sprigs in body cavity. Tie legs together and wings close to body.

Place chicken, breast side down, in a 4- or 5-quart slow cooker. Cover and cook on LOW 6 or 7 hours or until juices are clear when thick part of chicken is pierced with a knife.

Remove chicken from slow cooker and discard garlic and rosemary. Cut chicken into individual pieces and serve.

Per serving: Cal 198 · Carb 1 gm · Prot 26 gm · Total fat 9 gm · Sat fat 3 gm · Cal from fat 81 · Chol 55 mg · Sodium 92 mg

# Potato- and Celery-Stuffed Chicken

*This* was a traditional family favorite at my friend Grace Wheeler's house when her children were growing up. ■ MAKES 4 TO 6 SERVINGS

1 (2½- to 3-lb.) whole broiler-fryer
  chicken
1 cup instant mashed-potato flakes
1 cup finely chopped celery
¼ cup finely chopped onion
1 tablespoon minced fresh parsley
2 tablespoons margarine, melted
½ teaspoon poultry seasoning

¼ teaspoon salt
¼ teaspoon ground black pepper
2 teaspoons olive oil
1 clove garlic, minced
Paprika, salt and ground black pepper
  for seasoning
Water
1 tablespoon cornstarch

Remove excess fat from chicken. Remove giblets from chicken and refrigerate for another use. Rinse and drain chicken. In a small bowl, combine potato flakes, celery, onion, parsley, margarine, poultry seasoning, salt and pepper. Spoon into chicken cavities. Secure openings with wooden picks. Tie legs together and wings close to body. Combine olive oil and garlic; rub on outside of chicken. Sprinkle with paprika, salt and pepper.

Place chicken, breast side up, in slow cooker. Cover and cook on LOW 5 to 6 hours or until juices are clear when thick part of chicken is pierced with a knife.

Remove chicken from cooker. Pour drippings into a 2-cup glass measuring cup; add enough water to equal 1 cup. Stir in cornstarch. Microwave on HIGH, stirring once, about 1½ minutes, or until slightly thickened. Skim off excess fat. Remove string and wooden picks from chicken. Carve and serve with dressing and gravy.

Per serving: Cal 589 · Carb 18 gm · Prot 58 gm · Total fat 30 gm · Sat fat 7 gm · Cal from fat 270 · Chol 124 mg · Sodium 456 mg

# Roasted Chicken Stuffed with Water Chestnuts and Bean Sprouts

If roasting chickens are not available at your market, purchase a large whole fryer.

■ MAKES 4 TO 6 SERVINGS

1 (5-lb.) whole roasting chicken
3 tablespoons soy sauce
1 (8-oz.) can water chestnuts, drained and chopped
1 cup (about 3 oz.) fresh bean sprouts
½ cup chopped celery
1 slice bread, toasted and chopped

Remove excess fat from chicken. Remove giblets from chicken and refrigerate for another use. Rinse and drain chicken. Set aside 1 tablespoon of the soy sauce. Combine remaining 2 tablespoons soy sauce with water chestnuts, bean sprouts, celery, and bread. Stuff mixture into chicken.

Place chicken, breast side down, in a 4- or 5-quart slow cooker. Brush chicken with reserved 1 tablespoon soy sauce. Cover and cook on LOW 4 or 5 hours or until juices are clear when thick part of chicken is pierced with a knife. Carve chicken and serve with stuffing.

Per serving: Cal 363 · Carb 9 gm · Prot 51 gm · Total fat 12 gm · Sat fat 3 gm · Cal from fat 108 · Chol 94 mg · Sodium 711 mg

# Cashew Chicken

*F*or an appetizing and colorful addition to this recipe, garnish each serving with thin slices of mango. ■ MAKES 5 TO 6 SERVINGS

6 boneless skinless chicken breast halves, cut into 1-inch strips (optional)
4 to 5 mushrooms, sliced
3 green onions, sliced into 1/2-inch pieces
1/4 cup soy sauce
2 teaspoons grated gingerroot
1/2 cup chicken broth
1/4 teaspoon salt

1/8 teaspoon pepper
1 (8-oz.) can sliced bamboo shoots, drained
1/2 cup toasted cashews (see Note, page 3)
1/2 cup Chinese pea pods
2 tablespoons cornstarch
3 tablespoons water
Cooked rice

Place chicken and mushrooms in a slow cooker. Add green onions, soy sauce, ginger, broth, salt and pepper. Cover and cook on LOW about 4 hours. Add bamboo shoots, cashews and pea pods; turn control to HIGH. In a small bowl, dissolve cornstarch in water. Stir into chicken mixture in cooker. Cover and cook on HIGH 20 to 30 minutes or until thickened, stirring at least once. Serve over cooked rice.

# Caribbean "Jerked" Chicken

※※※※※※※※※※※※※※※※※※※※※※※※※※※※※※※※※※※※※※

*T*o crisp the "jerked" coating on the cooked chicken, broil or grill for several minutes or until bubbly. ■ MAKES 5 SERVINGS

½ cup sliced green onions
2 tablespoons grated gingerroot
1 teaspoon ground allspice
3 fresh jalapeño chiles, seeded and
   coarsely chopped
1 teaspoon vegetable oil
2 teaspoons seasoned pepper

½ teaspoon salt
1 clove garlic
1 tablespoon honey
5 chicken thighs and drumsticks
   (joined together)
Cooked rice
Papaya (optional), peeled and sliced

In a blender or food processor, combine onions, ginger, allspice, jalapeño chiles, oil, seasoned pepper, salt and garlic. Process until finely chopped. Stir in honey to form a paste. Brush on all sides of chicken. Place a rack in a slow cooker. Place chicken on rack. Cover and cook on LOW 4 to 4½ hours or until chicken is tender. Serve with rice. Garnish with papaya, if desired.

# Honey-Hoisin Chicken

※※※※※※※※※※※※※※※※※※※※※※※※※※※※※※※※※※※※※※※※※※

*T*he combination of Asian ingredients with traditional seasonings results in an exciting flavor for an attractive main dish. ■ MAKES 5 TO 6 SERVINGS

| | |
|---|---|
| 2½ to 3 lb. chicken pieces | ¼ teaspoon salt |
| 2 tablespoons soy sauce | ⅛ teaspoon ground black pepper |
| 2 tablespoons hoisin sauce | 2 tablespoons cornstarch |
| 2 tablespoons honey | 2 tablespoons cold water |
| 2 tablespoons dry white wine | Toasted sesame seeds (see Note, |
| 1 tablespoon grated gingerroot | below) |

Rinse chicken and pat dry with paper towels. Combine soy sauce, hoisin sauce, honey, wine, ginger, salt and pepper. Dip each piece of chicken into sauce; then place in a 3½-quart slow cooker. Pour remaining sauce over chicken. Cover and cook on LOW about 4 or 5 hours or until chicken is tender.

Turn control to HIGH. Remove chicken from slow cooker and keep warm. Dissolve cornstarch in cold water. Stir mixture into juices in slow cooker. Cover and cook on HIGH 15 to 20 minutes or until slightly thickened. Spoon sauce over chicken and sprinkle with sesame seeds.

Per serving: Cal 243 · Carb 11 gm · Prot 30 gm · Total fat 7 gm · Sat fat 2 gm · Cal from fat 63 · Chol 56 mg · Sodium 630 mg

NOTE: To toast sesame seeds, spread seeds in a 9-inch pie or cake pan. Heat in a 350F (175C) oven about 5 minutes or until golden. Or toast seeds in a dry skillet over low heat 3 or 4 minutes.

# Raspberried Drumsticks

*T*his is an ideal dish to prepare at home and take to a potluck supper. ■ MAKES 5 MAIN-DISH
SERVINGS OR 10 POTLUCK SERVINGS

5 drumsticks with thighs attached
3 tablespoons soy sauce
⅓ cup red raspberry fruit spread or
  jam
1 teaspoon prepared mustard

¼ teaspoon ground black pepper
2 tablespoons cornstarch
2 tablespoons cold water
Cooked rice

Rinse chicken and pat dry with paper towels. In a small bowl, combine soy sauce, fruit
spread, mustard and pepper. Brush soy mixture on chicken. Place chicken in a 3½-quart
slow cooker. Pour remaining soy mixture over chicken. Cover and cook on LOW 5 to 6
hours or until chicken is tender.

Remove chicken from slow cooker and keep warm. Turn control to HIGH. In a small
bowl, dissolve cornstarch in cold water. Stir into cooking juices in slow cooker. Cook on
HIGH, stirring occasionally, 10 to 15 minutes or until thickened. Spoon over chicken.
Serve over cooked rice.

Per serving without rice: Cal 356 · Carb 10 gm · Prot 30 gm · Total fat 20 gm ·
Sat fat 6 gm · Cal from fat 180 · Chol 83 mg · Sodium 780 mg

# Old-Fashioned Chicken 'n' Noodles

×◇×◇×◇×◇×◇×◇×◇×◇×◇×◇×◇×◇×◇×◇×◇×◇×◇×◇×◇×◇×◇×◇×◇×◇×◇×◇×◇×◇×◇×◇×◇×

*R*eminiscent of grandma's house, this dish is easy to put together in your slow cooker.

■ MAKES 6 TO 8 SERVINGS

| | |
|---|---|
| 2½ to 3 lb. chicken pieces | ½ teaspoon chopped fresh thyme |
| 1 small onion, finely chopped | 1 (10½-oz.) can condensed chicken |
| ½ cup thinly sliced celery | broth |
| 1 clove garlic, minced | ¼ cup cornstarch |
| ½ teaspoon salt | ⅓ cup cold water |
| ⅛ teaspoon ground black pepper | 8 to 12 ounces medium egg noodles |
| ½ teaspoon poultry seasoning | Chopped fresh parsley |

Rinse chicken and pat dry with paper towels. Combine chicken, onion, celery, garlic, salt, pepper, poultry seasoning and thyme in a 3½-quart slow cooker. Add chicken broth. Cover and cook on low 4 or 5 hours or until chicken is tender.

Remove chicken from slow cooker. Discard skin and bones; cut chicken into bite-size pieces and set aside.

Turn control to HIGH. Dissolve cornstarch in cold water. Stir into juices in slow cooker. Cover and cook on HIGH 15 to 20 minutes or until slightly thickened. Stir in chicken.

Meanwhile, cook noodles according to package directions and drain. Spoon mixture over cooked noodles. Sprinkle with chopped parsley.

Per serving: Cal 477 · Carb 35 gm · Prot 45 gm · Total fat 16 gm · Sat fat 4 gm · Cal from fat 144 · Chol 83 mg · Sodium 638 mg

# Kowloon Chicken

XXXXXXXXXXXXXXXXXXXXXXXXXXXXXXXXXXXXXXXXXXXXXXXXXXXXXXXXX

*T*he success of this popular dish depends on the contrast of the ginger and soy with the sweet mango flavor. ■ MAKES 5 TO 6 SERVINGS

3 to 3½ lb. chicken parts
1 teaspoon grated gingerroot
1 clove garlic, minced
1 cup chicken broth
¼ teaspoon salt
⅛ teaspoon pepper
1 mango, peeled and diced

1 (4-oz.) can sliced water chestnuts, drained
4 green onions, diagonally sliced
¼ cup cornstarch
¼ cup soy sauce
Cooked rice or noodles

Place chicken in a slow cooker. In a small bowl, combine ginger, garlic, broth, salt and pepper. Pour mixture over chicken. Cover and cook on LOW 4½ to 5 hours or until chicken is tender. Turn control to HIGH. Add mango, water chestnuts and green onions. In a small bowl, dissolve cornstarch in soy sauce; stir into cooking juices in cooker. Cover and cook on HIGH 15 to 20 minutes or until slightly thickened. Serve with cooked rice or noodles.

# Soy Chicken Legs

So quick and easy to put together, it cooks without any attention and is then enjoyed at dinnertime. ■ MAKES 5 TO 6 SERVINGS

5 or 6 chicken drumsticks with thighs attached
½ cup soy sauce
¼ cup packed light brown sugar
1 clove garlic, crushed
1 (8-oz.) can tomato sauce
1 tablespoon toasted sesame seeds (see Note, page 166)

Rinse chicken and pat dry with paper towels. Place chicken in a 3½-quart slow cooker. In a medium bowl, combine soy sauce, brown sugar, garlic and tomato sauce. Pour sauce over chicken. Cover and cook on LOW about 5 hours or until chicken is tender.

Remove to a platter; sprinkle with sesame seeds.

Per serving: Cal 393 · Carb 17 gm · Prot 32 gm · Total fat 21 gm · Sat fat 6 gm · Cal from fat 189 · Chol 83 mg · Sodium 2055 mg

# Chicken Cacciatore

XXXXXXXXXXXXXXXXXXXXXXXXXXXXXXXXXXXXXXXXXXXXXXXXXXXXXXX

*F*or a change serve this dish over strands of steamed spaghetti squash. The texture and colors are great together. ■ MAKES 5 TO 6 SERVINGS

1 (2½- to 3½-lb.) broiler-fryer
  chicken, cut up
1 onion, chopped
1 teaspoon dried basil or oregano
½ teaspoon lemon pepper
¼ teaspoon salt
2 garlic cloves, minced

¼ cup rosé wine
1 tablespoon sugar
½ green bell pepper, sliced
1 (8-oz.) can tomato sauce
1 cup sliced fresh mushrooms
Cooked pasta

Combine all ingredients except mushrooms and pasta in a slow cooker. Cover and cook on LOW 5 to 6 hours. Turn control to HIGH and add mushrooms. Cover and cook about 10 minutes. Serve over pasta.

# Chicken and Mango with Ginger-Curry Topping

*A* combination of popular tropical flavors results in a new way to present chicken.

■ MAKES 5 TO 6 SERVINGS

1 large mango
2 teaspoons fresh lemon juice
1 teaspoon honey
1 clove garlic, crushed

⅛ teaspoon paprika
¼ teaspoon salt
⅛ teaspoon ground black pepper
2½ to 3 lb. chicken pieces

GINGER-CURRY TOPPING

⅓ cup plain low-fat yogurt
¼ teaspoon curry powder
¼ teaspoon grated gingerroot

1 teaspoon brown sugar
⅛ teaspoon grated orange peel

Peel mango and remove flesh from seed; mash in a small bowl. Stir in lemon juice, honey, garlic, paprika, salt and pepper. Rinse chicken and pat dry with paper towels. Place chicken in a 3½-quart slow cooker. Spoon mango mixture over chicken. Cover and cook on LOW about 4 hours or until chicken is tender. While chicken cooks, prepare Ginger-Curry Topping.

To serve, arrange chicken in a serving dish and spoon drippings over chicken. Top each serving with a dab of Ginger Curry Topping.

# Ginger-Curry Topping

Combine ingredients in a small bowl and refrigerate.

Per serving: Cal 333 · Carb 9 gm · Prot 38 gm · Total fat 15 gm · Sat fat 4 gm · Cal from fat 135 · Chol 83 mg · Sodium 236 mg

# Venetian Chicken

*R*obust flavors of sun-dried tomatoes and mushrooms complement the chicken. ▪ MAKES
5 TO 6 SERVINGS

1 teaspoon sweet paprika
1/4 cup all-purpose flour
1 teaspoon dried basil
1/4 teaspoon salt
1/4 teaspoon pepper
1 (2 1/2- to 3 1/2-lb.) broiler-fryer
   chicken, cut up
3 to 4 dried mushrooms
1/4 cup chopped sun-dried tomatoes

1 small onion, chopped
2 tablespoons red wine (optional)
1 (8-oz.) can tomato sauce
1 tablespoon freshly grated lemon
   peel
Cooked pasta
Grated Parmesan cheese
Chopped fresh parsley

In a large bowl, combine paprika, flour, basil, salt and pepper. Coat chicken pieces with
mixture; set aside. Rinse mushrooms and break into small pieces; remove and discard thick
stems. Place mushrooms, sun-dried tomatoes and onion in a slow cooker. Place chicken
pieces on top. In a bowl, combine wine, if using, tomato sauce and lemon peel; pour over
chicken. Cover and cook on LOW 5 to 6 hours or until chicken is tender. Serve over pasta;
top with Parmesan cheese and parsley.

# Plum-Glazed Chicken

*T*ender pieces of chicken are seasoned with a sweet-sour plum sauce. ■ MAKES 5 TO 6 SERVINGS

| | |
|---|---|
| 2½ to 3 lb. chicken pieces, skinned | ¼ teaspoon ground allspice |
| ½ cup plum preserves | ¼ teaspoon ground black pepper |
| ¼ cup minced onion | Hot cooked rice |
| 1 clove garlic, minced | 1 tablespoon cornstarch |
| 3 tablespoons chili sauce | 2 tablespoons dry sherry |
| 2 tablespoons balsamic vinegar | Diagonally sliced green onions, |
| 1 tablespoon soy sauce | including some tops |
| ½ teaspoon ground ginger | |

Rinse chicken and pat dry with paper towels. Place half of chicken in a 3½-quart slow cooker. In a small bowl, combine preserves, onion, garlic, chili sauce, vinegar, soy sauce, ginger, allspice and pepper. Spoon half of the mixture over chicken in slow cooker. Top with remaining chicken; then remaining preserves mixture. Cover and cook on LOW 7 to 8 hours or until chicken is tender.

Arrange chicken pieces over hot cooked rice. Skim fat from cooking juices and discard. Pour remaining liquid into a small saucepan. Dissolve cornstarch in sherry. Stir into cooking juices; cook, stirring constantly, over medium-high heat until thickened slightly. Pour glaze over chicken and sprinkle with green onions.

Per serving: Cal 478 · Carb 29 gm · Prot 46 gm · Total fat 17 gm · Sat fat 5 gm · Cal from fat 153 · Chol 99 mg · Sodium 496 mg

# Orange and Ginger Chicken

*T*he flavors of this dish are similar to those of favorite traditional Asian chicken recipes but require a lot less work.  ■ MAKES 5 TO 6 SERVINGS

2 to 3 lb. chicken pieces
1 (8-oz.) can sliced water chestnuts, drained
½ cup orange juice
1 teaspoon grated orange peel
3 tablespoons soy sauce

2 teaspoons grated gingerroot
1 clove garlic, crushed
3 tablespoons cornstarch
3 tablespoons cold water
Cooked rice

Rinse chicken and pat dry with paper towels. Place chicken pieces in a 3½-quart slow cooker. Top with water chestnuts. In a small bowl, combine orange juice, orange peel, soy sauce, ginger and garlic. Pour over chicken. Cover and cook on low about 4 hours or until chicken is tender.

Remove chicken and water chestnuts and keep warm. Dissolve cornstarch in water; stir into cooking juices in slow cooker. Cover and cook on HIGH, stirring occasionally, 10 to 15 minutes or until slightly thickened. Spoon sauce over chicken and rice.

Per serving without rice: Cal 362 · Carb 14 gm · Prot 36 gm · Total fat 17 gm · Sat fat 5 gm · Cal from fat 153 · Chol 83 mg · Sodium 758 mg

# Chicken Tetrazzini

*T*he chicken absorbs interesting flavors from other ingredients in the slow cooker. Add finishing touches at the last minute. ■ MAKES 5 TO 6 SERVINGS

4 boneless skinless chicken breast
   halves, cut into 2 × ½-inch strips
1 cup chicken broth
½ cup dry white wine
1 onion, finely chopped
½ teaspoon salt
¼ teaspoon dried thyme
¼ teaspoon pepper

2 tablespoons minced fresh parsley
6 to 8 mushrooms, sliced
3 tablespoons cornstarch
¼ cup water
½ cup half-and-half
8 oz. spaghetti, broken into 2-inch
   pieces, cooked and drained
½ cup grated Parmesan cheese

In a slow cooker, combine chicken, broth, wine, onion, salt, thyme, pepper and parsley. Cover and cook on LOW 4 to 5 hours. Turn control to HIGH. Add mushrooms. In a small bowl, dissolve cornstarch in water; stir into slow cooker. Cover and cook on HIGH 20 minutes. Stir in half-and-half, cooked spaghetti, and half the cheese. Cover and heat on HIGH 5 to 10 minutes. Spoon into serving dish; sprinkle with remaining cheese.

Top to bottom: Greek Lamb, Vegetables, and Feta Cheese (page 132) with couscous and pita bread, and Cranberry-Port Pork Roast (page 119) with steamed asparagus

Left to right: Three-Pepper Steak (page 98) with rice, and Jicama-Cilantro Round Steak (page 93) with steamed baby carrots

Clockwise from top: Taste-of-Italy Beans 'n' Sausage (page 154), Curried Lentils and Vegetables (page 160), and Cannellini and Salmon Salad Toss (page 150)

Clockwise from left: Sunshine Carrot Pudding with Lemon Sauce (page 190), Rhubarb-Apple Compote (page 186), and Garden of Eden Apples (page 194)

# Chicken with Cabbage and Apples

✕◇✕◇✕◇✕◇✕◇✕◇✕◇✕◇✕◇✕◇✕◇✕◇✕◇✕◇✕◇✕◇✕◇✕◇✕◇✕◇✕◇✕◇✕◇✕◇✕◇✕◇✕◇✕◇✕◇✕◇✕◇✕◇

*R*ice or noodles are the perfect accompaniment for dishes with Asian-accented seasonings. ■ MAKES ABOUT 5 SERVINGS

3 to 3½ lb. chicken pieces
½ head cabbage, shredded (about 3 cups)
1 small onion, sliced
2 apples, cored and cut into wedges
2 tablespoons soy sauce
2 teaspoons grated fresh gingerroot
⅛ teaspoon red pepper flakes

Rinse chicken and pat dry with paper towels. Place cabbage in bottom of a 3½-quart slow cooker. Top with onion, chicken and apples. Combine soy sauce, ginger and pepper flakes. Spoon over chicken and vegetables. Cover and cook on LOW about 6 hours or until chicken is tender.

Per serving: Cal 492 · Carb 13 gm · Prot 55 gm · Total fat 23 gm · Sat fat 6 gm · Cal from fat 207 · Chol 122 mg · Sodium 622 mg

# Cranberry-Orange Chicken

⬥⬥⬥⬥⬥⬥⬥⬥⬥⬥⬥⬥⬥⬥⬥⬥⬥⬥⬥⬥⬥⬥⬥⬥⬥⬥⬥⬥⬥⬥⬥⬥⬥⬥⬥⬥⬥⬥⬥⬥⬥

*T*o reduce fat, remove and discard the skin from the chicken before cooking. ■ MAKES ABOUT 6 SERVINGS

2½ to 3 lb. chicken pieces
1 (8-oz.) can whole-berry cranberry
    sauce
2 tablespoons orange juice
1 teaspoon grated orange peel
⅛ teaspoon ground nutmeg

1 tablespoon sweet-hot mustard
½ teaspoon salt
⅛ teaspoon ground black pepper
3 tablespoons cornstarch
3 tablespoons cold water

Rinse chicken and pat dry with paper towels. Place cut-up chicken in a 3½-quart slow cooker. In small bowl, combine cranberry sauce, orange juice and peel, nutmeg, mustard, salt and pepper. Stir until blended but not smooth. Pour over chicken. Cover and cook on LOW for 4 or 5 hours or until chicken is tender.

Remove chicken and keep warm. Turn control to HIGH. Dissolve cornstarch in water. Stir into pot with juices. Cook on HIGH, stirring occasionally, 10 to 15 minutes or until thickened. Spoon over chicken.

Per serving: Cal 370 · Carb 19 gm · Prot 38 gm · Total fat 14 gm · Sat fat 4 gm · Cal from fat 126 · Chol 83 mg · Sodium 333 mg

# Arroz con Pollo

*A* delightful chicken and rice dish from Spain and Mexico is very popular here. ▪ MAKES 4 TO 5 SERVINGS

½ teaspoon salt
¼ teaspoon pepper
1 clove garlic, crushed
1 teaspoon dried oregano
2 teaspoons chili powder
1 (2½- to 3½-lb.) broiler-fryer
   chicken, cut up

½ cup chicken broth
2 tablespoons red wine
1 (10-oz.) package frozen green peas,
   thawed
½ cup pimiento-stuffed olives
2 cups cooked rice
2 tablespoons chopped fresh cilantro

In a small bowl, combine salt, pepper, garlic, oregano and chili powder. Sprinkle spice mixture over both sides of chicken pieces. Place chicken in a slow cooker. Pour broth and wine over chicken. Cover and cook on LOW 5 to 6 hours. Remove chicken and cover to keep warm. Turn control to HIGH. Add peas and olives. Cover and cook on HIGH 7 to 10 minutes. Stir in cooked rice and chicken until combined. Sprinkle with cilantro and serve.

# Peanut Butter 'n' Ginger Chicken

*A* whisk is the best tool to efficiently mix the sauce. ■ MAKES 5 TO 6 SERVINGS

3½ lb. chicken pieces
¼ cup peanut butter
2 tablespoons soy sauce
1 teaspoon grated gingerroot
½ teaspoon grated orange peel

2 tablespoons orange juice
⅛ teaspoon hot sauce
2 green onions, including some green
   tops, sliced
Cooked noodles or rice

Rinse chicken and pat dry with paper towels. Place chicken in a 3½-quart slow cooker. In a small bowl, whisk together peanut butter, soy sauce, ginger, orange peel, juice and hot sauce until well blended. Stir in green onions. Spoon over chicken. Cover and cook on LOW about 5 hours or until chicken is tender.

Serve chicken over cooked noodles or rice.

Per serving without noodles: Cal 606 · Carb 4 gm · Prot 65 gm · Total fat 35 gm · Sat fat 9 gm · Cal from fat 315 · Chol 144 mg · Sodium 709 mg

# Chile-Citrus Chicken with Sun-Dried Tomatoes

*H*ot chile adds a spark to a traditional chicken dish that's good with noodles or rice.

■ MAKES 5 TO 6 SERVINGS

3 lb. chicken pieces
6 dried tomato halves, coarsely chopped
1 small dried red chile, seeded and finely chopped
2 green onions, including some tops, sliced

½ teaspoon salt
½ cup orange juice
1 teaspoon grated orange peel
2 tablespoons cornstarch
2 tablespoons cold water

Rinse chicken and pat dry with paper towels. Place chicken in a 3½-quart slow cooker. In a medium bowl, combine tomatoes, chile, green onions, salt, orange juice and orange peel. Stir until blended. Pour over chicken. Cover and cook on LOW 4 to 5 hours or until chicken is tender.

Remove chicken and keep warm. Dissolve cornstarch in water. Stir into the cooking juices in slow cooker. Cook on HIGH 15 to 20 minutes or until slightly thickened. Spoon over chicken.

Per serving: Cal 478 · Carb 9 gm · Prot 54 gm · Total fat 23 gm · Sat fat 6 gm · Cal from fat 207 · Chol 121 mg · Sodium 421 mg

# Peanutty Chicken 'n' Rice

*T*he peanut mixture will be rather thick when spread on the chicken, but it is thinned down during the cooking process and can be spooned over the finished dish.  ■ MAKES 4 TO 6 SERVINGS

3½ lb. chicken pieces
½ cup roasted shelled peanuts
2 tablespoons soy sauce
1 clove garlic
⅛ teaspoon red pepper flakes
1 tablespoon red wine vinegar
Cooked rice

Rinse chicken and pat dry with paper towels. Place chicken in a 3½-quart slow cooker. Combine peanuts, soy sauce, garlic, red pepper flakes and red wine vinegar in a blender. Process until finely chopped. Spread sauce over chicken. Cover and cook on low about 5 hours or until chicken is tender.

Spoon chicken and cooking juices over cooked rice.

Per serving without rice: Cal 765 · Carb 5 gm · Prot 82 gm · Total fat 44 gm · Sat fat 11 gm · Cal from fat 396 · Chol 180 mg · Sodium 811 mg

# Touch-of-the-Orient Chicken Rolls

*I*ndividually wrapped servings of chicken make an unusual presentation on a bed of cooked rice. ■ MAKES 6 SERVINGS

¼ cup soy sauce
1 tablespoon sesame oil
¼ teaspoon dried red pepper flakes
1 tablespoon chopped chives
2 tablespoons chopped fresh cilantro
2 teaspoons grated gingerroot
1 (8-oz.) can sliced water chestnuts, drained

6 boneless skinless chicken breast halves
6 large lettuce leaves
3 tablespoons cornstarch
¼ cup water
1 (10-oz.) can mandarin oranges, drained

In a medium bowl, combine soy sauce, sesame oil, pepper flakes, chives, cilantro, ginger and water chestnuts; set aside. Wrap each chicken piece in a lettuce leaf; place in a slow cooker. Pour sauce with water chestnuts over chicken. Cover and cook on LOW 4 to 4½ hours or until chicken is tender. Remove chicken and cover to keep warm. Turn control to HIGH. In a small bowl, dissolve cornstarch in water; stir into sauce in cooker. Cover and cook on HIGH 15 to 20 minutes or until slightly thickened. Stir in oranges. To serve, spoon sauce over each serving.

# Chicken Chop Suey

*N*o need to buy takeout chop suey—make this dish, bring out the chopsticks, and enjoy.

■ MAKES 5 TO 6 SERVINGS

2 boneless skinless chicken breast
   halves
1/2 cup chopped celery
4 green onions, cut into 1-inch pieces
1/2 teaspoon salt
1 tablespoon chopped gingerroot
2/3 cup chicken broth
1/4 cup soy sauce

1/2 teaspoon sugar
1 cup sliced fresh mushrooms
1 cup fresh bean sprouts
1 teaspoon sesame oil
2 tablespoons cornstarch
2 tablespoons water
Cooked rice

Cut chicken into strips about 1½ inches long and ¼ inch wide. Place in a slow cooker with celery, green onions, salt and ginger. In a small bowl, combine broth, soy sauce and sugar; pour mixture over chicken. Cover and cook on LOW 5 to 6 hours. Turn control to HIGH. Add mushrooms and bean sprouts. Cover and cook on HIGH about 5 minutes. Drizzle sesame oil over mixture; stir to mix. Dissolve cornstarch in water and stir into chicken mixture in cooker. Cover and cook on HIGH 10 to 15 minutes. Serve with cooked rice.

# Spiced Chicken with Brown Rice

*A* yogurt-orange sauce laced with an intriguing blend of spices is spooned over chicken and brown rice, giving this dish the flavors of India.  ◗ MAKES 4 TO 5 SERVINGS

6 boneless, skinless chicken thighs
1/4 teaspoon salt
1/2 teaspoon ground black pepper
1/4 teaspoon paprika
1 small onion, chopped
1 large clove garlic, finely minced or crushed
1 teaspoon sugar
1/2 teaspoon ground coriander

1/2 teaspoon ground cumin
1/8 teaspoon ground cardamom
1 1/2 teaspoons grated orange peel
1/3 cup orange juice
1 tablespoon cornstarch
1/2 cup plain nonfat yogurt
2 cups cooked brown rice
Chopped fresh cilantro

Rinse chicken and pat dry with paper towels. Remove any excess fat from chicken. Tuck ends under on each thigh to make a small bundle. Place, seam side down, on bottom of a slow cooker. Sprinkle with salt, pepper and paprika. Combine onion, garlic, sugar, coriander, cumin, cardamom, orange peel and orange juice in a small bowl. Spoon evenly over chicken. Cover and cook on LOW about 4 hours or until chicken is tender.

Remove chicken from slow cooker and keep warm. Pour cooking juices into a small saucepan. Combine cornstarch with yogurt in a small bowl. Stir into pan juices. Cook over medium heat, stirring constantly, until mixture thickens slightly.

Place chicken on cooked rice; spoon sauce over all. Sprinkle with cilantro.

Per serving: Cal 276 · Carb 31 gm · Prot 25 gm · Total fat 5 gm · Sat fat 1 gm · Cal from fat 45 · Chol 87 mg · Sodium 412 mg

# Curried Island Chicken

*L*et people choose their favorite combination of toppings.  ■ MAKES 4 TO 5 SERVINGS

1 (2½- to 3½-lb.) broiler-fryer
    chicken, cut up
1 (8-oz.) can pineapple chunks in
    juice
4 teaspoons curry powder
1 clove garlic, crushed
1 teaspoon chicken bouillon granules
1 tablespoon grated onion

½ teaspoon salt
⅛ teaspoon pepper
2 tablespoons cornstarch
2 tablespoons water
3 cups cooked rice
Shredded coconut, dates, raisins
    and/or chopped banana or papaya
Favorite chutney

Place chicken in a slow cooker. Drain pineapple and reserve juice and chunks separately. In a small bowl, combine reserved juice with curry powder, garlic, bouillon granules, onion, salt and pepper. Pour mixture over chicken. Cover and cook on LOW 4½ to 5 hours or until chicken is tender. Remove chicken from pot and keep warm. Turn control to HIGH. In a small bowl, dissolve cornstarch in water; stir cornstarch mixture and reserved pineapple chunks into slow cooker. Cover and cook on HIGH 15 to 20 minutes. Serve chicken and sauce over cooked rice. Sprinkle with your choice of accompaniments.

# Chicken with Fresh Herbs

XXXXXXXXXXXXXXXXXXXXXXXXXXXXXXXXXXXXXXXXXXXXXXXXXXXXXXXXX

*T*he chicken is seasoned with fresh herbs and layered with fresh vegetables. ■ MAKES 6 SERVINGS

2 leeks, sliced and rinsed
6 boneless, skinless chicken breast
  halves or thighs
4 ears of corn
1 large carrot, shredded
2 tomatoes, coarsely chopped

2 teaspoons chopped fresh oregano
1 teaspoon chopped fresh thyme
½ teaspoon salt
¼ teaspoon ground black pepper
1 clove garlic, crushed

Place leeks on bottom of a slow cooker. Top with chicken. Cut corn kernels off the cobs. Sprinkle corn over chicken. Layer carrot over corn and chicken. Combine tomatoes, oregano, thyme, salt, pepper and garlic in a small bowl. Spoon into slow cooker. Cover and cook on LOW about 5 hours or until chicken is tender.

Per serving: Cal 197 · Carb 15 gm · Prot 29 gm · Total fat 2 gm · Sat fat 0 gm · Cal from fat 18 · Chol 41 mg · Sodium 274 mg

# Creamy Chicken 'n' Leeks

*I*f desired, use thighs for guests who prefer dark pieces of chicken. ■ MAKES 8 SERVINGS

8 boneless, skinless chicken breast
 halves
½ teaspoon salt
⅛ teaspoon ground black pepper
3 leeks, cut into 1-inch crosswise
 pieces and rinsed

¼ cup dried currants
¼ cup dry white wine
½ cup fat-free chicken broth
¼ cup cornstarch
½ cup nonfat milk

Rinse chicken and pat dry with paper towels. Sprinkle chicken with salt and pepper. Place leeks in bottom of a slow cooker. Top with chicken breasts and currants. Add wine and broth. Cover and cook on LOW 6 to 7 hours or until chicken is tender.

Turn control to HIGH. Remove chicken, leeks and currants; keep warm. In a small bowl, dissolve cornstarch in milk; gradually stir into cooking juices in slow cooker. Cover and cook on HIGH, stirring occasionally, about 15 minutes or until thickened. Serve over cooked chicken mixture.

Per serving: Cal 198 · Carb 14 gm · Prot 29 gm · Total fat 1 gm · Sat fat 0 gm · Cal from fat 9 · Chol 41 mg · Sodium 262 mg

# Mission Chicken

※※※※※※※※※※※※※※※※※※※※※※※※※※※※※※※※※※※※※※※※※※※

*S*eedless grapes and almonds add crunch to the slightly spicy orange sauce. ■ MAKES 4 TO 5 SERVINGS

1 (2½- to 3½-lb.) broiler-fryer
   chicken, cut up
¼ teaspoon ground cinnamon
¼ teaspoon ground cloves
¼ teaspoon salt
½ teaspoon seasoned salt
¼ teaspoon lemon pepper
1 (6-oz.) can frozen orange juice
   concentrate, thawed

2 or 3 drops hot pepper sauce
3 tablespoons cornstarch
3 tablespoons water
1 cup seedless grapes, halved
¼ cup toasted slivered almonds
   (see Note, page 3)

Place chicken in a slow cooker. In a small bowl, combine cinnamon, cloves, salt, seasoned salt, lemon pepper, orange juice concentrate and hot pepper sauce. Pour mixture over chicken. Cover and cook on LOW about 5 hours or until chicken is tender. Turn control to HIGH. In a small bowl, dissolve cornstarch in water; stir into cooking juices in cooker. Cover and cook on HIGH 15 to 20 minutes or until thickened. Stir in grapes. Sprinkle with almonds.

# Thai Chicken

*T*urmeric turns this dish a beautiful golden color, and peanuts add crunchiness. Adjust the seasonings to suit your taste.  ■ MAKES 8 SERVINGS

| | |
|---|---|
| 4 whole chicken breasts | 1 (8-oz.) can pineapple chunks, |
| 1 tablespoon grated gingerroot | drained |
| 3 green onions, sliced | 2 tablespoons cornstarch |
| 1 (14-oz.) can coconut milk | 2 tablespoons water |
| ½ to ¾ teaspoon turmeric | Cooked rice |
| ¼ to ½ teaspoon dried red pepper | ½ cup chopped peanuts |
| flakes | |

Cut chicken breasts in half, making 8 pieces. Place chicken in a slow cooker. Add ginger, green onions, coconut milk, turmeric and pepper flakes. Cover and cook on LOW 4 to 5 hours or until chicken is tender. Turn control to HIGH; add pineapple. In a small bowl, dissolve cornstarch in water; stir into chicken mixture in cooker. Cover and cook on HIGH about 15 minutes. Serve over rice and sprinkle with peanuts.

# Savory Chicken and Vegetables

✖✖✖✖✖✖✖✖✖✖✖✖✖✖✖✖✖✖✖✖✖✖✖✖✖✖✖✖✖✖✖✖✖✖✖✖✖✖✖✖✖✖✖✖✖

*A* delicious way to eat and enjoy your vegetables. ■ MAKES 5 TO 6 SERVINGS

1 lb. boneless, skinless chicken breasts, cut into bite-size pieces
1 (16-oz.) package frozen mixed vegetables
1 small onion, chopped
1 cup sliced fresh mushrooms
1 large potato, peeled and cut into ¼-inch cubes
1¼ cups water
2 tablespoons quick-cooking tapioca

1 tablespoon fresh lemon juice
2 teaspoons chicken bouillon granules
½ teaspoon ground white pepper
¼ teaspoon ground mustard
¼ teaspoon crushed sage
¼ teaspoon salt
⅛ teaspoon garlic powder
Pinch of turmeric
⅓ cup nonfat dry milk powder
Fresh minced parsley

Rinse chicken and pat dry with paper towels. Combine chicken, mixed vegetables, onion, mushrooms and potato in a 3½-quart slow cooker. In a small bowl, combine water, tapioca, lemon juice, bouillon granules, white pepper, mustard, sage, salt, garlic powder and turmeric. Pour over chicken mixture. Mix well. Cover and cook on LOW 6 to 7 hours.

Stir in dry milk and cook 15 minutes. Sprinkle each serving with parsley.

Per serving: Cal 237 · Carb 30 gm · Prot 26 gm · Total fat 1 gm · Sat fat 0 gm · Cal from fat 9 · Chol 32 mg · Sodium 225 mg

# Nostalgic Chicken & Herbed Dumplings

*T*his dish is a time-honored favorite that's designed for today's busy families. ■ MAKES 5 TO 6 SERVINGS

2 whole cloves
8 to 10 small white onions, halved
1 (2½- to 3½-lb.) broiler-fryer
  chicken, cut up
½ teaspoon salt
¼ teaspoon pepper
1 clove garlic, minced
½ teaspoon dried marjoram, crushed
½ teaspoon dried thyme, crushed

1 bay leaf
½ cup chicken broth
½ cup dry white wine
3 tablespoons cornstarch
¼ cup water
1 cup packaged biscuit mix
1 tablespoon chopped fresh parsley
6 tablespoons milk

Insert cloves in one onion. Place all onions in a slow cooker. Add chicken, salt, pepper, garlic, marjoram, thyme, bay leaf, broth and wine. Cover and cook on LOW 4 to 5 hours or until chicken is tender. Remove bay leaf and onion with cloves; discard. Turn control to HIGH. In a small bowl, dissolve cornstarch in water; stir into chicken mixture in cooker. Cover and cook while making dumplings; stir once. In a medium bowl, combine biscuit mix with parsley and milk, mixing with a fork until moistened. Drop by teaspoonfuls on chicken mixture around edges of pot. Cover and cook on HIGH 30 minutes or until dumplings are cooked in centers when tested with a fork.

# Tarragon Chicken Thighs

Cooked chicken thighs are moist and juicy and rich with flavor. ■ MAKES 8 SERVINGS

½ teaspoon salt
⅛ teaspoon pepper
¼ cup margarine or butter, melted
1 tablespoon plus 1 teaspoon finely chopped fresh tarragon
8 chicken thighs

1 large tomato, peeled, seeded and chopped
1 green onion, chopped
¼ cup dry white wine
2 tablespoons cornstarch
½ cup half-and-half

In a medium bowl, combine salt, pepper, margarine or butter and 1 tablespoon tarragon. Roll chicken pieces in melted butter mixture. Place in a slow cooker. Top with tomato, onion and wine. Cover and cook on LOW 5 to 6 hours. Remove chicken and cover to keep warm. Turn control to HIGH. In a small bowl, dissolve cornstarch in half-and-half; stir into cooking juices in cooker. Cover and cook on HIGH 20 minutes or until thickened. Add remaining teaspoon of fresh tarragon. Spoon sauce over chicken.

# Red & Gold Sweet-Sour Chicken

*You'll* be proud to present this colorful dish on a bed of rice. ■ MAKES 4 TO 6 SERVINGS

1 (2½- to 3½-lb.) broiler-fryer
    chicken, cut up
1 small onion, thinly sliced
1 cup chicken broth
¼ cup packed brown sugar
¼ cup vinegar
1 tablespoon hoisin sauce

½ teaspoon salt
⅓ cup cornstarch
⅓ cup water
1 red bell pepper, cut into chunks
1 mango, peeled and cut into chunks
½ cup jícama strips

Place chicken and onion in a slow cooker. In a small bowl, combine broth, brown sugar, vinegar, hoisin sauce and salt. Pour mixture over chicken. Cover and cook on LOW about 5 hours or until chicken is tender. Turn control to HIGH. In a small bowl, dissolve cornstarch in water; stir into chicken mixture in cooker. Add bell pepper. Cover and cook on HIGH 15 to 20 minutes. Stir in mango and jícama. Cover and cook 5 minutes.

# Chicken Olé

*Try* this creamy casserole that's highlighted with fresh orange and avocado slices.
■ MAKES 8 SERVINGS

1 (10¾-oz.) can condensed cream of
    chicken soup
1 (10¾-oz.) can condensed cream of
    mushroom soup
1 (7-oz.) can green chile
    salsa
1 cup sour cream
1 tablespoon grated onion

12 corn tortillas, cut into 6 or 8 pieces
    each
4 cups coarsely chopped cooked
    chicken or turkey
¾ cup (3 oz.) shredded Cheddar
    cheese
Orange slices
Avocado slices

Lightly grease sides and bottom of a slow cooker. Combine soups, salsa, sour cream and onion in a bowl. In the slow cooker, arrange alternating layers of tortillas with chicken and soup mixture. Cover and cook on LOW 4 to 5 hours. Sprinkle with cheese. Cover and cook on LOW another 5 or 10 minutes or until cheese melts. Serve with orange and avocado slices.

# Chicken Tortilla Casserole

*T*his is a wonderful way to turn leftover chicken into a special meal in a dish. It fits nicely into the smaller slow cookers. ■ MAKES 4 TO 5 SERVINGS

| | |
|---|---|
| 1 teaspoon dried oregano | 2 cups chopped cooked chicken |
| 1/4 teaspoon garlic powder | 3/4 cup shredded Monterey Jack |
| 1 (4-oz.) can chopped green chiles, | cheese |
| drained | 3 tablespoons raw pumpkin seeds |
| 1 (8-oz.) can tomato sauce | Salsa |
| 6 corn tortillas | |

Grease a 6-cup baking dish that fits in slow cooker. In a small bowl, combine oregano, garlic powder, chiles and tomato sauce. Place 2 tortillas in bottom of greased baking dish. Layer 1 cup chicken over tortillas, 1/2 cup tomato mixture, 1/4 cup cheese and 1 tablespoon pumpkin seeds. Tear 2 tortillas into bite-size pieces and spread over mixture. Repeat with remaining ingredients, ending with cheese and pumpkin seeds on top. Place baking dish in the slow cooker. Cover and cook on HIGH 4 to 5 hours. Serve with salsa.

# Chicken-Vegetable Pinwheels

*B*e careful not to tear chicken with mallet when pounding it.  ■ MAKES 6 SERVINGS

6 boneless, skinless chicken breast
 halves
1 egg, beaten slightly
¼ pound Italian turkey sausage
2 slices finely chopped bread, crusts
 removed
1 small carrot, peeled and shredded

2 green onions, including tops,
 chopped
1 stalk celery, finely chopped
¼ teaspoon salt
⅛ teaspoon fresh ground pepper
¼ cup sliced green onions, including
 some tops

Rinse chicken and pat dry with paper towels. Place each breast half between waxed paper or plastic wrap. Carefully flatten chicken with meat mallet to about ¼-inch thickness.

In a small bowl, combine egg, sausage, bread, carrot, chopped onions, celery, salt and pepper. Spread about ¼ cup stuffing mixture down the center of each chicken piece. Roll up; secure with a wooden pick or small skewer. Place chicken rolls in a 3½-quart slow cooker. Cover and cook on LOW 4½ to 5 hours. To serve, transfer chicken to plates; spoon a small amount of cooking juice over each chicken pinwheel. Garnish with green onions.

Per serving: Cal 203 · Carb 6 gm · Prot 32 gm · Total fat 4 gm · Sat fat 1 gm · Cal from fat 36 · Chol 86 mg · Sodium 377 mg

# North-of-the-Border Pozole

*A* hearty Americanized version of the popular Mexican dish featuring hominy. ■ MAKES
ABOUT 6 SERVINGS

2 boneless skinless chicken breast
halves, cut into strips
4 pork steaks, trimmed and cut into
strips
1 (15-oz.) can hominy, drained
1 small onion, chopped

1 (4-oz.) can diced green chiles, drained
½ teaspoon salt
¼ teaspoon pepper
1 teaspoon chili powder
Sliced radishes
Chopped cilantro

Combine chicken, pork, hominy, onion, chiles, salt, pepper and chili powder. Cover and
cook on LOW about 4 hours. Spoon into a serving bowl; sprinkle with sliced radishes and
chopped cilantro.

# Chicken Breasts, Saltimbocca Style

*M*y version of a famous Italian dish. ■ MAKES 6 CHICKEN ROLLS

6 boneless skinless chicken breast
halves
6 small slices ham
6 small slices Swiss cheese
¼ cup all-purpose flour
¼ cup grated Parmesan cheese
1 teaspoon salt
½ teaspoon ground dried sage

¼ teaspoon pepper
⅓ cup vegetable oil
1 (10½-oz.) can condensed cream of
chicken soup
½ cup dry white wine
¼ cup cornstarch
¼ cup water
Cooked rice

Pound chicken breast halves until thin between two sheets of waxed paper or foil. Place a
slice of ham and cheese on each chicken piece. Roll up and tuck ends in; secure with small

skewers or wooden picks. Combine flour, Parmesan cheese, salt, sage and pepper in a shallow bowl. Coat chicken rolls in flour mixture. Refrigerate chicken at least 1 hour.

In a large skillet, heat oil over medium heat. Add chicken rolls and cook, turning, until browned on all sides. Place browned chicken in a slow cooker. Combine soup and wine and pour over chicken rolls. Cover and cook on LOW 4 to 5 hours or until chicken is tender. Turn control to HIGH. In a small bowl, dissolve cornstarch in water; stir into cooking juices in cooker. Cover and cook on HIGH 10 minutes. Serve with hot rice.

# Sorrento Chicken Roll-Ups

*E*ntertaining is a breeze when you prepare these roll-ups ahead of time; let them cook while you are busy with other chores. ■ MAKES 6 SERVINGS

| | |
|---|---|
| 6 boneless skinless chicken breast halves | ¼ cup dry white wine |
| 6 slices prosciutto | ½ cup chicken broth |
| 2 tablespoons Dijon mustard | ¾ cup chopped mushrooms |
| ½ teaspoon ground dried sage | 3 tablespoons cornstarch |
| ½ teaspoon salt | ½ cup milk or half-and-half |
| ⅛ teaspoon pepper | Cooked pasta or rice |

Place chicken between 2 sheets of waxed paper or foil. Pound with a meat mallet until about ½ inch thick. Place each chicken piece on a prosciutto slice. Spread top of each chicken piece with mustard and sprinkle with sage. Starting at short end, roll up each "sandwich" jellyroll style. Place in a slow cooker. Sprinkle with salt and pepper. Add wine and broth. Cover and cook on LOW 5 to 6 hours. Remove chicken rolls and keep warm. Add mushrooms to cooking juices in cooker. Turn control to HIGH. In a small bowl, dissolve cornstarch in milk or half-and-half; stir into mushroom mixture in cooker. Cover and cook on HIGH 20 to 30 minutes or until thickened, stirring once. Serve chicken rolls over pasta or rice. Top each serving with sauce.

# Paella

❈❈❈❈❈❈❈❈❈❈❈❈❈❈❈❈❈❈❈❈❈❈❈❈❈❈❈❈❈❈❈❈❈❈❈

*S*affron is the classic flavoring for this dish, but turmeric has been substituted for it here. If you have saffron, use a pinch in place of the turmeric. ▪ MAKES 6 TO 8 SERVINGS

| | |
|---|---|
| 4 chicken pieces, skinned | ¾ cup chicken broth |
| 1 carrot, peeled and thinly sliced | 2 tablespoons chopped pimiento |
| ½ onion, finely chopped | ¼ lb. shelled raw shrimp |
| 2 tomatoes, chopped | 6 to 8 small clams in shells or 1 |
| 1 small smoked sausage, sliced (about | (6½-oz.) can whole clams, drained |
| 1 cup) | ½ cup green peas |
| 1 teaspoon turmeric | Salt and pepper, to taste |
| 1 teaspoon dried oregano | 2 cups cooked rice |
| 3 cloves garlic, minced | |

In a slow cooker, combine chicken, carrot, onion, tomatoes, sausage, turmeric, oregano, garlic and chicken broth. Cover and cook on LOW 5 to 6 hours or until chicken is tender. Turn control to HIGH. Add pimiento, shrimp, clams and peas. Cover and cook on HIGH 30 minutes. Season with salt and pepper to taste. Stir in rice and serve.

# Jambalaya

❧f you enjoy spicy food, you can add some more heat to this Creole favorite with chiles or cayenne pepper after trying it as it is.  ▪ MAKES 5 TO 6 SERVINGS

1 (2½- to 3½-lb.) broiler-fryer
  chicken, cut up
1 onion, chopped
½ cup finely chopped green bell
  pepper
1 carrot, peeled and thinly sliced
1 clove garlic, minced
1 teaspoon dried oregano

1 teaspoon dried basil
½ teaspoon salt
¼ teaspoon black pepper
¼ teaspoon paprika
¼ teaspoon dried red pepper flakes
1 (14-oz.) can tomatoes, cut up
1 lb. shelled raw shrimp
2 cups cooked rice

In a slow cooker, combine chicken, onion, bell pepper, carrot, garlic, oregano, basil, salt, black pepper, paprika, pepper flakes and tomatoes. Cover and cook on LOW 4 to 5 hours. Turn control to HIGH. Add shrimp and rice. Cover and cook on HIGH 30 to 40 minutes or until shrimp are pink.

# Polenta-Chili Casserole

❧t's easy to make your own polenta lining for a chili casserole in the slow cooker.  ▪ MAKES ABOUT 6 SERVINGS

¾ cup yellow cornmeal
2¾ cups cold water
1 (15-oz.) can low-fat turkey chili with beans
¼ cup chopped leeks
2 boneless, skinless chicken breast halves, cubed
About 1 cup (4 oz.) shredded Monterey Jack cheese

In a 2-quart saucepan, combine cornmeal and cold water. Bring to a boil over medium heat, reduce heat to low, and cook, stirring, about 5 minutes or until thickened. Remove from heat; cool about 10 minutes. Spread over bottom and 1½ to 2 inches up sides of a 3½-quart slow cooker.

In a medium bowl, combine turkey chili, leeks, and chicken. Spoon into center of polenta mixture. Cover and cook on LOW about 5 hours. About 15 minutes before serving, sprinkle top of bean mixture with cheese.

> Per serving: Cal 255 · Carb 22 gm · Prot 19 gm · Total fat 11 gm · Sat fat 5 gm · Cal from fat 99 · Chol 42 mg · Sodium 504 mg

# Orange-Cranberry Turkey Fettuccine

*A* memorable main dish to serve during the holiday season or any time during the year.

■ MAKES ABOUT 4 SERVINGS

| | |
|---|---|
| 1 lb. boneless skinless turkey breast and/or thighs | 1 tablespoon Worcestershire sauce |
| 1 green onion, chopped | ⅛ teaspoon freshly grated nutmeg |
| 2 oranges, peeled and cut into small chunks | ¼ teaspoon salt |
| ½ cup dried cranberries | ⅛ teaspoon pepper |
| ½ cup orange juice | 2 tablespoons cornstarch |
| 2 tablespoons brown sugar | 3 tablespoons water |
| | Cooked fettuccine |
| | Chopped pecans |

Cut turkey into thin strips. In a slow cooker, combine turkey with green onion, oranges, cranberries, orange juice, brown sugar, Worcestershire sauce, nutmeg, salt and pepper. Cover and cook on LOW about 4 hours or until turkey is tender. Turn control to HIGH. In a small bowl, dissolve cornstarch in water; stir into turkey mixture. Cover and cook on HIGH 15 to 20 minutes, stirring once. Serve over hot cooked fettuccine. Sprinkle with chopped pecans.

# Turkey with Jícama-Ginger Salsa

*A* whole turkey breast will not fit into most slow cookers, so use half of the breast or about 2½ pounds. ▪ MAKES ABOUT 6 SERVINGS

1 (2½-lb.) turkey breast half with
    bone and skin
½ teaspoon salt
⅛ teaspoon ground black pepper

2 tablespoons white wine
2 stalks celery, sliced
¼ cup chopped fresh parsley

### JÍCAMA-GINGER SALSA

½ cup finely chopped
    jícama
2 tablespoons finely chopped fresh
    cilantro
¼ cup finely chopped green onions,
    including some tops

2 teaspoons finely chopped
    gingerroot
2 teaspoons finely chopped jalapeño
    chile
1 small tomato, peeled and finely
    chopped

Rinse turkey and pat dry with paper towels. Sprinkle turkey with salt and pepper. Insert meat thermometer into turkey and place in a slow cooker. Add wine. Sprinkle with celery and parsley. Cover and cook on LOW 4 to 5 hours or until turkey is tender and an instant-read thermometer registers 180F (80C). While turkey cooks, prepare Jícama-Ginger Salsa. Slice turkey and serve with Jícama-Ginger Salsa.

# Jícama-Ginger Salsa

Combine ingredients in a small bowl and refrigerate.

Per serving: Cal 311 · Carb 2 gm · Prot 42 gm · Total fat 13 gm · Sat fat 4 gm · Cal from fat 117 · Chol 122 mg · Sodium 308 mg

# Tijuana Turkey

※※※※※※※※※※※※※※※※※※※※※※※※※※※※※※※※※※

*I*nspired by the flavors of mole, a popular Mexican sauce, the cocoa in this dish imparts a richness and mysterious nuance. Peanut butter replaces the usual ground nuts. ■ MAKES ABOUT 4 SERVINGS

1 lb. turkey breast, cut into ¾-inch cubes
1 small green bell pepper, finely chopped
1 small onion, minced
1 clove garlic, minced
1 tablespoon brown sugar
1 tablespoon chili powder
2 tablespoons cornmeal
3 tablespoons unsweetened cocoa powder
1 teaspoon ground cumin

1 teaspoon dried oregano leaves, crushed
½ teaspoon salt
¼ teaspoon ground cinnamon
⅛ teaspoon ground red pepper
1 (8-oz.) can tomato sauce
1½ cups water
1½ tablespoons smooth peanut butter
3 cups hot cooked rice
¼ cup chopped fresh cilantro

Combine turkey, bell pepper, onion and garlic in a 3½-quart slow cooker. In a small bowl, mix brown sugar, chili powder, cornmeal, cocoa powder, cumin, oregano, salt, cinnamon and red pepper. Stir into turkey mixture. Whisk tomato sauce with water and peanut butter; pour over turkey mixture, mixing well. Cover and cook on LOW 4 to 5 hours.

Serve over hot cooked rice. Sprinkle with cilantro.

Per serving: Cal 339 · Carb 58 gm · Prot 42 gm · Total fat 5 gm · Sat fat 1 gm · Cal from fat 45 · Chol 90 mg · Sodium 758 mg

# Stuffed Turkey Breast

*P*repare the stuffing first and the croutons will absorb all the delicious flavors while you prepare the turkey. ■ MAKES 8 TO 9 SERVINGS

¼ cup margarine or butter, melted
1 small onion, finely chopped
1 celery stalk, finely chopped
2 cups herb-seasoned croutons (about 3½ oz.)
½ cup chicken broth

2 tablespoons minced fresh parsley
½ teaspoon poultry seasoning
1 whole uncooked turkey breast (about 5 lb.)
Salt and pepper
½ cup dry white wine

Place a rack in a slow cooker. In a medium bowl, combine margarine or butter, onion, celery, croutons, broth, parsley and poultry seasoning. Slice turkey breast crosswise, from breastbone to ribcage, leaving slices attached to the bone. Sprinkle with salt and pepper.

Cut a piece of cheesecloth about 30 inches long. Soak cheesecloth in ¼ cup of the wine; place turkey on cheesecloth. Stuff bread mixture into slits of turkey. Fold cheesecloth over top of turkey. Place turkey on a rack in slow cooker. Pour remaining ¼ cup white wine over turkey. Cover and cook on LOW 7 to 8 hours or until tender. Remove turkey from cooker; discard cheesecloth. Serve each person one or more slices of turkey with dressing, plus some of the drippings.

# Turkey Tostada Crisps

✕✕✕✕✕✕✕✕✕✕✕✕✕✕✕✕✕✕✕✕✕✕✕✕✕✕✕✕✕✕✕✕✕✕✕✕✕✕✕✕

*A* topping of shredded jícama provides a pleasant crispy texture and flavor contrast.

■ MAKES 6 SERVINGS

1 medium onion, finely chopped
1 medium yellow bell pepper, seeded and chopped
1 large tomato, seeded and chopped
½ lb. uncooked turkey breast, diced
½ teaspoon salt
1 (4-oz.) can diced green chiles, drained

1 (1.62-oz.) package spices and seasonings for enchilada sauce
1 tablespoon vegetable oil
6 (7-inch) flour tortillas
¼ cup shredded Monterey Jack cheese
1 medium jícama, peeled and shredded

Combine onion, bell pepper, tomato, turkey, salt, green chiles and seasoning mix in a 3½-quart slow cooker. Cover and cook on LOW about 5 hours or until turkey and vegetables are tender.

Heat oil in a medium skillet. Add tortillas, one at a time, and cook until lightly browned on both sides and crispy. Spoon sauce on crisp tortillas. Top each with cheese and jícama.

Per serving: Cal 179 · Carb 24 gm · Prot 16 gm · Total fat 6 gm · Sat fat 1 gm · Cal from fat 54 · Chol 34 mg · Sodium 338 mg

# Five-Spice Turkey Thighs

*F*ive-spice is a reddish brown powder usually made of ground star anise, cloves, cinnamon, fennel and Szechwan peppercorns. ■ MAKES ABOUT 6 SERVINGS

1½ to 1¾ lb. boneless, skinless
  turkey thighs
2 green onions, including tops,
  minced
2 tablespoons soy sauce
2 tablespoons sherry
1 tablespoon sugar
1 teaspoon Chinese five-spice powder
1 teaspoon sesame oil

¼ teaspoon ground black pepper
1½ tablespoons cornstarch
2 tablespoons cold water
1 tablespoon toasted sesame seeds
  (see Note, page 166)
1 tablespoon thin, diagonally sliced
  green onions
Hot cooked rice

Trim thighs of excess fat; tuck ends under to make a bundle. Place in a 3½-quart slow cooker. Combine minced onions, soy sauce, sherry, sugar, Chinese five-spice powder, sesame oil and pepper; mix well. Pour over turkey thighs. Cover and cook on LOW about 6 hours or until turkey is tender. Remove turkey from slow cooker and keep warm. Combine cornstarch and water until smooth and stir into cooking juices in slow cooker. Cover and cook on HIGH 15 to 20 minutes or until slightly thickened. Slice turkey; sprinkle with sesame seeds and sliced onions. Serve with rice and sauce.

Per serving: Cal 82 · Carb 5 gm · Prot 7 gm · Total fat 3 gm · Sat fat 0.5 gm · Cal from fat 27 · Chol 23 mg · Sodium 369 mg

# Turkey with Leek & White Wine Sauce

*I*f your favorite turkey parts are not available, substitute cut-up chicken. ■ MAKES 4 TO 6 SERVINGS

| | |
|---|---|
| 2 leeks, trimmed and thinly sliced | 1/4 teaspoon salt |
| 2 teaspoons instant chicken bouillon granules | 1/8 teaspoon pepper |
| | 2 turkey thighs or 1 turkey breast half |
| 1 tablespoon margarine or butter, room temperature | 1/4 cup dry white wine |
| | 2 tablespoons cornstarch |
| 1/3 cup finely chopped watercress | 1/2 cup nonfat sour cream |

Place leeks in a slow cooker. Combine bouillon granules, margarine or butter, watercress, salt and pepper. Remove skin from turkey. Pat watercress mixture on all sides of turkey. Place turkey on top of leeks. Pour wine over turkey. Cover and cook on LOW 4½ to 5 hours or until turkey is tender. Remove turkey and keep warm. Turn control to HIGH. Stir cornstarch into sour cream and stir into cooking juices with leeks. Cover and cook on HIGH 10 to 15 minutes. Slice turkey; spoon leeks and sauce over turkey slices.

# Turkey, Yam and Apple Stew

*T*urkey breast can be substituted for the thighs in this slightly sweet dish.  ■ MAKES ABOUT
6 SERVINGS

¾ lb. boneless, skinless turkey thighs,
   cut into bite-size pieces
2 medium green apples, cored and
   diced
2 lb. yams, peeled and cut into 1-inch
   chunks
¼ cup diced onion
1 cup chicken broth or bouillon
½ cup apple juice

2 tablespoons quick-cooking tapioca
1 tablespoon maple-flavored syrup
½ teaspoon ground cinnamon
½ teaspoon poultry seasoning
¼ teaspoon salt
¼ teaspoon ground white pepper
½ cup light sour cream or plain
   nonfat yogurt

Combine all ingredients, except sour cream or yogurt, in a 3½-quart slow cooker. Cover
and cook on LOW 6 to 7 hours or until yams are tender.

Serve in bowls with a dollop of light sour cream or plain nonfat yogurt.

Per serving: Cal 274 · Carb 58 gm · Prot 7 gm · Total fat 2 gm · Sat fat 0.5 gm ·
Cal from fat 18 · Chol 12 mg · Sodium 172 mg

# Tarragon-Mustard Turkey with Fettuccine

*If turkey is not available, substitute uncooked chicken.* ■ MAKES 4 TO 6 SERVINGS

1 lb. boneless, skinless turkey breast
2 leeks
2 stalks celery, chopped
1 tablespoon chopped fresh
   tarragon
2 tablespoons Dijon mustard
1 tablespoon fresh lemon juice
1 tablespoon brown sugar
1 teaspoon instant chicken bouillon
   granules
¼ teaspoon salt
⅛ teaspoon ground black pepper
2 tablespoons cornstarch
2 tablespoons cold water
6 to 8 ounces fettuccine or medium
   pasta shells

Cut turkey into thin strips, about 1 × ¼ inches. Trim leeks; halve lengthwise. Rinse and slice. Combine turkey and leeks in a 3½-quart slow cooker with celery.

In a small bowl, combine tarragon, mustard, lemon juice, brown sugar, bouillon granules, salt and pepper. Spoon over turkey. Cover and cook on LOW 4½ to 5 hours or until turkey and vegetables are tender.

Turn control to HIGH. Dissolve cornstarch in cold water in a small bowl. Stir into cooking juices in slow cooker. Cover and cook on HIGH 20 to 30 minutes or until thickened.

Cook pasta according to package directions and drain. Spoon turkey mixture over cooked pasta.

Per serving: Cal 271 · Carb 48 gm · Prot 41 gm · Total fat 1 gm · Sat fat 0 gm · Cal from fat 9 · Chol 90 mg · Sodium 280 mg

# Pasta with Easy Turkey-Vegetable Sauce

*D*ouble the recipe and freeze half of mixture for another time.  ■ MAKES 5 TO 6 SERVINGS

1 green bell pepper, diced
1 red onion, thinly sliced
8 to 10 ounces uncooked turkey
   breast, cut into strips
1 (14½-oz.) jar chunky pizza sauce
3 small plum tomatoes, seeded and
   chopped
½ teaspoon dried oregano leaves

1 tablespoon chopped fresh basil, plus
   additional for garnish
¼ teaspoon ground black pepper
8 ounces medium pasta shells or
   fettuccine
About 1 cup (4 ounces) shredded
   light mozzarella cheese

Combine bell pepper, onion, turkey, pizza sauce, tomatoes, oregano, basil and black pepper in a 3½-quart slow cooker. Cover and cook on LOW 5 to 6 hours or until turkey and vegetables are tender.

Cook pasta according to package directions and drain. Spoon sauce over cooked pasta. Top with cheese and additional basil.

Per serving: Cal 288 · Carb 44 gm · Prot 27 gm · Total fat 5 gm · Sat fat 3 gm · Cal from fat 45 · Chol 49 mg · Sodium 187 mg

# Turkey Fillets, Barbecue Style

*A*n easy way to prepare barbecued poultry, without worrying about lighting the charcoal and watching the fire. ■ MAKES 6 TO 7 SERVINGS

6 or 7 boneless turkey fillets or cutlets
¼ cup molasses
¼ cup red wine vinegar
¼ cup ketchup
2 tablespoons Worcestershire sauce
½ teaspoon hickory smoke salt
1 tablespoon grated onion
½ teaspoon salt
⅛ teaspoon pepper
Cooked basmati or brown rice

Place turkey fillets in a slow cooker. In a small bowl, combine remaining ingredients except rice. Pour over turkey. Cover and cook on LOW about 4 hours. Serve with basmati or brown rice.

# Spinach and Prosciutto Turkey Roulades

*F*or an impressive presentation, serve individual servings of sliced turkey roulade over cooked white or wild rice. ■ MAKES 6 TO 7 SERVINGS

| | |
|---|---|
| 6 or 7 turkey cutlets (about 1 lb.) | ½ teaspoon ground black pepper |
| 1 (10-oz.) package chopped frozen spinach, thawed | 3 (3½ × 6¼-inch) thin slices prosciutto or ham |
| 2 tablespoons minced fresh parsley | ¼ teaspoon salt |
| ¼ cup dry bread crumbs | ¼ teaspoon paprika |
| 3 tablespoons shredded Parmesan cheese | ¼ cup dry vermouth or white wine |
| 3 tablespoons toasted pine nuts (see Note, page 3) | ¾ cup chicken bouillon or broth |
| | 1 tablespoon all-purpose flour |
| 2 teaspoons dried sage leaves, crushed | 2 tablespoons water |
| | Cooked rice |

Pound turkey cutlets between plastic wrap to about ¼-inch thickness; set aside. Drain spinach; press out excess moisture with back of a large spoon. Combine spinach, parsley, bread crumbs, Parmesan cheese, pine nuts, 1 teaspoon of the sage and ¼ teaspoon pepper; mix well.

Halve prosciutto lengthwise. Place a half slice on each cutlet. Spoon about ½ cup spinach mixture on each. Starting at short end, roll up. Place in a 3½-quart slow cooker, seam side down. Sprinkle each with salt, remaining ¼ teaspoon pepper and paprika. Pour vermouth or wine and bouillon around turkey rolls. Cover and cook on LOW 4 to 6 hours or until turkey is tender.

Remove turkey from slow cooker and keep warm. Turn control to HIGH. Add remaining teaspoon sage. In a small bowl, dissolve flour in water and add to slow cooker. Cook, stirring, on HIGH 10 to 15 minutes or until thickened. Slice each turkey roll and serve on cooked rice, topped with sauce.

Per serving without rice: Cal 113 · Carb 7 gm · Prot 29 gm · Total fat 3 gm · Sat fat 1 gm · Cal from fat 27 · Chol 68 mg · Sodium 503 mg

# Malaysian Turkey Cutlets

※◇※◇※◇※◇※◇※◇※◇※◇※◇※◇※◇※◇※◇※◇※◇※◇※◇※◇※◇※◇※◇※◇※◇※◇※

*B*uying a package of turkey breast cutlets or slices is a shortcut to an intriguing flavor combination highlighted by mint. ■ MAKES 5 TO 6 SERVINGS

    1 cup fresh cilantro leaves
    1/3 cup fresh mint leaves
    2 tablespoons soy sauce
    1 tablespoon vegetable oil
    1/2 teaspoon chili oil
    1 clove garlic, crushed
    1 lb. turkey breast cutlets

Process cilantro, mint, soy sauce, vegetable oil, chili oil and garlic in a food processor until finely chopped. Brush on all sides of turkey and place in a 3½-quart slow cooker. Pour any remaining sauce over turkey. Cover and cook on **LOW** about 4 hours or until turkey is tender.

Per serving: Cal 73 · Carb 2 gm · Prot 29 gm · Total fat 4 gm · Sat fat 1 gm · Cal from fat 36 · Chol 72 mg · Sodium 493 mg

# Southeast Asian–Style Meatballs

*E*njoy these main-dish meatballs or make them smaller for appetizers. ■ MAKES 8 TO 10 MEATBALLS

1 lb. uncooked ground turkey or lean
   pork
½ cup dry bread crumbs
1 egg, slightly beaten
2 tablespoons soy sauce
2 tablespoons hoisin sauce

2 teaspoons grated gingerroot
¼ teaspoon pepper
2 tablespoons toasted sesame seeds
   (see Note, page 166)
Cooked noodles

### PLUM GLAZE

½ cup plum jelly
1 tablespoon white wine vinegar

1 tablespoon ketchup
1 tablespoon sweet hot mustard

Place a rack in a slow cooker. In a medium bowl, combine ground turkey or pork, bread crumbs, egg, soy sauce, hoisin sauce, ginger and pepper. Form into 8 to 10 balls about 2 inches in diameter. Place on rack in slow cooker. If all meatballs don't fit in a single layer, poke small holes in 2 sheets of foil about 7 inches square. Cover bottom layer of meatballs with one sheet of foil; repeat with second layer of meatballs and another piece of foil. Cover and cook on LOW 3½ to 4 hours. While meatballs cook, prepare Plum Glaze.

Transfer meatballs to a serving dish. Spoon Plum Glaze over meatballs. Sprinkle with sesame seeds. Serve over cooked noodles.

# Plum Glaze

Combine ingredients in a small bowl. Heat in microwave or in a small saucepan over low heat until smooth.

# My Favorite Pasta Sauce

✳✳✳✳✳✳✳✳✳✳✳✳✳✳✳✳✳✳✳✳✳✳✳✳✳✳✳✳✳✳✳✳✳✳✳✳✳✳✳✳✳

*B*y using lean ground turkey and lean beef, you cut the cholesterol and calorie count, while creating an appealing flavor combination. Serve over cooked pasta or rice. ■ MAKES ABOUT 6 SERVINGS

½ lb. lean ground turkey
½ lb. lean ground beef
1 stalk celery, chopped
2 medium carrots, peeled and chopped
1 clove garlic, crushed
1 medium onion, chopped

1 (28-oz.) can diced tomatoes with juice
1 (6-oz.) can tomato paste
½ teaspoon salt
⅛ teaspoon ground black pepper
¼ teaspoon dried thyme

Combine ground turkey, beef, celery, carrots, garlic and onion in a 3½-quart slow cooker. Stir in diced tomatoes, tomato paste, salt, pepper and thyme. Cover and cook on LOW 7 to 8 hours or until meat and vegetables are tender.

Per serving: Cal 212 · Carb 15 gm · Prot 16 gm · Total fat 10 gm · Sat fat 1 gm · Cal from fat 90 · Chol 56 mg · Sodium 487 mg

# Taste-of-the-Southwest Turkey Loaf

*V*arious combinations of fresh salsa are usually found in the deli case of your supermarket.

■ MAKES 5 TO 6 SERVINGS

½ cup refrigerated fresh salsa
2 tablespoons chopped fresh cilantro
1 green onion, including top,
  chopped
1 egg, slightly beaten

¼ teaspoon ground cumin
¼ teaspoon salt
1 zucchini, shredded
1¼ lb. ground turkey or chicken

In a medium bowl, combine salsa, cilantro, green onion, egg, cumin, salt, zucchini and turkey. Form into a 6-inch-round loaf. Place loaf on a trivet in a 3½-quart slow cooker. Cover and cook on LOW 4 to 4½ hours.

Remove loaf from slow cooker. Cut into wedges and serve.

Per serving: Cal 199 · Carb 4 gm · Prot 21 gm · Total fat 10 gm · Sat fat 3 gm · Cal from fat 90 · Chol 134 mg · Sodium 404 mg

# Round Sesame Turkey Loaf

*T*he uncooked mixture will be fairly soft, but it will become firmer as it cooks. ■ MAKES 5 TO 6 SERVINGS

1 lb. ground turkey
1 egg, slightly beaten
2 green onions, including some tops, chopped
2 tablespoons soy sauce
½ teaspoon grated gingerroot

¼ cup chopped water chestnuts
2 tablespoons prepared sweet-and-sour sauce
1 cup cooked rice
1 tablespoon toasted sesame seeds (see Note, page 166)

In a medium bowl, combine all ingredients except sesame seeds. Form into a 6-inch-round loaf. Press sesame seeds into top. Place loaf in a 3½-quart slow cooker. Cover and cook on LOW about 4 hours.

Remove loaf from slow cooker. Cut into wedges and serve.

Per serving: Cal 228 · Carb 15 gm · Prot 18 gm · Total fat 9 gm · Sat fat 2 gm · Cal from fat 81 · Chol 115 mg · Sodium 530 mg

# Turkey Lasagna

※※※※※※※※※※※※※※※※※※※※※※※※※※※※※※※※※※※※※※※※※※※

*T*urkey adds an exciting new flavor to lasagna, and a lower fat content. ■ MAKES 8 TO 10 SERVINGS

| | |
|---|---|
| 1 lb. uncooked ground turkey | ½ teaspoon salt |
| 1 onion, chopped | 1 tablespoon chopped fresh basil |
| 1 clove garlic | 1 (15-oz.) container low-fat ricotta |
| 1 (16-oz.) can peeled, diced tomatoes | cheese |
| in juice | ½ cup grated Parmesan cheese |
| 1 (8-oz.) can tomato sauce | 1 teaspoon minced fresh oregano |
| 1 beef bouillon cube, crushed | 8 oz. lasagna noodles, cooked and |
| 1 tablespoon minced fresh parsley | drained |
| 2 teaspoons sugar | 8 oz. mozzarella cheese, thinly sliced |

In a slow cooker, combine turkey, onion, garlic, tomatoes, tomato sauce, bouillon cube, parsley, sugar, salt and basil. Cover and cook on LOW 6 to 7 hours. In a medium bowl, mix ricotta cheese, ¼ cup of the Parmesan cheese and oregano.

Preheat oven to 350F (175C). In a 13 × 9-inch pan, layer half of the cooked noodles, sauce, mozzarella cheese and ricotta cheese mixture and repeat, reserving enough sauce to layer on top. Sprinkle with remaining ¼ cup Parmesan cheese. Bake in preheated oven 45 minutes.

# Teriyaki Turkey Loaf

*F*lavors of the Far East enhance this more traditional turkey loaf. ■ MAKES ABOUT 6 SERVINGS

1¼ lb. ground turkey
¼ cup fine dry bread crumbs
1 egg, beaten slightly
½ cup finely chopped celery
2 green onions, including some tops,
  finely chopped
¼ teaspoon salt

⅛ teaspoon ground black pepper
¼ cup finely chopped green bell
  pepper
½ cup teriyaki sauce
1 (8-oz.) can sliced water chestnuts,
  drained

In a medium bowl, combine turkey, bread crumbs, egg, celery, green onions, salt and black pepper. Form into a 5½- to 6-inch-round loaf. Place loaf in a 3½-quart slow cooker.

In a small bowl, combine bell pepper, teriyaki sauce and water chestnuts. Spoon over loaf. Cover and cook on low about 4 hours.

Remove loaf from slow cooker. Cut into thin wedges or slices.

Per serving: Cal 186 · Carb 7 gm · Prot 18 gm · Total fat 9 gm · Sat fat 2 gm · Cal from fat 81 · Chol 111 mg · Sodium 628 mg

# Raspberry-Glazed Turkey Meatballs

*Y*our friends will love this sweet-sour sauce with its intriguing raspberry flavor. ■ MAKES ABOUT 45 MEATBALLS

½ cup seedless raspberry fruit spread
   or preserves
2 tablespoons raspberry vinegar
2 tablespoons chili sauce
½ teaspoon ground cardamom
¾ teaspoon salt
⅜ teaspoon ground black pepper
1¼ lb. lean ground turkey

⅓ cup quick-cooking oats
¼ cup minced onion
1 large egg, slightly beaten
1 tablespoon Worcestershire sauce
1 teaspoon cornstarch
1 tablespoon cold water
Minced green onion

In a small bowl, whisk raspberry spread, vinegar, chili sauce, cardamom, ¼ teaspoon salt and ⅛ teaspoon pepper. Spread 3 tablespoons of mixture over bottom of a slow cooker; set remainder aside.

In a medium bowl, combine turkey, oats, onion, egg, Worcestershire sauce, remaining ½ teaspoon salt and remaining ¼ teaspoon pepper. Shape into 1- to 1½-inch balls. Place in sauce in slow cooker. Spoon remaining sauce over meatballs. Cover and cook on LOW 6 hours.

Turn control to HIGH. In a small bowl, dissolve cornstarch in water. Spoon over meatballs. Cover and cook on HIGH 5 to 10 minutes or until thickened. Sprinkle with green onions.

Per meatball: Cal 30 · Carb 2 gm · Prot 3 gm · Total fat 1 gm · Sat fat 0 gm · Cal from fat 9 · Chol 15 mg · Sodium 64 mg

# Ground Turkey Vegetable Round

*L*eftovers can be served cold or used for sandwiches. ■ MAKES 6 TO 8 SERVINGS

1½ lb. uncooked ground turkey
1 cup soft bread crumbs
⅓ cup toasted pine nuts (see Note, page 3)
2 eggs, slightly beaten
¼ cup chopped green onions
1 tablespoon Dijon mustard

1 teaspoon prepared horseradish
1 tablespoon Worcestershire sauce
½ teaspoon salt
⅛ teaspoon pepper
1 medium zucchini
1 carrot, peeled

In a large bowl, combine turkey, bread crumbs, pine nuts, eggs, onions, mustard, horseradish, Worcestershire sauce, salt and pepper. In a food processor, shred zucchini and carrot. Stir vegetables into turkey mixture. Shape into a 6-inch ball. Place a metal rack in slow cooker. Place turkey round on 16-inch-long double thickness of cheesecloth. Gently lift into cooker and place on rack. Fold cheesecloth over meat. Cover and cook on LOW about 4½ hours. Lift out meat with ends of cheesecloth. Cut into 6 to 8 wedges. Spoon drippings over top.

# Turkey Porcupines in Enchilada Sauce

*T*he popular meat and rice meatballs turn Mexican and spicy! ■ MAKES 19 MEATBALLS OR 4 TO 5 SERVINGS

1¼ lb. lean ground turkey
½ cup white long-grain rice
½ cup finely chopped green bell pepper
2 tablespoons minced onion

½ teaspoon salt
¼ teaspoon ground black pepper
1 (19-oz.) can enchilada sauce
¼ cup water

In a medium bowl, combine turkey, rice, bell pepper, onion, salt and black pepper; mix well. Shape mixture into balls about 1½ inches in diameter; place in slow cooker. Combine enchilada sauce and water; pour over meatballs. Cover and cook on LOW about 6 hours or until rice is tender. To serve, spoon sauce over meatballs.

Per meatball: Cal 70 · Carb 5 gm · Prot 5 gm · Total fat 3 gm · Sat fat 1 gm · Cal from fat 27 · Chol 24 mg · Sodium 231 mg

# Cranberry-Orange Turkey Roll

� decorative border✱

*N*one of your guests will suspect that this impressive dish is so simple to prepare.

■ MAKES 6 SERVINGS

¼ cup sugar
2 tablespoons cornstarch
¾ cup orange marmalade
1 cup fresh cranberries, ground or finely chopped
1 (2- to 2½-lb.) frozen turkey roll, partially thawed
Salt and pepper

In a small saucepan, blend sugar and cornstarch; stir in marmalade and cranberries. Cook and stir until mixture is bubbly and slightly thickened. Place turkey roll in a slow cooker. Sprinkle lightly with salt and pepper. Pour sauce over turkey. Cover and cook on LOW 9 to 10 hours. Insert a meat thermometer in turkey roll during the last 2 or 3 hours of cooking and cook until temperature reaches 185F (85C). Slice turkey roll. Spoon sauce over turkey slices.

# Sausage Polenta Pie

*A* spicy mixture is hidden beneath a polenta topping. ■ MAKES 5 TO 6 SERVINGS

1 (14-oz.) package reduced-fat smoked turkey sausage, cut into ½-inch slices
1 onion, finely chopped
1 clove garlic, crushed
1 tomato, peeled, seeded and chopped
1 (8-oz.) jar picante sauce

2 teaspoons chopped fresh basil
1 teaspoon chopped fresh oregano
1 tablespoon chopped fresh parsley
1 cup cornmeal
3¾ cups chicken broth
1 tablespoon margarine or butter
¼ cup grated Parmesan cheese

Combine sausage, onion, garlic, tomato, picante sauce, basil, oregano and parsley in a slow cooker; set aside. In a medium saucepan, combine cornmeal and broth. Bring to a boil; cook, stirring, over medium heat until thick, about 5 minutes. Stir in margarine or butter and half the cheese. Spoon on top of sausage mixture in slow cooker. Sprinkle with remaining cheese. Cover and cook on LOW about 6 hours. Serve with a large spoon directly onto plates.

# Chunky Spaghetti 'n' Turkey Meatballs

*T*urkey-flavored sausage plus fresh herbs add texture and flavor to this spaghetti recipe.

■ MAKES 6 SERVINGS

1 medium onion, chopped
1 carrot, peeled and chopped
2 stalks celery, chopped
1 clove garlic, crushed
1 (8-oz.) can tomato sauce
1 tablespoon chopped fresh basil
2 teaspoons chopped fresh oregano
1 teaspoon chopped fresh thyme
1 teaspoon Worcestershire sauce
1/8 teaspoon ground black pepper

1 (28-oz.) can diced tomatoes with juice
1/2 lb. mild Italian turkey sausage
1/2 lb. extra-lean ground beef
1/3 cup seasoned dry bread crumbs
1 egg, beaten slightly
2 tablespoons milk
1 pound spaghetti, cooked and drained
Grated Parmesan cheese (optional)

Combine onion, carrot, celery, garlic, tomato sauce, basil, oregano, thyme, Worcestershire sauce, pepper and tomatoes in a 3 1/2-quart slow cooker.

In a medium bowl, combine turkey sausage, ground beef, bread crumbs, egg and milk. Form mixture into about 18 meatballs. Carefully place meatballs in sauce in slow cooker. Cover and cook on LOW about 7 hours or until meat and vegetables are tender.

Cook spaghetti according to package directions and drain. Spoon meatball mixture over cooked spaghetti. Sprinkle with grated Parmesan cheese, if desired.

Per serving: Cal 803 · Carb 145 gm · Prot 37 gm · Total fat 14 gm · Sat fat 1 gm · Cal from fat 126 · Chol 82 mg · Sodium 3638 mg

# South-of-the-Border Lasagna

*U*se turkey sausage and low-fat ricotta cheese to produce lasagna with lower fat and fewer calories. ■ MAKES 7 TO 8 SERVINGS

¾ lb. turkey sausage
2 tomatoes, seeded and chopped
3 fresh tomatillos, husked and chopped
1 (19-oz.) can green enchilada sauce
1 clove garlic, crushed
¼ teaspoon salt

⅛ teaspoon ground black pepper
8 ounces lasagna noodles
1 cup low-fat or nonfat ricotta cheese
1 cup shredded reduced-fat jalapeño Jack cheese
Chopped fresh cilantro

Crumble sausage into a slow cooker. Stir in tomatoes, tomatillos, enchilada sauce, garlic, salt and pepper. Cover and cook on LOW 5½ to 6 hours.

Preheat oven to 350F (175C). Grease a 13 × 9-inch baking dish. Cook lasagna noodles according to package directions and drain. Spread about ½ cup turkey mixture in bottom of prepared pan; arrange alternate layers of noodles, ricotta cheese, and hot turkey mixture. Top with Jack cheese. Bake 25 to 30 minutes or until bubbly around edges. Sprinkle with cilantro.

Per serving: Cal 340 · Carb 36 gm · Prot 21 gm · Total fat 13 gm · Sat fat 3 gm · Cal from fat 117 · Chol 56 mg · Sodium 817 mg

# Cornish Hens with Cherry Sauce

*Only* three hens fit into a 3½-quart slow cooker; four fit into a 4- or 5-quart pot.  ■ MAKES
3 TO 4 SERVINGS

3 or 4 Cornish hens
1 (6-oz.) package Stove Top
   cornbread stuffing
1½ cups hot water
¼ cup plus 2 tablespoons margarine
   or butter

¾ cup red currant jelly
¼ cup pitted dried red cherries,
   coarsely chopped
2 teaspoons fresh lemon juice
½ teaspoon salt
¼ teaspoon ground allspice

Thaw hens if frozen. Place a rack in a slow cooker. In a medium bowl, combine stuffing
mix with seasoning packet, water and ¼ cup of the margarine or butter. Stuff hens and
place on rack in slow cooker. In a small saucepan, combine jelly, cherries, remaining 2
tablespoons margarine or butter, lemon juice, salt and allspice. Cook over LOW heat, stirring until jelly is melted. Reserve ⅔ cup sauce. Brush remaining sauce on hens in cooker.
Cover and cook on LOW 6 to 7 hours. Serve whole or cut hens in half with kitchen shears.
Spoon reserved sauce over hens at serving time.

# Tuscan-Style Cornish Hens

*T*hese are enhanced by flavorful herbs and seasonings. ■ MAKES 6 SERVINGS

3 Cornish hens, thawed if frozen and
    cut in half
2 to 3 ounces thinly sliced prosciutto,
    chopped
2 cloves garlic, crushed
12 fresh sage leaves, chopped
2 tablespoons chopped fresh fennel
    leaves

½ teaspoon salt
¼ teaspoon ground pepper
2 tablespoons vegetable oil
5 teaspoons cornstarch
2 tablespoons cold water
Fresh fennel tops

Rinse hens and pat dry. In a food processor, combine prosciutto, garlic, sage, fennel, salt, pepper and oil; process until finely chopped. Brush or pat mixture on skin and inside hens. Place hens on a trivet in a 4- to 5-quart slow cooker. Cover and cook on LOW 5 to 5½ hours or until hens are tender.

Pour 1½ cups cooking juices into a 2-cup measuring cup. Skim off and discard fat. In a small saucepan, dissolve cornstarch in cold water. Add cooking juices. Cook, stirring, over medium heat until slightly thickened. Spoon sauce over hens and garnish with fennel tops.

Per serving: Cal 167 · Carb 3 gm · Prot 26 gm · Total fat 5 gm · Sat fat 1 gm · Cal from fat 45 · Chol 115 mg · Sodium 383 mg

# Cornish Hens with Lime Glaze

✖✖✖✖✖✖✖✖✖✖✖✖✖✖✖✖✖✖✖✖✖✖✖✖✖✖✖✖✖✖✖✖✖✖✖✖✖✖✖✖

*H*ere is the ideal entrée for an elegant meal. Serve with a fresh green vegetable and sliced tomatoes. ■ MAKES 4 SERVINGS

2 Cornish hens
2 slices cinnamon bread, cubed
1 celery stalk, chopped
½ teaspoon dried tarragon
2 tablespoons chopped walnuts
1 green onion, chopped
⅓ cup vermouth or white wine

3 tablespoons margarine or butter, melted
2 tablespoons sugar
2 tablespoons fresh lime juice
1 tablespoon soy sauce
3 tablespoons cornstarch
3 tablespoons water

Thaw hens if frozen. In a bowl, combine bread cubes, celery, tarragon, walnuts and green onion. Sprinkle with vermouth or white wine and toss. Spoon mixture into cavity of each hen. In a bowl, mix together margarine or butter, sugar, lime juice and soy sauce. Brush hens with sauce. Place a rack or trivet in a slow cooker. Place hens on end, neck down, on rack. Cover and cook on LOW 6 to 7 hours or until hens are tender. Remove hens and cover to keep warm. Turn control to HIGH. In a small bowl, dissolve cornstarch in water; stir into cooking juices. Cover and cook on HIGH 10 minutes or until thickened. With shears, cut hens in half. Spoon sauce over each.

# Cornish Hens with Fresh Salsa

*C*ornish hens are perfect for cooking in a slow cooker. They come out moist and succulent.

■ MAKES 6 SERVINGS

3 Cornish hens, thawed if frozen and
   cut in half
1/2 teaspoon salt

1/4 teaspoon ground pepper
1/4 teaspoon seasoned salt
3 cloves garlic, cut in half

FRESH SALSA

3 medium tomatoes, peeled, seeded
   and chopped
3 green onions, including tops,
   chopped
1/4 cup coarsely chopped fresh
   cilantro

2 tablespoons chopped fresh parsley
1 small jalapeño chile, seeded and
   finely chopped
1/4 teaspoon salt

Rinse hens and pat dry with paper towels. Season hens with salt, pepper and seasoned salt. Insert a piece of garlic in cavity of each hen. Place hens in a 4- to 5-quart slow cooker. Cover and cook on LOW 5 to 5½ hours or until hens are tender. While hens cook, prepare Fresh Salsa.

Serve Fresh Salsa with hens.

# Fresh Salsa

Combine ingredients in a small bowl and refrigerate several hours for flavors to blend.

Per serving: Cal 157 · Carb 4 gm · Prot 24 gm · Total fat 4 gm · Sat fat 1 gm · Cal from fat 36 · Chol 110 mg · Sodium 440 mg

# Burgundy-Basted Duckling

*F*or a golden brown duckling, place on broiler pan after cooking it in the slow cooker; then brown it in a 400F (205C) oven 15 to 20 minutes.  ■ MAKES 4 SERVINGS

| | |
|---|---|
| 1 (4- to 5-lb.) ready-to-cook duckling | 1 clove garlic, minced |
| ¼ cup Burgundy wine | 1 teaspoon salt |
| 1 tablespoon fresh lemon juice | 1 teaspoon dried marjoram, crushed |
| ½ teaspoon grated lemon peel | ¼ teaspoon pepper |
| 1 tablespoon Worcestershire sauce | 2 or 3 drops bottled hot pepper sauce |

Place a rack in a 4-quart or larger slow cooker. With a fork, prick skin of duckling all over at approximately 2-inch intervals. Place duckling breast side down on rack in slow cooker. In a bowl, combine remaining ingredients. Brush half of wine mixture over duckling. Cover and cook on LOW 6 to 7 hours. If possible, remove fat with a bulb baster. Turn duckling and baste with more wine mixture once during cooking. Cut into serving pieces and serve hot.

# Imperial Duckling

*A* rosy sauce gives the duck a festive touch and delicious flavor.  ■ MAKES 4 SERVINGS

1 (4- to 5-lb.) ready-to-cook duckling
2 tablespoons grated onion
¼ teaspoon dried tarragon
½ cup orange juice
⅛ teaspoon salt
⅛ teaspoon dry mustard

¼ cup currant jelly
2 tablespoons grated orange peel
2 tablespoons port wine
2 teaspoons cornstarch
1 orange, peeled, sectioned and cut
   into chunks

Place a rack in a 4-quart or larger slow cooker. With a fork, prick skin of duckling all over at approximately 2-inch intervals. Place duckling on rack in slow cooker. (When cooking duckling in a 3½-quart (or smaller) slow cooker, cut the duckling into quarters or halves before putting it into the pot.) In a small saucepan, combine onion, tarragon, orange juice, salt, mustard, jelly, orange peel, wine and cornstarch. Cook over medium heat until thickened. Brush ⅓ cup sauce over duckling, reserving remaining sauce. Cover and cook on LOW 6 to 7 hours or until duckling is tender, turning once during cooking. If possible, remove fat with a bulb baster. Stir orange sections into remaining sauce, heat and pour over duck just before serving.

# BEANS & GRAINS

Because slow cookers are newer electric cousins of the old-fashioned bean pot, bean dishes cook especially well in them. Today's cooks like to prepare beans in slow cookers because they can spend the day away from home while long, slow cooking is mingling compatible flavors to create traditional favorites or regional dishes.

Dried beans and peas are legumes, which include lentils, black-eyed peas, garbanzo or chickpeas, pinto beans, black beans, and many other types. Legumes are the richest source of vegetable protein and are a good source of soluble fiber. Nutritionists encourage us to increase our intake of legumes and grains because of their many benefits. In this chapter we offer Red Beans & Rice and Refried Black Beans, which highlight ethnic flavors from the South and West. Favorite Baked Beans and Fresh Black-Eyed Peas add new zest to long-standing favorites.

You will notice that soaking is not called for in these recipes, but be sure to allow plenty of cooking time. Most bean recipes may be cooked longer than the times indicated or they may be cooked one day, refrigerated, and reheated for use the next day. Fiesta Turkey & Bean Salad is a two-day recipe that combines your slow-cooked beans with other ingredients in a hearty salad.

Most of the bean recipes serve six to eight people. You can double any of them for a party if the quantity will fit in your slow cooker. While you are getting everything else ready, the beans cook with no fuss or bother. Then they stay hot until serving time in the slow cooker. In case you hadn't guessed—slow cookers are ideal buffet servers.

To make beans easier to digest, there are a number of over-the-counter commercial products available at your pharmacy. These are food enzymes that are meant to be sprinkled on cooked beans or taken in tablet form.

# Red Beans & Rice

*A* slow-cooker version of a favorite traditional Southern dish. ∎ MAKES 4 TO 6 SERVINGS

1 lb. spicy smoked sausage, cut into ½-inch slices
2 (15-oz.) cans small red beans, drained
1 green or yellow bell pepper, chopped
1 jalapeño chile, seeded and finely chopped
1 (15-oz.) can peeled, diced tomatoes in juice
1 small red onion, chopped
1 cup uncooked rice

In a slow cooker, combine sausage, beans, bell pepper, jalapeño chiles, tomatoes and onion. Cover and cook on LOW 5½ to 6 hours. Meanwhile, cook rice according to package directions. Spoon cooked rice into individual soup bowls or one large serving dish. Top with bean mixture.

# Cannellini and Salmon Salad Toss

*F*or eye appeal, save a few of the large fennel leaves to use as a garnish.  ■ MAKES 6 TO 7 SERVINGS

| | |
|---|---|
| 1 lb. dried cannellini beans, sorted and rinsed | 2 carrots, peeled and thinly sliced |
| 7 cups water | 2 tablespoons chopped fresh dill |
| 1½ teaspoons salt | ⅓ cup vegetable oil |
| 1 small fennel bulb, finely chopped or sliced and leaves reserved for garnish | 2 tablespoons fresh lemon juice |
| | ⅛ teaspoon ground black pepper |
| | ½ lb. fresh salmon fillets or thin salmon steaks |
| 1 small red onion, chopped | |

Combine beans, water and 1 teaspoon salt in a 3½-quart slow cooker. Cover and cook on HIGH 9 to 10 hours or until beans are tender.

Dip out beans with slotted spoon, draining off liquid. Refrigerate beans until chilled.

In a large bowl, combine chilled beans, fennel, onion, carrots, dill, oil, lemon juice, remaining ½ teaspoon salt and pepper.

Preheat broiler. Rinse salmon and place on a broiler rack. Broil salmon until it just begins to flake when pierced with a fork, about 10 minutes. Break salmon into chunks and remove any bones. Sprinkle salmon over fennel mixture. Garnish with fennel leaves.

Per serving: Cal 450 · Carb 50 gm · Prot 23 gm · Total fat 18 gm · Sat fat 2 gm · Cal from fat 162 · Chol 21 mg · Sodium 412 mg

# Refried Black Beans

*These* beans are an appetizing accompaniment to traditional pork roast as well as to enchiladas or tacos.  ▪ MAKES 6 TO 8 SERVINGS

1 lb. dried black beans, rinsed
2 teaspoons chili powder
1 clove garlic, crushed
½ teaspoon ground cumin
1 small onion, chopped
½ teaspoon salt

6 cups water
1 tablespoon vegetable oil
4 oz. crumbled goat cheese (about ¾ cup)
2 tablespoons finely chopped fresh cilantro

In a slow cooker, combine beans, chili powder, garlic, cumin, onion, salt and water. Cover and cook on HIGH 6 to 7 hours or until beans are soft. Drain beans and partially mash with a potato masher or in a food processor, leaving about half of the beans whole. Just before serving, heat oil in a large skillet over medium heat. Add partially mashed beans, heat, and stir until fairly dry. Serve topped with goat cheese and cilantro.

# Hot Sausage & Bean Chili

*L*eave this hearty main dish cooking while you are working or doing errands. ■ MAKES 5 TO 6 SERVINGS

1 lb. dried pink beans
2 teaspoons chili powder
1 onion, chopped
1 yellow or orange bell pepper, chopped
1 clove garlic, crushed
2 tablespoons chopped cilantro

1 (15-oz.) can peeled diced tomatoes with juice
1 fresh jalapeño chile, seeded and chopped
3 cups hot water
¾ lb. spicy or hot bulk pork sausage

Combine all ingredients except sausage in a slow cooker. Meanwhile, lightly brown sausage in a medium skillet over medium heat; drain off fat. Add browned sausage to bean mixture. Cover and cook on LOW 8 or 9 hours or until beans are tender.

# Barbecued Limas and Beef

*C*hoose high or low cooking, depending on which method fits into your schedule.
■ MAKES 5 TO 6 SERVINGS

1 lb. dried small lima beans, sorted and rinsed
½ lb. beef stew meat, cut into ¼-inch cubes
1 small onion, chopped
2 stalks celery, chopped
1 carrot, coarsely shredded

¼ teaspoon salt
⅛ teaspoon ground black pepper
½ cup barbecue sauce
1 (6-oz.) can tomato paste
1 tablespoon prepared mustard
1 tablespoon honey
4 cups water

Combine beans, beef, onion, celery, carrot, salt and pepper in a 3½-quart slow cooker. Stir in barbecue sauce, tomato paste, mustard, honey and water. Cover and cook on LOW 10 hours or cook on HIGH 5½ to 6 hours, stirring once, or until beans and beef are tender.

Per serving: Cal 494 · Carb 71 gm · Prot 30 gm · Total fat 11 gm · Sat fat 2 gm · Cal from fat 99 · Chol 27 mg · Sodium 437 mg

# Slow-Cooker Cassoulet

*A* French cassoulet is a hearty peasant dish featuring a country combination of beans with chicken or duck and sausage or other meats. ■ MAKES 5 TO 6 SERVINGS

1 (2½- to 3½-lb.) broiler-fryer
  chicken, cut up
1 small leek, thinly sliced
1 clove garlic, crushed
3 tablespoons chopped fresh parsley
½ teaspoon salt

¼ teaspoon pepper
2 (15-oz.) cans white kidney beans,
  drained
½ lb. smoked sausage links, cut into
  ½-inch-thick slices
¼ cup dry white wine

In a slow cooker, combine chicken, leek, garlic, parsley, salt and pepper. Top with beans and sausage. Add wine. Cover and cook on LOW 5 to 6 hours or until chicken is tender.

# Fiesta Turkey & Bean Salad

*F*or an exciting main-dish salad, cook the beans a day ahead; cool and combine with other ingredients and refrigerate overnight. ■ MAKES 6 TO 8 SERVINGS

1 cup dried kidney beans
1 cup dried garbanzo beans
1/4 lb. smoked turkey, diced
5 cups water
2 tablespoons chopped fresh parsley
1 clove garlic, crushed
1 cup chopped cooked artichoke
   hearts or broccoli
1 small yellow or red bell pepper,
   chopped

1/2 cup olive oil
1/4 cup white wine vinegar
2 tablespoons Dijon mustard
2 teaspoons honey
2 tablespoons chopped fresh chives
1 teaspoon dried dill weed
1/4 teaspoon salt
1/8 teaspoon pepper
Lettuce
2 tablespoons watercress leaves

In a slow cooker, combine dried beans, turkey, water, parsley and garlic. Cover and cook on LOW 10 to 11 hours or until beans are tender but firm. Drain and discard liquid; cool drained bean mixture. Add artichokes or broccoli and bell pepper. In a medium bowl, combine oil, vinegar, mustard, honey, chives, dill weed, salt and pepper. Pour over bean mixture, cover and refrigerate. Line a serving bowl with lettuce; add bean mixture. Sprinkle with watercress.

Left to right: Pesto– and Turkey-Stuffed Pita Pockets (page 142), Rangoon Chicken Wraps (page 138), and Home-Style Barbecue Beef Wraps (page 140)

Clockwise from left: Sicilian Salsa (page 168), Curried Cauliflower Appetizer (page 169), and Corn– and Turkey-Stuffed Bell Peppers (page 177)

Clockwise from left: Chicken Vegetable Pinwheels (page 62) with broccoli and rice, Chicken and Mango with Ginger-Curry Topping (page 42) with green beans, and Sesame Turkey Loaf (page 86) with carrots and peas

Clockwise from top left: Italian Sausage and Vegetable Chowder (page 18), Chicken 'n' Vegetable Soup with Fresh Salsa (page 16), and Corn 'n' Bean Chili (page 29)

# Baked Beans with Canadian Bacon

*I*t is important to thoroughly stir the mixture at least once to ensure even cooking for all the beans. ■ MAKES 6 TO 8 SERVINGS

| | |
|---|---|
| 1 lb. dried small white beans, sorted and rinsed | 1 medium onion, chopped |
| | 1 tablespoon prepared mustard |
| 4 cups water | ½ teaspoon salt |
| ⅓ cup molasses | 2 ounces sliced Canadian bacon, cut |
| ¼ cup packed light brown sugar | into strips |

Thoroughly combine beans, water, molasses, brown sugar, onion, mustard and salt in a 3½-quart slow cooker. Place bacon strips on top. Cover and cook on HIGH about 5 hours. Stir mixture; cover and cook on HIGH 1 to 2 additional hours or until beans are tender.

Per serving: Cal 365 · Carb 66 gm · Prot 17 gm · Total fat 4 gm · Sat fat 0 gm · Cal from fat 36 · Chol 3 mg · Sodium 340 mg

# Picante Beef 'n' Beans

*T*ake this dish to your next potluck dinner and impress your friends.  ■ MAKES 6 TO 8 SERVINGS

1 lb. dried red kidney beans, sorted
  and rinsed
1 large red onion, thinly sliced
2 medium tomatoes, chopped
2 tablespoons chopped fresh cilantro

½ lb. lean beef round steak, cut into
  strips about ¼-inch thick
1 (8-oz.) jar picante sauce
2 (10½-oz.) cans condensed beef
  bouillon

Combine kidney beans, onion, tomatoes and cilantro in a 3½-quart slow cooker. Top with beef, then picante sauce and beef bouillon. Cover and cook on LOW 8 to 8½ hours or until beans and beef are tender.

Per serving: Cal 498 · Carb 66 gm · Prot 31 gm · Total fat 13 gm · Sat fat 3 gm · Cal from fat 117 · Chol 38 mg · Sodium 821 mg

# Confetti Bean Casserole

*C*orn teams up with beans for a very popular hearty combination.  ■ MAKES 5 TO 6 SERVINGS

1 lb. dried small red or pinto beans
3½ cups chicken broth
½ lb. small smoked cocktail sausage
  links, halved
1 clove garlic, crushed
1 small onion, finely chopped

1 red or green bell pepper, chopped
2 tablespoons chopped fresh parsley
½ teaspoon salt
⅛ teaspoon pepper
1 cup cooked whole-kernel corn

Combine all ingredients except corn in a slow cooker. Cover and cook on LOW 6 to 7 hours or until beans are tender. Add corn about 30 minutes before turning off heat. Serve hot.

# Easy Three-Bean Medley

*E*qually delicious whether served as a snack with chips or spread on tortillas as a favorite lunch, this dish cooks quickly because you start with canned beans. ■ MAKES ABOUT 6 CUPS

1 (15-oz.) can red beans, drained and rinsed
1 (15-oz.) can black beans, drained and rinsed
1 (8¾-oz.) can red kidney beans, drained and rinsed
1 large tomato, chopped
1 clove garlic, crushed

2 tablespoons chopped fresh cilantro
1 teaspoon chili powder
1 small cucumber
1 cup picante sauce
Tortillas or corn chips
Shredded reduced-fat Cheddar cheese or low-fat sour cream (optional)

Combine beans, tomato, garlic, cilantro and chili powder in a 3½-quart slow cooker. Peel cucumber and halve lengthwise. Scoop out and discard seeds. Dice cucumber and stir into beans. Stir in picante sauce. Cover and cook on LOW about 4 hours. Spoon beans onto tortillas or dip corn chips into warm mixture. Sprinkle with cheese or sour cream, if desired.

Per cup without tortillas: Cal 187 · Carb 36 gm · Prot 11 gm · Total fat 1 gm · Sat fat 0 gm · Cal from fat 9 · Chol 0 mg · Sodium 963 mg

# Favorite Baked Beans

*I*t is not necessary to soak beans ahead of time, but be sure to plan ahead and allow adequate cooking time. ■ MAKES 6 TO 8 SERVINGS

1 lb. dried small white beans, rinsed
3½ cups water
⅓ cup molasses
¼ cup brown sugar

1 onion, chopped
¼ lb. salt pork, cut into 1-inch cubes
1 tablespoon prepared mustard
½ teaspoon salt

Combine all ingredients in a slow cooker. Cover and cook on HIGH 6 to 7 hours or until beans are tender.

# Curried Lentils and Vegetables

*L*ightly cooking the spices together before they are added to the other ingredients is the secret to a very special flavor combination. Be very careful not to burn them. ■ MAKES 5 TO 6 SERVINGS

1½ cups baby carrots
1 cup thinly sliced celery
1 small onion, minced
2 medium yams, peeled and diced
1 cup dried lentils, sorted and rinsed
2 teaspoons vegetable oil
1 clove garlic, minced
1 tablespoon curry powder
1 teaspoon ground cumin
½ teaspoon salt

¼ teaspoon ground white pepper
1 teaspoon minced gingerroot
1 (14½-oz.) can fat-free chicken
    broth
1 tablespoon minced lemon peel
½ cup frozen green peas
½ cup nonfat plain yogurt
2 tablespoons minced green onion,
    including top

Combine carrots, celery, onion, yams and lentils in a 3½-quart slow cooker; set aside.

Heat oil in a small skillet over medium heat. Add garlic, curry powder, cumin, salt, pepper and ginger. Cook, stirring, 1 minute. Stir in chicken broth and lemon peel. Pour over vegetables in slow cooker. Cover and cook on LOW 6 to 7 hours or until vegetables are tender.

Turn control to HIGH. Place frozen peas in a strainer. Run hot water over them to thaw. Add peas to contents of slow cooker. Cover and cook on HIGH 15 minutes. Top each serving with a dab of yogurt and a sprinkle of green onion.

Per serving: Cal 182 · Carb 38 gm · Prot 10 gm · Total fat 3 gm · Sat fat 0.5 gm · Cal from fat 27 · Chol 1 mg · Sodium 491 mg

# Fresh Black-Eyed Peas

*H*ere's the perfect side dish to accompany broiled ham or chicken. ■ MAKES 4 TO 6 SERVINGS

| | |
|---|---|
| 3 to 4 slices uncooked bacon, chopped | ½ teaspoon salt |
| 3 cloves garlic, crushed | ¼ teaspoon pepper |
| 4 green onions, tops included, finely chopped | 1 teaspoon dried oregano |
| 1 cup chopped, peeled fresh or canned tomatoes | 1 cup water |
| | 1 lb. fresh or frozen black-eyed peas, thawed |

Combine all ingredients in a slow cooker. Cover and cook on HIGH 5 to 6 hours.

# Spiced Garbanzo Beans

✕◇✕◇✕◇✕◇✕◇✕◇✕◇✕◇✕◇✕◇✕◇✕◇✕◇✕◇✕◇✕◇✕◇✕◇✕◇✕◇✕◇✕◇✕◇✕◇✕◇

*T*his vegetarian delight features an exciting combination of spices to liven up garbanzo beans (also called chickpeas). ■ MAKES 6 TO 7 SERVINGS

2 (15-oz.) cans garbanzo beans
1 medium onion, chopped
1 (1-inch) piece fresh gingerroot, peeled and finely chopped
3 cloves garlic, minced
1 (14½-oz.) can diced tomatoes in juice
1 teaspoon ground black pepper
1 teaspoon ground cloves

½ teaspoon ground cardamom
½ teaspoon ground coriander
1 teaspoon ground cumin
2 bay leaves
1 (1-inch) cinnamon stick
3 dried red chiles
½ teaspoon salt
Chopped cilantro

Drain garbanzo beans; reserve ¾ cup liquid. Combine drained garbanzo beans, onion, ginger and garlic in a 3½-quart slow cooker. Add ¾ cup reserved liquid and diced tomatoes with juice. Stir in pepper, cloves, cardamom, coriander, cumin, bay leaves, cinnamon, dried chiles and salt. Cover and cook on LOW 8 to 9 hours. Remove and discard bay leaves, cinnamon stick, and chiles. Sprinkle with chopped cilantro.

Per serving: Cal 163 · Carb 29 gm · Prot 7 gm · Total fat 3 gm · Sat fat 0 gm · Cal from fat 37 · Chol 0 mg · Sodium 854 mg

# Pizza Beans

*I*f possible, stir beans once or twice while they are cooking to ensure that they all are coated with sauce. ■ MAKES 6 TO 8 SERVINGS

1 lb. dried great Northern beans
3½ cups water
4 tomatoes, peeled, seeded and
  chopped
1 onion, chopped
¼ cup chopped red or green bell
  pepper
1 clove garlic, crushed

1 teaspoon salt
½ teaspoon dried oregano, crushed
¼ teaspoon dried rosemary, crushed
1 cup (4 oz.) shredded mozzarella
  cheese
¼ cup grated Romano or Parmesan
  cheese

In a slow cooker, combine beans, water, tomatoes, onion, bell pepper, garlic, salt, oregano and rosemary. Cover and cook on HIGH 6 to 7 hours or until beans are tender. Top with mozzarella, then Romano cheese. Cover and cook another 10 minutes or until cheese melts.

# Taste-of-Italy Beans 'n' Sausage

*T*his is a slow-cooker version of a popular traditional main dish from the hill towns of Italy. ■ MAKES ABOUT 8 SERVINGS

1 lb. dried cannellini beans or lima
  beans, sorted and rinsed
4 cups water
1 clove garlic, crushed
1 (14½-oz.) can diced tomatoes with
  Italian seasoning

1 tablespoon chopped fresh sage
  leaves
½ to ¾ lb. sweet Italian turkey
  sausage, crumbled
½ teaspoon salt
¼ teaspoon ground black pepper

Combine all ingredients in a 3½-quart slow cooker. Cover and cook on HIGH 9 to 10 hours or until beans are tender.

Per serving: Cal 265 · Carb 39 gm · Prot 17 gm · Total fat 5 gm · Sat fat 0 gm · Cal from fat 45 · Chol 15 mg · Sodium 502 mg

# Sweet-Sour Bean Trio

*A* picnic wouldn't be complete without everyone's favorite bean salad. Serve hot or chilled. ■ MAKES 6 TO 8 SERVINGS

4 bacon slices
1 onion, chopped
¼ cup packed brown sugar
1 teaspoon prepared mustard
1 clove garlic, crushed

1 teaspoon salt
¼ cup vinegar
1 (1-lb.) can lima beans, drained
1 (1-lb.) can baked beans, drained
1 (1-lb.) can kidney beans, drained

Cook bacon in a skillet until crisp; reserve drippings. Crumble bacon. Combine bacon and 2 tablespoons bacon drippings with onion, brown sugar, mustard, garlic, salt and vinegar. Combine mixture with beans in a slow cooker. Cover and cook on LOW 6 to 8 hours.

# Vegetarian Soybeans

*A* garden of summer vegetables enhances this meatless dish. ■ MAKES 6 TO 8 SERVINGS

| | |
|---|---|
| 1 lb. dried soybeans, sorted and rinsed | 1 yellow bell pepper, chopped |
| 1 cup water | 1 jalapeño chile, seeded and minced |
| 4 cups vegetable juice | 1 onion, chopped |
| 2 zucchini, shredded | 2 tablespoons chopped fresh cilantro |
| 2 tomatoes, chopped | 2 teaspoons chili powder |
| | 1 clove garlic, crushed |

Combine all ingredients in a 3½-quart slow cooker. Cover and cook on HIGH 8 to 9 hours, stirring once after 7 hours if possible, or until beans are tender.

Per serving: Cal 382 · Carb 36 gm · Prot 29 gm · Total fat 15 gm · Sat fat 2 gm · Cal from fat 135 · Chol 0 mg · Sodium 146 mg

# Sour Cream Limas

*I*t is important to stir beans after 8 hours of cooking. This ensures a more even cooking of all the beans. ▪ MAKES 6 TO 8 SERVINGS

| | |
|---|---|
| 1 lb. dried baby lima beans | ¼ cup molasses |
| 4 cups water | 2 tablespoons prepared mustard |
| ¼ cup margarine or butter, melted | ½ teaspoon salt |
| ½ cup brown sugar | 1 cup sour cream |

Combine all ingredients except sour cream in a slow cooker. Cover and cook on LOW 8 hours. Stir beans; cover and continue cooking on LOW 3 to 4 hours or until beans are tender. Stir in sour cream.

# Savory Tomato Limas

*A* hearty accompaniment to hot dogs or burgers. ▪ MAKES 6 TO 8 SERVINGS

| | |
|---|---|
| 1 lb. dried large lima beans, rinsed | ½ teaspoon chili powder |
| 3 cups water | 1 (10¾-oz.) can condensed tomato |
| 1 onion, finely chopped | soup |
| 1 clove garlic, minced | 2 tablespoons vinegar |
| 1 tablespoon prepared mustard | 2 tablespoons brown sugar |
| 1 tablespoon Worcestershire sauce | ¼ lb. salt pork, cut into 1-inch cubes |
| ½ teaspoon salt | |

Combine all ingredients in a slow cooker. Cover and cook on HIGH about 5 hours or until beans are tender.

# Spicy Pintos on Tortillas

※※※※※※※※※※※※※※※※※※※※※※※※※※※※※※※※※※※※※※

*T*hese are designed for those who enjoy bean dishes with a chile accent.  ▪ MAKES 12 TORTILLAS

| | |
|---|---|
| 1 lb. dried pinto or kidney beans, sorted and rinsed | ½ teaspoon salt |
| 1 jalapeño chile, seeded and chopped | ¼ teaspoon ground black pepper |
| 1 mild green chile, seeded and chopped | 1 teaspoon chili powder |
| 1 medium red onion, chopped | 4 cups beef broth |
| 1 clove garlic, crushed | 1 cup water |
| ¼ cup chopped fresh parsley | 1 tablespoon vegetable oil |
| 2 tablespoons chopped fresh cilantro | 12 medium flour tortillas |
| | Shredded Cheddar cheese (optional) |

Combine beans, chiles, onion, garlic, parsley, cilantro, salt, pepper, chili powder, broth and water in a 3½-quart slow cooker. Cover and cook on HIGH about 6 hours or until beans are tender.

Heat oil in a large skillet over medium heat. Adding 1 or 2 tortillas at a time, heat until lightly browned; turn and brown other side. Repeat until all are browned. Dip out beans with a slotted spoon, draining off liquid. Use beans as a topping for tortillas. Sprinkle with cheese, if desired.

Per tortilla: Cal 254 · Carb 42 gm · Prot 12 gm · Total fat 5 gm · Sat fat 0.5 gm · Cal from fat 45 · Chol 0 mg · Sodium 363 mg

# Barbecued Pinto Beans

*T*hese beans are the perfect accompaniment for your favorite grilled steaks or burgers.

■ MAKES 6 TO 8 SERVINGS

1 pound dried pinto beans, sorted
   and rinsed
3 cups water
1 onion, chopped
1 green bell pepper, chopped

1 jalapeño chile, seeded and chopped
1 (18-oz.) bottle barbecue sauce
¼ cup molasses
¼ teaspoon salt

Combine all ingredients in a 3½-quart slow cooker. Cover and cook on HIGH 8 to 9 hours or until beans are tender.

Per serving: Cal 374 · Carb 66 gm · Prot 17 gm · Total fat 5 gm · Sat fat 0 gm · Cal from fat 45 · Chol 0 mg · Sodium 812 mg

# Mac's Kidney Beans

*O*ur friend Mac created a simple and thoroughly enjoyable recipe. ■ MAKES 8 TO 10 SERVINGS

4 bacon slices, chopped
3 (15-oz.) cans kidney beans, drained
1 cup bottled chili sauce
½ cup sliced green onions
⅓ cup packed brown sugar

In a small skillet, cook bacon until crisp; reserve drippings. In a slow cooker, combine bacon and 2 tablespoons drippings with drained kidney beans, chili sauce and green onions. Sprinkle top with brown sugar. Cover and cook on LOW 4 to 6 hours. Keep beans hot and serve from cooker.

# Lentil Casserole

*A* nutritious side dish that can become a main-dish salad by adding chopped cucumber and lettuce. ■ MAKES 6 TO 8 SERVINGS

> 1 cup lentils
> 2 bacon slices, chopped
> 1 cup stewed tomatoes, chopped, with juice
> 1 teaspoon Chinese five-spice powder
> ¼ teaspoon dried red pepper flakes
> 1 small onion, chopped
> 1 cup water

Rinse lentils; pick out any debris. Place all ingredients in a slow cooker. Cover and cook on LOW 7 to 8 hours or until all liquid is absorbed. Serve hot or cold.

# Corn-Bacon Pudding

*A* 4- or 5-cup metal mixing bowl makes a fine substitute for a mold or casserole dish.

■ MAKES 4 TO 6 SERVINGS

4 bacon slices, cooked and crumbled
3 eggs, separated
1 (16-oz.) can whole-kernel corn, drained
1 cup evaporated skim milk
2 teaspoons sugar

1 tablespoon all-purpose flour
1/4 teaspoon salt
1/4 teaspoon pepper
3/4 cup shredded Cheddar cheese
2 tablespoons chopped fresh parsley
2 cups hot water

Butter a 4- or 5-cup casserole dish or metal bowl that fits in your slow cooker. In a bowl, combine bacon, egg yolks, corn, milk, sugar, flour, salt and pepper. Stir in cheese. In a small bowl, beat egg whites until stiff but not dry. Fold egg whites and parsley into corn mixture. Spoon into prepared casserole dish. Cover top with foil, crimping edges to seal. Pour hot water into a slow cooker and add a rack. Set casserole on rack in cooker. Cover and cook on LOW 4 to 5 hours or until a knife inserted off-center comes out clean. Serve warm directly from casserole dish with a large spoon.

# Corn Stuffing Balls

*S*erve as an accompaniment to roast chicken or turkey, or grilled meats. ■ MAKES 8 SERVINGS

1 small onion, chopped
1/2 cup chopped celery with leaves
1 (17-oz.) can cream-style corn
1/4 cup water
1/8 teaspoon pepper

1 teaspoon poultry seasoning
2 cups herb-seasoned stuffing mix (about 8 oz.)
2 eggs, slightly beaten
1/4 cup margarine or butter, melted

In a bowl, combine onion, celery, corn, water, pepper, poultry seasoning, stuffing and eggs. Form into 8 balls. Place in bottom of a slow cooker; spoon margarine or butter over balls. Cover and cook on LOW 3½ to 4 hours.

# Mock Chile Relleno

*H*ow hot the chiles are will determine how spicy this flavorful Mexican combination is. Look for a "heat rating" on the side of the can. ■ MAKES 4 TO 5 SERVINGS

2 (4-oz.) cans whole green chiles, drained
½ cup (2 oz.) shredded Cheddar cheese
1½ cups (6 oz.) shredded Monterey Jack cheese

1 (14½-oz.) can tomatoes, drained and sliced
3 eggs, separated
½ cup evaporated milk
1½ tablespoons all-purpose flour

Grease sides and bottom of a slow cooker. Remove seeds from chiles and cut into strips. Place half the chiles in the bottom of the cooker. Sprinkle with Cheddar cheese, then layer with remaining chiles, Jack cheese and tomatoes. Beat egg whites until stiff but not dry. Beat egg yolks slightly. Fold egg yolks and milk into egg whites. Fold in flour. Pour mixture over tomatoes. Cover and cook on HIGH 2 to 3 hours or until mixture is set. Serve while piping hot.

# Curried Barley

✻✻✻✻✻✻✻✻✻✻✻✻✻✻✻✻✻✻✻✻✻✻✻✻✻✻✻✻✻✻✻✻✻✻✻✻✻✻✻✻✻✻

*E*njoy a tasty side dish that's high in fiber and delicious paired with grilled chicken.

■ MAKES 8 SERVINGS

| | |
|---|---|
| 4 cups chicken broth | ½ teaspoon curry powder |
| ⅔ cup barley | ½ cup raisins or dried currants |
| 1 to 2 carrots, peeled and chopped | ½ cup chopped onions |
| 2 garlic cloves, minced | Plain yogurt |
| ¼ teaspoon red (cayenne) pepper | |

Combine all ingredients except yogurt in a slow cooker. Cover and cook on HIGH 3 to 4 hours or until all liquid is absorbed and vegetables are tender. Serve topped with yogurt.

# Barley and Beef Stew

✻✻✻✻✻✻✻✻✻✻✻✻✻✻✻✻✻✻✻✻✻✻✻✻✻✻✻✻✻✻✻✻✻✻✻✻✻✻✻✻✻✻

*T*his chunky stew is hearty enough to serve as a main dish.  ■ MAKES ABOUT 6 SERVINGS

| | |
|---|---|
| ½ lb. beef stew meat or round steak, cut into ½-inch cubes | 2 turnips, peeled and cut into ½-inch cubes |
| ¾ cup pearl barley | 1 teaspoon dried thyme leaves |
| 4 carrots, peeled and sliced | ½ teaspoon salt |
| 2 stalks celery with leaves, chopped | ¼ teaspoon ground black pepper |
| 1 large onion, chopped | 5 cups beef broth |

Combine beef, barley, carrots, celery, onion, turnips, thyme, salt and pepper in a 3½-quart slow cooker. Pour in broth. Cover and cook on LOW 9 to 11 hours or until beef and barley are tender. Spoon into soup bowls.

Per serving: Cal 223 · Carb 30 gm · Prot 13 gm · Total fat 6 gm · Sat fat 2 gm · Cal from fat 54 · Chol 23 mg · Sodium 886 mg

# Orange Barley Casserole

*H*ere's an especially tasty accompaniment for broiled ham slices. ■ MAKES 6 TO 8 SERVINGS

2 cups orange juice
⅓ cup barley
¼ cup dried currants
¼ cup dried apricots, halved
¼ cup chopped dates

1 apple, peeled, cored and chopped
½ teaspoon ground allspice
2 to 3 tablespoons chopped walnuts
  or pecans

In a slow cooker, combine all ingredients. Cover and cook on LOW 3 to 4 hours. Serve warm.

# Couscous Provençal

*I*f using canned tomatoes, increase couscous to ½ cup. Enjoy this side dish hot or chilled.
■ MAKES 5 TO 6 SERVINGS

3 cups peeled, chopped fresh
   tomatoes or 1 (14-oz.) can
   tomatoes
3 green onions, chopped
4 cloves garlic, crushed

½ teaspoon dried thyme
1 teaspoon dried basil
⅓ cup couscous
½ cup ripe olives, sliced
Feta or blue cheese

In a slow cooker, combine tomatoes, green onions, garlic, thyme and basil. Cover and cook on LOW 5 to 6 hours. Stir in couscous and olives. Turn control to HIGH. Cover and cook on HIGH 25 to 30 minutes. Serve sprinkled with crumbled cheese.

# Stuffed Grape Leaves

*F*or a strictly vegetarian dish, substitute vegetable broth for the chicken broth. ■ MAKES 22 TO 25 GRAPE ROLLS

½ cup uncooked long-grain white
   rice
1 cup fat-free chicken broth
2 tablespoons chopped fresh parsley
1 small onion, finely chopped
¼ teaspoon salt
⅛ teaspoon ground black pepper

⅛ teaspoon ground allspice
¼ teaspoon grated lemon peel
¼ cup dried currants
2 tablespoons toasted pine nuts
   (see Note, page 3)
1 (8-oz.) jar grape leaves (40 to 45
   leaves)

In a medium saucepan, combine rice, broth, parsley, onion, salt, pepper, allspice and lemon peel. Cover and simmer gently over low heat 15 minutes or until rice is tender. Stir in currants and pine nuts; set aside.

Rinse and carefully separate grape leaves in a bowl of cold water. Remove stems, if necessary. Set aside 22 to 25 of the most perfect ones. Place a metal rack in bottom of a 3½-quart slow cooker. Top with the imperfect leaves.

On a work surface, lay perfect leaves out flat, rough or vein side up. Spoon about 1½ to 2 tablespoons stuffing near stem end of each leaf. Fold stem end up over filling, then both sides to middle. Roll up, rather tight, like a small cylinder. Stack rolls very close together on bed of leaves in slow cooker. Top with an inverted heavy plate to hold rolls in place. Add enough hot water to cover rolls. Cover and cook on LOW 6 to 7 hours or until leaves are tender. Drain and serve warm or at room temperature.

Per grape roll: Cal 26 · Carb 5 gm · Prot 1 gm · Total fat 0.5 gm · Sat fat 0 gm · Cal from fat 5 · Chol 0 mg · Sodium 74 mg

# Shades of Autumn Rice

*A* combination of popular fall flavors enhances rice in the slow cooker—an ideal accompaniment to roast pork or chicken. ■ MAKES 4 TO 6 SERVINGS

1 cup uncooked brown rice
1½ cups apple juice or cider
1 (10½-oz.) can condensed chicken
    broth
1 apple, peeled, cored and chopped
⅓ cup golden raisins

¼ cup chopped walnuts
1 tablespoon brown sugar
¼ teaspoon freshly grated nutmeg
½ teaspoon ground cinnamon
½ teaspoon salt

Combine all ingredients in a slow cooker. Cover and cook on LOW 4 to 5 hours or until rice is tender.

# Wild Rice with Portobello Mushrooms

*P*ortobello mushrooms add a meatlike flavor and texture. ■ MAKES 5 TO 6 SERVINGS

¾ cup wild rice, rinsed and drained
½ cup long-grain brown rice
½ lb. portobello mushrooms, stems
    removed
1 medium onion, diced
2 cups diced celery
½ lb. boneless lean pork, cut into
    ½-inch cubes
1 (10¾-oz.) can reduced-fat cream of
    mushroom soup

¼ teaspoon ground sage
¼ teaspoon ground black pepper
2 cups hot chicken broth or bouillon
¼ cup soy sauce
¼ cup minced fresh parsley
¼ cup toasted slivered almonds
    (optional) (see Note, page 3)

Combine rices in a 3½-quart slow cooker. Wipe mushrooms with a damp cloth. Cut into ⅜-inch-thick slices; add to slow cooker. Stir in onion, celery, pork, soup, sage and pepper. Stir in broth and soy sauce. Cover and cook on LOW 6 to 7 hours or until all the liquid is absorbed and rices are tender. Stir before serving. Garnish each serving with minced fresh parsley and toasted almonds, if desired.

Per serving: Cal 314 · Carb 44 gm · Prot 19 gm · Total fat 8 gm · Sat fat 2 gm · Cal from fat 72 · Chol 31 mg · Sodium 1576 mg

# VEGETABLES & SIDE DISHES

*W*ith an increased emphasis on the nutritional value of fresh vegetables in our diets, we have become interested in using them in a variety of ways. One of the greatest advantages of cooking vegetables in a slow cooker is being able to cook them ahead of time. It is not necessary to watch, stir or worry about boil-overs. You can be doing something else around the house or running errands. When you return, the vegetables are done. Serve them for dinner or combine them with other ingredients in a casserole that can be browned in the oven later and then served.

For an impressive, aromatic vegetable combination, you will enjoy Sorrento Potato and Cheese Packets. Potatoes, pearl onions and cherry tomatoes are packed in foil with herbs and cheese, then cooked on a trivet in the slow cooker.

Shells of many fresh vegetables make attractive, appetizing, and flavorful containers for main dishes. We especially enjoy red or green bell peppers stuffed with a well-seasoned combination of smoked turkey sausage and corn.

Rules for cooking vegetables vary almost as much as the vegetables themselves. For example, you will discover countless ways to prepare the squash family in your slow cooker. You can stuff acorn squash, mash banana squash and simmer zucchini. Herbed Squash Trio combines zucchini, crookneck and pattypan squash. Calabacitas is a spicy blend of zucchini, tomatoes, corn and chiles.

It is wise to turn the control to HIGH when you are cooking most vegetables in a slow cooker. Many of them have a tendency to dry out and discolor when left on LOW for a long time.

Dense vegetables like carrots, celery, turnips, parsnips, onions and beets take an extra-long time to cook in a slow cooker. Cut these kinds of vegetables into smaller pieces as suggested in the recipes for Carrots in Dilled Wine Sauce and Orange-Glazed Ginger Carrots. Strangely enough, these vegetables take as long or longer to cook than many meats. We suggest you thinly slice, chop, halve or quarter vegetables to ensure they get done in the specified cooking time. Be sure to consider this when combining vegetables with meat.

Recipes for sweet potatoes or yams may be interchanged. Use the one you prefer or whichever is available in your market. Sweet and white potatoes are delicious when "baked" in a slow cooker. Wash the potatoes but do not actually dry them. While still damp, place in the slow cooker and cook on LOW until soft and tender. Whole potatoes can be placed on top of a roast and will be done when the roast is. Try adding two or three potatoes to Dilled Pot Roast.

# Carrots in Dilled Wine Sauce

*C*arrots are attractive and easy to eat when cut into ¼-inch sticks about 3 inches long.
■ MAKES 6 TO 8 SERVINGS

8 medium carrots, peeled and cut into
  small sticks
½ cup chicken broth
½ cup dry white wine
1 teaspoon dried dill weed

3 tablespoons finely chopped shallots
½ teaspoon salt
1 tablespoon fresh lemon juice
2 tablespoons cornstarch
2 tablespoons water

Place carrots in a slow cooker. Combine broth, wine, dill weed, shallots, salt and lemon juice in a small bowl. Pour mixture over carrots. Cover and cook on HIGH 2 to 2½ hours or until carrots are tender. In a small bowl, dissolve cornstarch in water; stir into carrot mixture. Cover and cook on HIGH 10 to 15 minutes or until slightly thickened.

# Orange-Glazed Ginger Carrots

*T*ry this dish on friends who claim they don't like vegetables, and watch them change their minds. ■ MAKES 5 TO 6 SERVINGS

6 medium carrots, thinly sliced (about 3 cups)
3 tablespoons margarine or butter, melted
1 teaspoon grated gingerroot
3 tablespoons orange marmalade
2 tablespoons chopped pecans

Combine carrots, margarine or butter, ginger, marmalade and pecans in a slow cooker. Cover and cook on HIGH 2 to 3 hours or until carrots are tender.

# Lemon Parsnips & Carrots

*N*aturally sweet carrots and parsnips are enlivened with a refreshing lemon and mint sauce. ■ MAKES 4 TO 6 SERVINGS

5 to 6 parsnips, peeled and thinly sliced (3 cups)
4 to 5 carrots, peeled and thinly sliced (3 cups)
2 cups chicken broth
¼ cup fresh lemon juice
3 tablespoons cornstarch
3 tablespoons water
2 tablespoons chopped fresh mint leaves

Place parsnips and carrots in a slow cooker. Pour in broth and lemon juice. Cover and cook on HIGH 2 to 4 hours or until vegetables are tender. In a small bowl, dissolve cornstarch in water; stir into vegetables with mint. Cover and cook 10 to 15 minutes.

# Carrots with Dijon Mustard and Brown Sugar

*F*or an easy way to fix carrots for a family get-together, cook and serve in the slow cooker.
■ MAKES 10 TO 12 SERVINGS

12 to 14 medium carrots, cut into sticks about 2 × ½ inches
1 tablespoon margarine or butter, at room temperature
⅓ cup Dijon mustard
½ cup packed light brown sugar
1 teaspoon grated gingerroot

Place carrots in a 3½-quart slow cooker. In a small bowl, combine margarine or butter, mustard, brown sugar and ginger; stir into carrots. Cover and cook on HIGH for 2 to 3 hours or until carrots are tender.

Per serving: Cal 89 · Carb 19 gm · Prot 1 gm · Total fat 1 gm · Sat fat 0 gm · Cal from fat 9 · Chol 0 mg · Sodium 67 mg

# Green Beans, Portuguese Style

*T*his recipe has received high praise for many years. Try it and you too will receive compliments. ■ MAKES 8 SERVINGS

¼ lb. salt pork
2 lb. fresh green beans
2 medium tomatoes
2 cups beef bouillon
½ teaspoon salt
½ teaspoon sugar
¼ teaspoon pepper

Dice salt pork and spread over bottom of a slow cooker. Wash beans. Break each bean into 2 or 3 pieces; place in pot over salt pork. Peel, seed and cube tomatoes; spoon over beans. Add bouillon with salt, sugar and pepper. Cover and cook on HIGH 3 to 4 hours or until beans are tender. Drain and serve hot.

# Leeks au Gratin

*L*eeks are the mild members of the onion family; here they are combined with garlic and onion. ▪ MAKES 6 SERVINGS

2 leeks
1 small onion, chopped
3 cloves garlic, chopped
1 celery stalk
1¼ cups chicken broth

½ teaspoon dry mustard
¼ cup cornstarch
½ cup evaporated milk
1 cup shredded Cheddar cheese
Salt and pepper, to taste

Trim off tough green leaves from leeks. Cut leeks lengthwise and rinse to remove sand and dirt. Cut white part only into thin slices. Combine with onion, garlic, celery, broth and mustard in a slow cooker. Cook on LOW 6 to 7 hours. Turn control to HIGH. In a small bowl, dissolve cornstarch in milk; stir into leek mixture. Add cheese. Cover and cook on HIGH about 15 minutes until thickened and cheese has melted. Season with salt and pepper.

# Sweet-Sour Baby Onions

*F*or a special treat, try these with grilled chicken or chops. Put them on about 4 hours before serving time and let them cook unattended. ▪ MAKES 6 SERVINGS

2 (10-oz.) bags frozen small whole onions, thawed
2 tablespoons olive oil
2 tablespoons red wine vinegar
2 tablespoons brown sugar
1 teaspoon chicken bouillon granules or 1 bouillon cube
½ teaspoon salt
⅛ teaspoon pepper

In a bowl, combine onions and oil; toss until well coated. In a slow cooker, combine onions with vinegar, brown sugar, bouillon granules, salt and pepper. Cover and cook on LOW 4 to 4½ hours or until onions are soft.

# Baked Onions and Apples with Cinnamon

*T*his fills your kitchen with a wonderful aroma while it is cooking! ■ MAKES 6 TO 8 SERVINGS

2 large onions, cut in half from top to bottom, then crosswise in thin slices
½ teaspoon salt
¼ teaspoon ground black pepper
4 large baking apples, cored and thinly sliced

2 tablespoons sugar
1 teaspoon ground cinnamon
2 tablespoons margarine or butter
2 tablespoons chopped pecans (optional)

Arrange half of the onion slices in a 3½-quart slow cooker; sprinkle with half of the salt and pepper. Top with half of the apples; sprinkle with half the sugar and cinnamon. Repeat layers with remaining ingredients. Dot top with margarine or butter. Cover and cook on LOW 8 hours or until onions and apples are tender. Top with chopped pecans, if desired.

Per serving: Cal 137 · Carb 26 gm · Prot 1 gm · Total fat 4 gm · Sat fat 1 gm · Cal from fat 36 · Chol 0 mg · Sodium 224 mg

# Steamed Broccoli-Corn Pudding

*F*resh corn and broccoli are combined in this vegetable casserole. ■ MAKES 5 TO 6 SERVINGS

2 ears of corn
2 eggs, slightly beaten
1 cup evaporated skim milk
1 small bunch (about 1/2 lb.) fresh
  broccoli, finely chopped
1/4 cup yellow cornmeal

1/2 teaspoon chili powder
1/8 teaspoon ground black pepper
1/4 teaspoon salt
2 tablespoons grated Parmesan
  cheese
2 cups hot water

Grease bottom and sides of a 6-cup baking dish or metal bowl that fits into a slow cooker; set aside.

Cut corn kernels off cobs. In a medium bowl, combine corn, eggs, milk, broccoli, cornmeal, chili powder, pepper and salt. Pour into prepared dish. Sprinkle with Parmesan cheese. Cover with foil, crimping edges to seal.

Pour hot water into a 4- to 5-quart slow cooker and add a metal rack. Set casserole on rack in slow cooker. Cover and cook on HIGH 2 1/2 to 3 hours or until a knife inserted in mixture comes out clean. Serve warm from baking dish.

Per serving: Cal 151 · Carb 21 gm · Prot 10 gm · Total fat 4 gm · Sat fat 1 gm · Cal from fat 36 · Chol 89 mg · Sodium 262 mg

# Rhineland Sweet-Sour Cabbage

*A* popular accompaniment to spareribs or pork roast. In German families it's always served with Christmas dinner. ■ MAKES 5 TO 6 SERVINGS

4 bacon slices, diced
¼ cup packed brown sugar
2 tablespoons all-purpose flour
½ teaspoon salt
⅛ teaspoon pepper

¼ cup water
¼ cup vinegar
1 medium head red cabbage,
　shredded (about 8 cups)
1 small onion, finely chopped

In a skillet, cook bacon until crisp; reserve drippings. Combine 1 tablespoon drippings in a slow cooker with remaining ingredients, except cooked bacon. Cover and cook on LOW 6½ to 7 hours or until cabbage is tender. Spoon into a serving bowl; sprinkle with reserved bacon.

# Ragout of Red Cabbage with Port

*S*erve as an accompaniment to roast pork, ham or duck. ■ MAKES ABOUT 10 SERVINGS

1 medium head (about 2 lb.) red
　cabbage
1 large red onion, chopped
1 medium apple, cored and chopped
Peel of ½ large orange, orange part
　only, cut into fine slivers
2 tablespoons sugar
1 teaspoon salt

½ teaspoon ground black pepper
½ cup port or other sweet red wine
1 tablespoon cornstarch
¼ cup red wine vinegar
½ to 1 teaspoon caraway seeds,
　crushed (optional)

Finely shred cabbage. Combine cabbage, onion, apple, orange peel, sugar, salt, pepper and wine in a 3½-quart slow cooker. Cover and cook on LOW 7 to 8 hours or until vegetables are tender. Turn control to HIGH. In a small bowl, dissolve cornstarch in vinegar. Add to cabbage mixture and stir. Cover and cook on HIGH 15 to 20 minutes or until slightly thickened. Add caraway, if desired.

> Per serving: Cal 63 · Carb 12 gm · Prot 1 gm · Total fat 0 gm · Sat fat 0 gm · Cal from fat 0 · Chol 0 mg · Sodium 224 mg

# Eggplant-Artichoke Parmigiana

*I*f you prefer, use homemade tomato sauce rather than canned. ■ MAKES 4 TO 6 SERVINGS

| | |
|---|---|
| 1 medium eggplant | 2 tablespoons capers, drained |
| ½ teaspoon salt | 2 teaspoons snipped fresh rosemary |
| 1 (14-oz.) jar tomato pasta sauce |    or ½ teaspoon dried |
| 1 (10-oz.) package frozen artichoke | ¼ teaspoon pepper |
|    hearts, thawed and quartered | ⅓ cup grated Parmesan cheese |

Cut eggplant into ¾-inch slices. Cut slices in half; sprinkle with salt. Alternate layers of eggplant, pasta sauce, artichoke hearts and capers in a slow cooker. Sprinkle with rosemary and pepper. Cover and cook on HIGH 4 to 5 hours or until eggplant is tender. Sprinkle with cheese and serve.

# Spicy Eggplant with Pine Nuts

*An* exciting yet easy way to add interest to a vegetable dish. ▪ MAKES 6 TO 7 SERVINGS

| | |
|---|---|
| 1 large eggplant | ¼ teaspoon salt |
| 1 medium onion, thinly sliced | ⅛ teaspoon ground black pepper |
| 1 jalapeño chile, seeded and chopped | ¼ teaspoon ground cumin |
| 1 clove garlic, minced | 2 teaspoons vegetable or olive oil |
| 1 medium tomato, chopped | 3 tablespoons pine nuts |

Cut eggplant crosswise into ¾-inch slices; place in a 3½-quart slow cooker. Top with onion, jalapeño chile, garlic, tomato, salt, pepper and cumin. Cover and cook on LOW about 5 hours or until eggplant is tender.

While eggplant cooks, heat oil in a small skillet over medium heat. Add pine nuts and sauté, stirring, until golden, about 3 minutes. Transfer eggplant to a serving dish and sprinkle with pine nuts.

Per serving: Cal 61 · Carb 6 gm · Prot 1 gm · Total fat 4 gm · Sat fat 0 gm · Cal from fat 36 · Chol 0 mg · Sodium 93 mg

# Acorn Squash, Indonesian

*C*hoose your favorite chutney or try Nectarine Chutney (see page 333) or Fresh Mango Chutney (page 334).  ■ MAKES 6 SERVINGS

3 acorn squash
Salt and pepper
¼ cup margarine or butter, melted
⅓ cup chutney
⅓ cup flaked coconut

Cut each squash in half; remove seeds. Wash and drain excess water but do not dry. Sprinkle with salt and pepper. Place in a slow cooker. Cover and cook on LOW 3 to 5 hours or until tender. Remove from cooker and place cut side up on a broiler pan or heatproof platter.

Preheat oven to 400F (205C). Brush inside of squash with margarine or butter. Mix chutney and coconut; spoon mixture into cavities of squash. Bake about 15 minutes or until bubbly.

# Sweet-and-Sour Squash

*S*erve as a Moroccan-inspired vegetable dish with traditional meats or as an accompaniment to COUSCOUS.  ■ MAKES 4 TO 5 SERVINGS

¾-lb. uncooked unpeeled banana squash
2 large leaves uncooked kale
3 oz. Canadian bacon, chopped
¾ cup sweet-and-sour sauce

Remove and discard peel from squash; cut into ½-inch pieces. Place squash on bottom of a 3½-quart slow cooker. Trim kale and cut crosswise into ½-inch strips; add to squash.

Sprinkle the vegetables with bacon. Spoon sweet-and-sour sauce over all. Cover and cook on LOW 4 to 4 ½ hours or until squash is tender.

Per serving: Cal 118 · Carb 22 gm · Prot 4 gm · Total fat 2 gm · Sat fat 0 gm · Cal from fat 18 · Chol 8 mg · Sodium 358 mg

# Herbed Squash Trio

*T*his three-squash combination results in a colorful and appetizing vegetable dish.

■ MAKES 6 TO 8 SERVINGS

4 zucchini (about 1¼ lb.)
2 crookneck squash (about ½ lb.)
1 pattypan squash (about 2 oz.)
½ teaspoon salt
¼ teaspoon pepper
⅛ teaspoon garlic salt

¼ cup margarine or butter
¾ cup herb-seasoned croutons
3 tablespoons grated Parmesan cheese
1 tablespoon chopped fresh chives

Cut all the squash into ¾-inch pieces. Put squash in bottom of a slow cooker. Sprinkle with salt, pepper and garlic salt. Dot with margarine or butter. Sprinkle with croutons, then cheese and chives. Cover and cook on LOW 6 to 7 hours or until tender. Serve with a slotted spoon.

# Calabacitas

*A* versatile side dish by itself, or add cooked beans and use as a filling for vegetarian tacos or enchiladas. ■ MAKES 5 TO 6 SERVINGS

2 medium zucchini
1 (16-oz.) can stewed tomatoes with juice
1 small onion, chopped
1 cup cooked whole-kernel corn

1 (4-oz.) can roasted green chiles, chopped
1 teaspoon dried oregano
½ teaspoon sugar
Salt and pepper

Cut zucchini into ¾-inch pieces. Combine all ingredients in a slow cooker. Cover and cook on HIGH 2 to 3 hours or until zucchini is tender. Season with salt and pepper to taste.

# Creole Zucchini

*F*ortunately these ingredients are available year round. ■ MAKES 6 OR 7 SERVINGS

2 lb. zucchini
1 small green bell pepper, chopped
1 small onion, chopped
1 clove garlic, minced
1 teaspoon salt

¼ teaspoon pepper
4 tomatoes, peeled and chopped
2 tablespoons margarine or butter
2 tablespoons minced fresh parsley

Cut zucchini into ¼-inch slices. In a slow cooker, combine zucchini, bell pepper, onion, garlic, salt and pepper. Top with chopped tomatoes, then margarine or butter. Cover and cook on HIGH about 2 hours or until zucchini is tender. Sprinkle with chopped parsley.

# Sorrento Potato and Cheese Packets

✕◇✕◇✕◇✕◇✕◇✕◇✕◇✕◇✕◇✕◇✕◇✕◇✕◇✕◇✕◇✕◇✕◇✕◇✕◇✕◇✕◇✕◇

*T*he potatoes absorb the rich flavors of the Mediterranean, releasing a mouth-watering aroma when the packet is opened.  ■ MAKES 6 SERVINGS

6 medium red potatoes, cut into
   eighths
18 pearl onions, trimmed and peeled
18 cherry tomatoes
6 cloves garlic, thinly sliced
4 to 6 ounces goat or feta cheese,
   crumbled
About 2 tablespoons olive oil

1 tablespoon finely chopped fresh
   rosemary
1½ teaspoons dried oregano leaves,
   crushed
½ teaspoon salt
¼ teaspoon ground black pepper
¼ cup water

Cut 6 (15 × 12-inch) sheets of foil. For each serving, place 1 potato, 3 onions and 3 cherry tomatoes in center of each foil sheet. Sprinkle each serving with 1 garlic clove, then one-sixth of the cheese. Drizzle each with about ½ teaspoon olive oil, and then sprinkle with equal amounts of rosemary, oregano, salt and pepper. Bring short ends of foil together; fold over twice to seal. Insert trivet in bottom of a 3½-quart slow cooker; pour in water. Arrange foil packets on trivet. Cover pot and cook on LOW about 8 hours or until vegetables are tender. To serve, place 1 packet on each plate.

Per serving: Cal 262 · Carb 40 gm · Prot 7 gm · Total fat 9 gm · Sat fat 3 gm · Cal from fat 81 · Chol 17 mg · Sodium 406 mg

# Potato and Turnip Slices with Mustard and Horseradish

*T*his appealing combination will entice almost anyone to enjoy vegetables.  ■ MAKES 6 TO 7 SERVINGS

1 (5-oz.) can evaporated skim milk
1 tablespoon sweet-hot mustard
1 tablespoon prepared horseradish
½ teaspoon salt
⅛ teaspoon ground black pepper
⅛ teaspoon ground nutmeg

5 medium potatoes, peeled and thinly sliced
3 medium turnips, peeled and thinly sliced
1 tablespoon chopped fresh chives

In a small bowl, combine milk, mustard, horseradish, salt, pepper and nutmeg. Place half of the potatoes into a 3½-quart slow cooker; top with half the turnips. Spoon half of the milk mixture over all. Repeat with remaining potatoes, turnips, and milk mixture. Sprinkle with chopped chives. Cover and cook on LOW about 5 hours or until vegetables are tender.

Per serving: Cal 128 · Carb 28 gm · Prot 4 gm · Total fat 0 gm · Sat fat 0 gm · Cal from fat 0 · Chol 1 mg · Sodium 271 mg

# Golden Delicious Apples and Yam Scallop

*T*he cinnamon- and nutmeg-accented apples and yams are a perfect fall dish to accompany a ham or a pork roast. ■ MAKES 6 TO 8 SERVINGS

5 or 6 medium yams, peeled and cut into ½-inch-thick slices
3 medium Golden Delicious apples, cored and cut into ½-inch-thick slices
3 tablespoons fresh lemon juice
¾ cup lightly packed light brown sugar

1 tablespoon all-purpose flour
1 teaspoon ground cinnamon
¼ teaspoon ground nutmeg
¼ teaspoon salt
¼ teaspoon ground white pepper
¼ cup chopped pecans
1 tablespoon margarine or butter (optional)

In a large bowl, combine yams, apples and lemon juice; toss to coat. In a small bowl, combine brown sugar, flour, cinnamon, nutmeg, salt, pepper and pecans. Place half of the yam mixture in a 4- to 5-quart slow cooker; top with half of the brown sugar mixture. Repeat with remaining yam mixture and brown sugar mixture. Dot top with margarine or butter, if desired. Cover and cook on LOW 7 to 8 hours or until yams and apples are tender.

Per serving: Cal 275 · Carb 62 gm · Prot 2 gm · Total fat 3 gm · Sat fat 0 gm · Cal from fat 27 · Chol 0 mg · Sodium 107 mg

# Old-Fashioned Stewed Tomatoes

*S*easoned croutons top off this dish, which has been a family favorite for several generations. ■ MAKES 5 TO 6 SERVINGS

| | |
|---|---|
| 4 to 5 large ripe tomatoes | ½ teaspoon sugar |
| Boiling water | 1 tablespoon chopped fresh basil |
| Cold water | 1 tablespoon chopped fresh parsley |
| 2 tablespoons margarine or butter | 1 bay leaf |
| 1 onion, thinly sliced | ½ teaspoon salt |
| ½ cup chopped celery | ⅛ teaspoon pepper |
| ¼ cup chopped green bell pepper | 1 cup seasoned croutons |

Dip tomatoes in boiling water 20 to 30 seconds. Drop into cold water and remove skins. Halve tomatoes, remove seeds and core. Coarsely chop tomatoes.

Combine tomatoes in a slow cooker with margarine or butter, onion, celery, bell pepper, sugar, basil, parsley, bay leaf, salt and pepper. Cover and cook on LOW 6 to 7 hours. Remove bay leaf and discard. Top with croutons.

# Stuffed Green Peppers

*I*f all the peppers do not fit in the bottom of the slow cooker, carefully place three in one layer and two on top. ■ MAKES 5 SERVINGS

| | |
|---|---|
| 5 green bell peppers | 1 (11- or 12-oz.) can whole-kernel |
| ½ lb. lean ground beef | corn, drained |
| ¼ cup finely chopped onion | 1 tablespoon Worcestershire sauce |
| 1 tablespoon chopped | 1 teaspoon prepared mustard |
| pimiento | 1 (10¾-oz.) can condensed tomato |
| ½ teaspoon salt | soup |

Cut a slice off the top of each pepper. Remove core, seeds, and white membrane. In a bowl, combine beef, onion, pimiento, salt and corn. Spoon mixture into peppers. Stand peppers up in a slow cooker. Add Worcestershire sauce and mustard to undiluted soup; pour over peppers. Cover and cook on LOW 7 to 8 hours or until peppers are tender.

# Corn- and Turkey-Stuffed Bell Peppers

*T*his colorful main dish is loaded with important nutrients. ■ MAKES 6 SERVINGS

½ lb. smoked turkey sausage, finely chopped
1 medium onion, finely chopped
1 (11-oz.) can whole-kernel corn, drained
2 slices toasted bread, crusts removed and cubed
2 tablespoons chopped fresh parsley

½ teaspoon salt
⅛ teaspoon ground black pepper
1 teaspoon chopped fresh thyme or ¼ teaspoon dried
2 medium tomatoes, seeded, peeled and chopped
3 large red or green bell peppers, cut in half lengthwise and seeded

In a large bowl, combine turkey sausage, onion, corn, bread, parsley, salt, black pepper, thyme and tomatoes. Spoon into pepper halves. Arrange on bottom of a 3½-quart slow cooker, stacking if necessary. Cover and cook on LOW about 5 hours or until peppers are tender.

Per serving: Cal 150 · Carb 21 gm · Prot 9 gm · Total fat 4 gm · Sat fat 1 gm · Cal from fat 36 · Chol 20 mg · Sodium 665 mg

# Stuffed Potatoes

*B*e creative and add additional toppings such as chopped pimiento, salsa, nuts or herbs.

■ MAKES 5 TO 6 SERVINGS

| | |
|---|---|
| 5 to 6 large baking potatoes | 1/8 teaspoon pepper |
| 3 tablespoons margarine or butter | 2 tablespoons grated Parmesan |
| 1/2 cup milk | cheese |
| 1/2 cup sour cream | Chopped fresh chives |
| 1 teaspoon salt | |

Wash potatoes; drain but do not dry. Place damp potatoes in a slow cooker. Cover and cook on LOW 6 to 8 hours or until tender. Remove from cooker. Cut off top third of each potato lengthwise and scoop out interior, leaving a 1/4-inch shell. Mash potato pulp. Add margarine or butter, milk, sour cream, salt and pepper. Beat until fluffy, adding more milk if necessary. Spoon mixture into shells, mounding tops. Sprinkle with cheese.

Place potatoes in a shallow baking pan. Preheat oven to 425F (220C) if serving now or cover and refrigerate to serve later. Bake 15 minutes or until hot and lightly browned. Top with chopped chives.

# Stuffed Honeyed Sweet Potatoes

Cook and stuff the potatoes ahead of time, then heat in the oven at serving time. ■ MAKES 5 TO 6 SERVINGS

| | |
|---|---|
| 5 to 6 sweet potatoes | 2 tablespoons dark rum |
| 1/2 cup margarine or butter, room temperature | 1/2 teaspoon ground cardamom |
| 1/4 cup half-and-half | 1/4 teaspoon salt |
| 2 tablespoons honey | 2 tablespoons chopped walnuts |

Wash potatoes; place damp potatoes in a slow cooker. Cover and cook on LOW about 5 hours or until done. Cut off top third of each potato lengthwise and scoop out interior, leaving a 1/4-inch shell. Mash potato pulp with margarine or butter, half-and-half, honey, rum, cardamom and salt. Return mixture to shells. Top with walnuts.

Arrange potatoes on a shallow baking sheet. Preheat oven to 425F (220C) if serving now or cover and refrigerate to serve later. Bake 15 minutes or until hot and lightly browned.

# Pork- and Chutney-Stuffed Onions

*A*n appetizing way to use leftover roast pork—serve as a light main dish or as a side dish.

- MAKES 5 SERVINGS

5 medium (about 8 oz. each) onions
2 cups chopped cooked boneless pork roast or cutlets (about 8 oz.)
1/4 cup soft bread crumbs
1 tablespoon chopped fresh parsley
1/8 teaspoon Italian seasoning

2 tablespoons fruit chutney, fruit finely chopped
1/4 teaspoon salt
1/8 teaspoon ground black pepper
1 to 2 tablespoons toasted coconut (see Note, page 134) or chopped cashews

Cut off about a 1/2-inch slice from top of each onion. Peel onions and scoop out centers, leaving about 1/2-inch-thick sides and bottoms. In a medium bowl, combine pork, bread crumbs, parsley, Italian seasoning, chutney, salt and pepper. Spoon into onion shells. Place onions on bottom of a 4- to 5-quart slow cooker. Cover and cook on LOW 7 to 8 hours or until onions are done. Sprinkle with coconut or cashews.

Per serving: Cal 168 · Carb 23 gm · Prot 12 gm · Total fat 3 gm · Sat fat 1 gm · Cal from fat 27 · Chol 30 mg · Sodium 200 mg

# Marinara Sauce

*F*or an Italian-style seafood sauce, add 1 pound cooked shrimp, clams or scallops at the end and cook on HIGH 10 to 15 minutes. ■ MAKES ABOUT 3 CUPS

1 (16-oz.) can peeled tomatoes, cut up
1 (6-oz.) can tomato paste
1 clove garlic, minced
2 tablespoons minced fresh parsley
1 teaspoon dried oregano

½ teaspoon dried basil
1 teaspoon salt
¼ teaspoon pepper
½ teaspoon seasoned salt
Cooked spaghetti
Grated Parmesan cheese

In a slow cooker, combine tomatoes, tomato paste, garlic, parsley, oregano, basil, salt, pepper and seasoned salt. Cover and cook on LOW 6 to 7 hours. Serve over cooked spaghetti. Top with Parmesan cheese.

# Sicilian Salsa

*F*or a change, try this salsa with your favorite pasta.  ■ MAKES 6 TO 8 SERVINGS

2 medium eggplants, peeled and diced
½ cup chopped onion
½ cup diced celery
3 large cloves garlic, minced
1 (6-oz.) can tomato paste
3 tablespoons red wine vinegar
1 tablespoon olive oil
½ teaspoon dried oregano leaves, crushed
½ teaspoon dried basil leaves, crushed

½ teaspoon ground black pepper
¼ cup capers, drained
¼ cup small pimiento-stuffed olives, thinly sliced
3 tablespoons minced fresh parsley
1½ tablespoons toasted pine nuts (see Note, page 3)
1 loaf French or Italian bread, thinly sliced

Combine eggplant, onion, celery, garlic, tomato paste, vinegar, olive oil, oregano, basil and pepper in a 3½-quart slow cooker. Cover and cook on LOW 6 to 8 hours or until eggplants are tender. Stir in capers, olives, parsley and pine nuts. Serve at room temperature or chilled. To serve, spoon on sliced French or Italian bread.

Per serving: Cal 288 · Carb 46 gm · Prot 9 gm · Total fat 9 gm · Sat fat 1 gm · Cal from fat 288 · Chol 0 mg · Sodium 767 mg

# Vegetarian Sauce

*U*se this tasty sauce as a topping for pasta or rice, or spoon over an omelet. ■ MAKES 6 TO 8 SERVINGS

1/3 cup dried mushrooms, rinsed
6 sun-dried tomatoes, cut in halves
1 (28-oz.) can crushed tomatoes
1/2 medium onion, finely chopped
2 cloves garlic, crushed
1 (15-oz.) can white kidney beans
   (cannellini), drained
1/2 cup red wine

2 tablespoons chopped green bell
   pepper
1/3 cup green peas, fresh or frozen
   and thawed
1 tablespoon chopped fresh parsley
Salt and pepper
Cooked pasta or rice
Crumbled goat or blue cheese

Break dried mushrooms in pieces; discard tough stems. In a slow cooker, combine mushrooms with sun-dried tomatoes, crushed tomatoes, onion, garlic, beans, wine and bell pepper. Cover and cook on HIGH 2½ to 3½ hours. Add peas and parsley. Cover and cook 15 minutes. Season with salt and pepper to taste. Serve over pasta or rice; sprinkle with crumbled goat or blue cheese.

# Classic Tomato-Vegetable Pasta Sauce

*S*tir in 1 tablespoon fresh basil when making the sauce, then sprinkle an extra teaspoon on top of the finished dish for extra eye appeal and flavor. ■ MAKES 4 TO 5 SERVINGS

| | |
|---|---|
| 1 (28-oz.) can tomato puree | 1 tablespoon chopped fresh basil |
| 2 stalks celery, chopped | ¼ teaspoon salt |
| 2 medium leeks, chopped and rinsed | ⅛ teaspoon ground black pepper |
| 1 cup sliced fresh mushrooms | 12 ounces spaghetti or noodles |
| 1 clove garlic, crushed | 1 teaspoon finely chopped fresh basil |
| ¼ cup dry red wine | |

Combine tomato puree, celery, leeks, mushrooms, garlic, wine, 1 tablespoon chopped basil, salt and pepper in a 3½-quart slow cooker. Cover and cook on LOW 6 to 7 hours or until vegetables are tender.

Cook pasta according to package directions. Drain and transfer to a serving bowl. Spoon sauce over pasta. Sprinkle sauce with finely chopped basil.

Per serving: Cal 453 · Carb 94 gm · Prot 16 gm · Total fat 2 gm · Sat fat 0 gm · Cal from fat 18 · Chol 0 mg · Sodium 963 mg

# PUDDINGS, CAKES & BREADS

## ✕✕✕✕✕✕✕✕✕✕✕✕✕✕✕✕✕✕✕✕✕✕✕✕✕

*S*teamed breads and "puddings," such as Banana Nut Bread and Persimmon Pudding, are moist and delicious when made in your slow cooker. An old holiday favorite from England, Traditional Plum Pudding is filled with dried fruits and nuts. With the even temperature in your slow cooker, you don't need to constantly check for water or worry about cakes and breads drying out on the surface.

There are a few tricks to remember when "baking" in one of these pots. First, turn the control to HIGH. The LOW setting is too low to give breads and cakes the texture you expect. With breads and cakes, you will need an additional container inside the slow cooker, covered with a lid or foil. The container is placed on a metal rack or trivet inside the pot. If you don't have a metal rack or trivet to fit your slow cooker, crumple foil and place it in the bottom of the cooker to support the baking container. Pour 2 cups of hot water around the container to provide steam for cooking the bread.

As a rule, it is not a good idea to remove the lid or foil from the bread container during the first 2 hours of cooking. After that, check the bread by inserting a wooden pick in the mixture. If the pick comes out clean, the bread is done.

For some recipes, such as Blueberry Coffee Cake and Cornbread, the procedure is slightly different. Cakes are "baked" in a pan set directly on the bottom of the slow cooker, similar to the way you would do it in an oven. It is not necessary to use a trivet or water. Instead of covering the uncooked cake mixture with foil or a lid, cover the top with four or five layers of paper towels. Because there is more moisture in a slow cooker than in an oven, it is necessary to compensate for this with the paper towels to help absorb the moisture on top of the cake. Also, leave the lid of your slow cooker slightly open to let extra moisture escape.

The type and kind of container to use for breads and cakes will depend on the size of your pot. In addition to molds and coffee cans, metal mixing bowls, springform or small Bundt pans make excellent containers. The following containers hold approximately the same amount of batter so you can substitute one for another:

1 (2-lb.) coffee can  
1 (6- or 7-cup) mold  
2 (1-lb.) coffee cans

1 (1½-quart) baking dish  
3 (16-oz.) vegetable cans

# Traditional Plum Pudding

*C*elebrate the holiday season in grand style by presenting this triumph at the end of dinner. ■ MAKES 6 TO 8 SERVINGS

4 slices bread, torn into pieces
1 cup milk
2 eggs
1 cup packed brown sugar
¼ cup orange juice
1 teaspoon vanilla extract
½ cup finely chopped or ground suet
   or vegetable shortening
1 cup all-purpose flour
1 teaspoon baking soda

½ teaspoon salt
2 teaspoons ground cinnamon
1 teaspoon ground cloves
1 teaspoon ground mace
2 cups raisins
1 cup chopped pitted dates
½ cup chopped mixed candied fruits
   and peels
½ cup coarsely chopped walnuts
Hot water

Place a metal rack or trivet in a slow cooker. Grease a 2-quart mold; set aside. In a medium bowl, soak bread in milk 10 minutes. Beat in eggs, sugar, juice and vanilla. Stir in suet or shortening. In a large bowl, combine flour, soda, salt and spices. Add raisins, dates, candied fruit and peels and walnuts, and mix well. Add bread mixture. Pour into prepared mold. Cover with foil. Add 1 inch hot water to slow cooker. Place mold on rack in slow cooker. Cover and cook on HIGH 5 to 6 hours. Remove from slow cooker; cool in pan 10 minutes. Loosen pudding from sides of mold with a small spatula. Invert on plate to unmold. Serve warm, plain or with Brandy Hard Sauce (page 307).

# Persimmon Pudding

*T*he bright orange, fig- or heart-shaped Hachiya persimmon should be very soft. The reddish orange, tomato-shaped Fuyu can be slightly firm. ■ MAKES 6 TO 8 SERVINGS

| | |
|---|---|
| 1½ cups all-purpose flour | ⅓ cup milk |
| 1 cup sugar | 1 egg |
| 1 teaspoon baking powder | 2 tablespoons maple syrup |
| 1 teaspoon baking soda | ¼ cup margarine or butter, melted |
| 1 teaspoon ground cinnamon | ½ cup chopped dried apricots |
| ¼ teaspoon freshly grated nutmeg | ¼ cup chopped pistachios |
| 2 persimmons | Boiling water |
| 1 tablespoon fresh lemon juice | |

### HOT LIME SAUCE

| | |
|---|---|
| 2 tablespoons cornstarch | 2 tablespoons margarine or butter |
| ½ cup sugar | ¼ teaspoon grated lime peel |
| ½ cup water | 3 tablespoons fresh lemon juice |
| ½ cup fresh lime juice | |

Place a metal rack or trivet in a slow cooker. Grease a 6- or 8-cup heatproof mold. In a large bowl, combine flour, sugar, baking powder, soda, cinnamon and nutmeg; set aside. Cut persimmons in half; scoop out pulp. Process lemon juice and pulp in a blender or food processor until pureed. Add milk, egg, maple syrup and margarine or butter; process until well blended. Stir liquid into flour mixture. Add apricots and pistachios. Spoon into prepared mold; cover with foil. Place on rack in slow cooker. Pour in boiling water until it comes halfway up the sides of the mold. Cover and steam on HIGH 3 hours. Remove mold from cooker. Loosen sides by inserting a thin knife between pudding and sides of mold. Invert on a platter. Prepare Hot Lime Sauce. Serve pudding warm with Hot Lime Sauce.

# Hot Lime Sauce

In a small saucepan, combine cornstarch and sugar. Add water and lime juice, and stir until smooth. Cook, stirring, over medium-low heat until thickened and translucent. Add margarine or butter; stir until melted. Remove from heat. Stir in lime peel and lemon juice. Makes about 1½ cups.

# Steamed Pumpkin-Date Pudding with Rum Sauce

*If* you don't have pumpkin pie spice, use ½ teaspoon cinnamon and ¼ teaspoon *each* allspice, cloves, and ginger. ■ MAKES 10 SERVINGS

| | |
|---|---|
| 1½ cups all-purpose flour | ¼ teaspoon salt |
| ½ cup packed light brown sugar | 1 cup canned pumpkin |
| 1 teaspoon baking powder | 2 tablespoons lemon yogurt |
| ½ teaspoon baking soda | 1 teaspoon vanilla extract |
| 1½ teaspoons pumpkin pie spice | ½ cup chopped dates |

RUM SAUCE

| | |
|---|---|
| ⅓ cup sugar | ⅔ cup water |
| 4 teaspoons cornstarch | ¼ cup light rum |
| ¼ teaspoon ground nutmeg | 1 teaspoon margarine or butter |
| Pinch of salt | |

Spray a 6-cup metal mold with vegetable cooking spray; set aside. Place a trivet in bottom of a 4- to 5-quart or larger slow cooker.

In a medium bowl, stir together flour, brown sugar, baking powder, baking soda, pumpkin pie spice and salt. Add pumpkin, yogurt and vanilla and mix until combined. Stir in dates. Spoon batter into prepared mold; cover with a lid or foil secured with string. Place mold

293

on trivet in slow cooker. Cover and cook on HIGH 3 hours or until a wooden pick inserted in center comes out clean. While pudding cooks, prepare Rum Sauce.

Remove mold from slow cooker and remove string and foil. Cool pudding on a wire rack 10 minutes. Loosen edges and turn out pudding onto a serving plate. Slice and serve warm or at room temperature with Rum Sauce.

# Rum Sauce

In a small saucepan, combine sugar, cornstarch, nutmeg, and salt. Gradually stir in water and rum. Cook and stir over low heat until mixture is thickened, about 3 minutes. Remove from heat; stir in margarine or butter. Makes 1⅛ cups.

Per serving: Cal 167 · Carb 35 gm · Prot 3 gm · Total fat 1 gm · Sat fat 0 gm · Cal from fat 9 · Chol 0 mg · Sodium 190 mg

# Grandma's Rice Pudding

*W*hen I was a child, my mother would sometimes make this for my lunch.  ■ MAKES 6 TO 8 SERVINGS

| | |
|---|---|
| ⅔ cup uncooked long-grain rice | 2 eggs, beaten |
| 1⅓ cups water | 1 teaspoon vanilla extract |
| 2 cups milk | ¾ cup raisins |
| 2 tablespoons margarine or butter | 1 cup hot water |
| ¼ teaspoon salt | Ground cinnamon |
| ⅓ cup sugar | |

Place a metal rack or trivet in a slow cooker. Grease a 5- or 6-cup baking dish. Cook rice according to package directions using 1⅓ cups water. Combine cooked rice with milk, margarine or butter, salt, sugar, eggs, vanilla and raisins. Pour into prepared baking dish. Cover baking dish with foil. Add 1 cup hot water to slow cooker. Place baking dish on trivet. Cover and cook on HIGH 4 hours. Sprinkle with cinnamon. Serve warm. Refrigerate any leftovers and serve chilled.

# Sunshine Carrot Pudding with Lemon Sauce

*T*his pudding can be eaten immediately, but the flavor improves if it is allowed to rest 8 hours before serving. ■ MAKES 8 TO 10 SERVINGS

1 cup whole-wheat flour
1/2 cup all-purpose flour
1/2 cup packed dark brown sugar
1/4 cup granulated sugar
1 teaspoon baking powder
1 teaspoon baking soda
1 teaspoon ground cinnamon
1/2 teaspoon ground nutmeg
1/8 teaspoon ground cloves

1/2 teaspoon salt
2 tablespoons diced candied ginger
2 cups lightly packed shredded carrots
1 (8-oz.) can crushed pineapple in juice
1/2 cup golden raisins
1 teaspoon vanilla extract
1 cup hot water

## LEMON SAUCE

1/2 cup sugar
1 1/2 tablespoons cornstarch
3 to 4 tablespoons fresh lemon juice

1 cup water
1 to 2 drops yellow food coloring (optional)
1 teaspoon margarine or butter

Grease and flour a 5- to 6-cup metal mold; set aside. Place a trivet in bottom of a 4- to 5-quart or larger slow cooker.

In a medium bowl, stir together whole-wheat and all-purpose flours, brown and granulated sugars, baking powder, baking soda, cinnamon, nutmeg, cloves and salt. Add ginger, carrots, pineapple with juice, raisins and vanilla and mix until combined. Batter will be thick. Transfer batter to prepared mold; cover mold with a lid or foil secured with string.

Place on trivet in slow cooker. Pour about 1 cup hot water around mold. Cover and cook on HIGH 3 hours or until a wooden pick inserted in center comes out clean.

Remove pudding mold from slow cooker. Remove string and foil. Cool pudding on a wire rack 15 to 20 minutes. While pudding cools, prepare Lemon Sauce.

Loosen edges and turn out pudding onto a serving plate. Slice and serve warm or at room temperature with warm Lemon Sauce.

# Lemon Sauce

In a small saucepan, combine sugar and cornstarch. Stir in lemon juice and water. Cook over medium heat, stirring constantly, until mixture comes to a boil and thickens. Remove from heat; stir in food coloring, if using, and butter. Serve warm. Makes about 1⅓ cups.

Per serving: Cal 198 · Carb 46 gm · Prot 4 gm · Total fat 1 gm · Sat fat 0 gm · Cal from fat 9 · Chol 0 mg · Sodium 298 mg

# Steamed Cranberry Pudding with Orange Blossom Sauce

*U*se fresh or frozen cranberries. Freeze fresh cranberries when they are in season for dishes such as this. ■ MAKES 8 TO 10 SERVINGS

1⅓ cups all-purpose flour
1 teaspoon baking soda
½ teaspoon salt
½ teaspoon ground allspice
¼ teaspoon ground nutmeg

2 cups coarsely chopped fresh cranberries
½ cup honey
1⅓ cup hot water

## ORANGE BLOSSOM SAUCE

2 tablespoons liquid egg substitute
2 tablespoons sugar
1/3 cup frozen orange juice
    concentrate, thawed

1/3 cup water
1 teaspoon margarine or butter

Grease and flour a 1-quart metal mold; set aside.

In a large bowl, stir together flour, baking soda, salt, allspice and nutmeg. Add cranberries, honey and 1/3 cup of the hot water and mix until combined. Spoon into prepared mold. Cover with a lid or foil secured with string. Place mold in a 4-quart or larger slow cooker. Pour the remaining 1 cup hot water around mold in slow cooker. Cover and cook on HIGH 3 hours or until a wooden pick inserted in center comes out clean.

Remove pudding mold from slow cooker. Remove string and foil. Cool on a wire rack 15 minutes. While pudding cools, prepare Orange Blossom Sauce.

When pudding has cooled, loosen edges and turn out onto a serving plate. Slice pudding and serve warm or at room temperature. Top each serving with hot Orange Blossom Sauce.

# Orange Blossom Sauce

In a medium saucepan, whisk together egg substitute, sugar, orange juice concentrate and water. Cook over medium-low heat, stirring constantly, until sauce is thick and creamy, about 5 minutes. Remove from heat, stir in margarine or butter. Serve hot. Makes about 1 cup.

Per serving: Cal 185 · Carb 42 gm · Prot 3 gm · Total fat 1 gm · Sat fat 0 gm · Cal from fat 9 · Chol 0 mg · Sodium 250 mg

# Home-Style Bread Pudding

*H*ere's a basic pudding that you can vary by using other dried fruit or even substituting chocolate chips. ■ MAKES 6 SERVINGS

| | |
|---|---|
| 1 (14-oz.) can sweetened condensed milk | ½ teaspoon ground cinnamon |
| 1¾ cups water | 3½ cups 1-inch bread cubes |
| 2 eggs, slightly beaten | ½ cup chopped dates or raisins |
| 1 teaspoon vanilla extract | ½ cup water |

RUM SAUCE

| | |
|---|---|
| 2 tablespoons sugar | 1 cup apple juice |
| 2 tablespoons cornstarch | ½ cup rum |

Place a metal rack or trivet in a slow cooker. Grease a 1-quart baking dish or metal bowl. In a large bowl, beat together milk, water, eggs, vanilla and cinnamon. Add bread cubes and dates or raisins. Thoroughly mix; let stand 10 minutes. Spoon into prepared baking dish. Add water to slow cooker. Set baking dish on rack. Cover and cook on HIGH 2½ to 3 hours. Remove from slow cooker and let stand 15 minutes before serving. Prepare Rum Sauce and serve with pudding.

# Rum Sauce

In a saucepan, mix together sugar, cornstarch and apple juice. Cook over low heat, stirring, until slightly thickened. Remove from heat; stir in rum. Serve warm or cold. Makes about 1½ cups.

# Kahlua Bread Pudding

*If* you have a 4- or 5-quart slow cooker, create this updated version of a traditional dessert.

■ MAKES 6 TO 8 SERVINGS

½ (16-oz.) loaf unsliced French bread
2 (12-oz.) cans evaporated skim
  milk or 3 cups half-and-half
¼ cup Kahlua liqueur
3 eggs
⅓ cup sugar

1 tablespoon powdered instant coffee
¼ teaspoon ground cinnamon
Toasted slivered or sliced almonds
  (see Note, page 3)
2 cups hot water

Place a metal rack or trivet in a slow cooker. Grease an 8- to 9-cup baking dish that fits into a 4- or 5-quart slow cooker. With a sharp knife, remove crust from bread; discard or make into bread crumbs for another use. Cut bread into 1-inch cubes; set aside. In a blender or food processor, combine milk or half-and-half, Kahlua, eggs, sugar, powdered coffee and cinnamon. Process until well mixed. Add to bread cubes. Stir to blend.

Fill prepared baking dish with mixture; cover with foil. Add hot water to slow cooker. Place mold on rack in slow cooker. Cover and cook on HIGH 2 to 2½ hours or until a knife inserted in the pudding comes out clean. Serve warm or cool. Sprinkle with toasted almonds.

# Almond Bread Pudding with Brandied Cherry Sauce

*T*he sauce adds flavor and color to this dessert.  ■ MAKES 6 TO 8 SERVINGS

3 cups 1/2-inch French bread cubes
2 1/4 cups low-fat milk
2 eggs
1/2 cup sugar
1/2 teaspoon vanilla extract

1/2 teaspoon almond extract
1/2 cup boiling water
3 tablespoons toasted sliced almonds
  (see Note, page 3)

### BRANDIED CHERRY SAUCE

1 (20-oz.) can light cherry pie filling
2 1/2 tablespoons brandy

1/4 teaspoon almond extract

Place bread cubes in a 1 1/2 quart casserole that fits into a 4- or 5-quart cooker. In a medium bowl, whisk together milk, eggs, sugar, vanilla and almond extract. Pour over bread; cover dish with foil and place in slow cooker. Pour 1/2 cup boiling water around casserole. Cover and cook on HIGH 2 hours. While pudding cooks, make Brandied Cherry Sauce.

Sprinkle pudding with almonds and serve warm or cold with Brandied Cherry Sauce.

# Brandied Cherry Sauce

Combine ingredients in small bowl; cover and chill at least 1 hour. Makes about 2 cups.

Per serving: Cal 220 · Carb 30 gm · Prot 7 gm · Total fat 6 gm · Sat fat 2 gm · Cal from fat 54 · Chol 78 mg · Sodium 160 mg

# Chocolate Pudding Cake

*C*hocolate sauce gives an even richer flavor to this chocolate lovers' fantasy come true.

- MAKES 6 TO 8 SERVINGS

2 cups all-purpose flour
2 teaspoons baking powder
¼ teaspoon salt
½ cup unsweetened cocoa powder
½ cup margarine or butter, room
   temperature

½ cup sugar
4 eggs
1 cup milk
1½ cups fresh bread crumbs
Chocolate or fudge sauce
Whipped cream (optional)

Place a metal rack or trivet in a slow cooker. Grease a 1½-quart mold or baking dish. Sift flour, baking powder, salt and cocoa into a bowl. In a large bowl, cream margarine or butter and sugar. Add eggs, one at a time, alternating with half the flour mixture, beating well after each addition. Add milk, alternating with remaining flour. Stir in bread crumbs. Pour into prepared mold and cover with foil. Add 2 cups hot water to slow cooker. Place mold with cake mixture on rack in cooker. Cover and cook on HIGH 3 to 4 hours. Serve warm or cold. To serve, slice cake and top each serving with chocolate or fudge sauce and whipped cream, if desired.

# Blueberry Coffee Cake

*This* dense blueberry coffee cake tastes great and would be ideal for Sunday brunch.

■ MAKES 4 TO 6 SERVINGS

| | |
|---|---|
| 1 cup all-purpose flour | 2 tablespoons milk |
| 1/2 cup sugar | 1/2 teaspoon vanilla extract |
| 2 teaspoons baking powder | 1 cup fresh or thawed frozen |
| 1/4 teaspoon salt | blueberries, drained |
| 1 egg, beaten | Cinnamon sugar or powdered sugar |
| 1/4 cup vegetable oil | |

Grease a 1 1/2-quart mold or baking dish. In a bowl, combine flour, sugar, baking powder and salt. Add egg, oil, milk and vanilla; beat until smooth. Fold in blueberries. Pour into prepared mold. Place in a slow cooker. Cover mold with 4 or 5 paper towels. Cover and cook on HIGH 3 to 4 hours. Cool on rack 5 minutes. Remove from mold and sprinkle with cinnamon sugar or powdered sugar. Serve warm.

# Carrot Coffee Cake

*N*ot quite as sweet or rich as traditional carrot cake, this version is just right for brunch. For special occasions, drizzle with powdered-sugar frosting. ■ MAKES 4 TO 6 SERVINGS

| | |
|---|---|
| 2 eggs | 1/2 teaspoon baking soda |
| 3/4 cup sugar | 1/8 teaspoon salt |
| 1/3 cup vegetable oil | 1 teaspoon ground cinnamon |
| 1 1/2 cups all-purpose flour | 1 cup grated carrot (2 medium) |
| 1 teaspoon baking powder | 2 cups hot water |

Place a metal rack or trivet in a slow cooker. Grease and flour a 6-cup mold. In a large bowl, beat eggs. Add sugar gradually, beating until slightly thickened. Add oil gradually and continue beating until thoroughly combined. Stir dry ingredients together and stir into liquid mixture until smooth. Stir in carrots. Pour into prepared mold. Cover with foil. Pour hot water into slow cooker. Place covered mold on rack. Cover and cook on HIGH about 3½ hours or until firm. Remove from slow cooker. Let stand at room temperature 10 minutes. Loosen cake from sides of mold with a small spatula. Invert onto cooling rack. Cut into thin wedges to serve.

# Banana Nut Bread

*A* great way to use ripe bananas. Serve slices of this bread plain, or spread with peanut butter, cream cheese or marmalade. ■ MAKES ABOUT 6 SERVINGS

| | |
|---|---|
| ⅓ cup vegetable shortening | ½ teaspoon salt |
| ½ cup sugar | 1 cup mashed ripe bananas (2 |
| 2 eggs | medium) |
| 1¾ cups all-purpose flour | ½ cup chopped walnuts |
| 1 teaspoon baking powder | 2 cups hot water |
| ½ teaspoon baking soda | |

Place a metal rack or trivet in a slow cooker. Grease a 5- or 6-cup mold; set aside. Cream shortening and sugar in a large bowl. Add eggs and beat well. Combine dry ingredients; add to creamed mixture alternately with mashed banana, blending well after each addition. Stir in nuts. Pour into prepared mold. Cover mold with foil. Add hot water to slow cooker. Place mold on rack in cooker. Cover and cook on HIGH about 3 hours or until bread is firm. Remove from cooker. Let stand 10 minutes in mold. Loosen edges with a small spatula; invert on plate. Slice and serve warm.

# Blueberry & Orange Bread

*B*egin with a mix and make it doubly good with two types of blueberries, accented with orange. ■ MAKES 6 SERVINGS

1 (14-oz.) package blueberry muffin mix
½ cup orange juice
1 egg
⅓ cup dried blueberries
⅓ cup chopped walnuts
1 tablespoon grated orange peel

Grease a 5- to 6-cup mold or baking dish. Drain canned blueberries from mix in a strainer; set aside. Pour mix into a large bowl. Stir in orange juice and egg. Mix to combine; fold in drained blueberries, dried blueberries, walnuts and orange peel. Spoon mixture into greased mold. Place mold in a slow cooker. Cover mold with 2 to 3 pieces of paper towel. Cover and cook on HIGH 2½ to 3 hours. Remove from pot and let stand 20 minutes. Invert mold onto a serving dish; let cool before slicing.

VARIATION: If using a mix with dried rather than canned blueberries, add to mixture with walnuts and orange peel.

# Cornbread

*A* tasty moist bread to serve with beans and a green salad. ■ MAKES 4 TO 6 SERVINGS

1 cup cornmeal
1 cup all-purpose flour
2 tablespoons sugar
1 tablespoon baking powder

½ teaspoon chili powder
1 egg
3 tablespoons vegetable oil
1 cup milk

Grease a 6- to 7-cup baking dish. In a bowl, stir all dry ingredients together. In a small bowl, beat together egg, oil and milk. Pour liquid ingredients into cornmeal mixture and stir to combine. Pour batter into prepared baking dish. Place dish in bottom of slow cooker. Cover with 2 to 3 pieces paper towel. Cover and cook on HIGH 4½ to 5 hours or until firm. Serve warm.

# Steamed Molasses Bread

Cut warm bread into slices or thin wedges and spread with plain or orange-flavored butter. ■ MAKES 6 SERVINGS

| | |
|---|---|
| 2 cups All-Bran cereal | 1 cup raisins |
| 2 cups whole-wheat flour | 1 egg |
| 2 teaspoons baking powder | 1¾ cups buttermilk |
| 1 teaspoon baking soda | ½ cup molasses |
| ½ teaspoon salt | 2 cups hot water |

Place a metal rack or trivet in a slow cooker. Grease and flour an 8-cup mold; set aside. In a medium bowl, combine cereal, flour, baking powder, soda, salt and raisins. In a large bowl, beat egg. Add milk and molasses, and stir to combine. Stir in dry ingredients; do not overbeat. Pour into prepared mold. Cover with foil. Pour hot water into slow cooker. Place covered mold on rack. Cover slow cooker and cook on HIGH 3½ to 4 hours. Remove mold from pot. Let stand 5 minutes. Loosen edges with small spatula, then invert on plate. Serve warm.

# Peanut Butter Bread

*A*ll-American flavors that have been favorites for many generations.  ■ MAKES 6 SERVINGS

2¾ cups hot water
¾ cup peanut butter
¾ cup milk
⅓ cup sugar
¼ teaspoon salt

1 egg, slightly beaten
2 cups all-purpose flour
4 teaspoons baking powder
¾ cup chopped salted peanuts

Place a metal rack or trivet in a slow cooker. Grease a 5- or 6-cup mold. In a large bowl, pour ¾ cup hot water over peanut butter. Stir in milk, sugar, salt, egg, flour, baking powder and peanuts. Stir well. Spoon batter into prepared mold. Cover with foil. Pour 2 cups hot water into slow cooker. Place mold on rack. Cover and cook on HIGH about 5 hours. Remove mold and let stand 10 minutes. Turn out on cooling rack. Slice and serve warm or cool. Spread with butter, marmalade or jam.

# Tropical Bread with Brandy Hard Sauce

*F*ragrant fresh mangoes are combined with other tropical flavors to create an exciting dessert.  ■ MAKES 6 SERVINGS

1 cup mango pulp
¾ cup orange juice
1 egg, beaten
¼ cup chopped dried persimmon or papaya
½ cup dried banana chips
½ cup pine nuts or pecans
¼ cup golden raisins

2 cups all-purpose flour
2 teaspoons baking soda
½ cup sugar
1 tablespoon margarine or butter, melted
½ teaspoon vanilla extract
1½ cups water

BRANDY HARD SAUCE

| | |
|---|---|
| 2 cups powdered sugar | 2 to 3 tablespoons brandy or brandy |
| ½ cup butter, room temperature | extract, to taste |

Place a metal rack or trivet in a slow cooker. Grease a 6-cup baking dish or mold. In a large bowl, beat together mango pulp, orange juice and egg. Stir in and thoroughly combine remaining ingredients. Pour into prepared baking dish or mold; set on rack in slow cooker. Add water to slow cooker. Cover and cook on HIGH 3 to 3½ hours. Remove mold from slow cooker; let stand 20 minutes. Invert onto serving dish. Prepare Brandy Hard Sauce and serve with warm or cold pudding.

# Brandy Hard Sauce

In a small bowl, combine sugar, butter and brandy extract. Mix until smooth and thoroughly combined. Makes about 1¼ cups.

# Blueberry Brown Bread

*D*ried blueberries and cherries are available in many supermarkets and gourmet stores. They contribute a welcome flavor without additional liquid. ■ MAKES 6 SERVINGS

| | |
|---|---|
| 1 cup cornmeal | ½ cup dried blueberries or cherries |
| 1 cup rye flour | ¾ cup molasses |
| 1 cup whole-wheat flour | 2 cups buttermilk |
| 1½ teaspoons baking soda | 2 cups hot water |
| ½ teaspoon salt | |

Place a metal rack or trivet in a slow cooker. Grease an 8-cup mold. In a large bowl, combine cornmeal, rye flour, whole-wheat flour, baking soda, salt and dried blueberries or cherries. Add molasses and buttermilk, stirring just until blended. Spoon into prepared mold. Cover with foil. Add hot water to slow cooker. Place mold on rack. Cover and cook on HIGH 3 to 3½ hours. Remove mold from cooker. Let stand on cooling rack 5 to 10 minutes. Unmold; slice and serve warm.

NOTE: To make a buttermilk substitute, add 1 tablespoon lemon juice for each cup of milk or follow the instructions on package of dry buttermilk mix.

# Pumpkin Nut Bread

※※※※※※※※※※※※※※※※※※※※※※※※※※※※※※※※※※※※※※※※※※※※※※※※※※※※

*M*ake this unusual bread when you have canned pumpkin left over from the holidays, or any time during the year. ■ MAKES 6 TO 8 SERVINGS

| | |
|---|---|
| 1½ cups all-purpose flour | ½ cup buttermilk |
| 1¼ teaspoons baking soda | 1 egg |
| ½ teaspoon salt | 2 tablespoons margarine or butter, |
| 1 teaspoon ground cinnamon | room temperature |
| ½ teaspoon freshly grated nutmeg | 1 cup chopped pecans |
| 1 cup canned pumpkin | 2 cups hot water |
| 1 cup sugar | |

Place a metal rack or trivet in a slow cooker. Grease and flour a 5- to 6-cup mold. In a large bowl, combine all ingredients except pecans and beat until well blended. Stir in nuts. Spoon into prepared mold. Cover with foil. Pour hot water in cooker. Place covered mold on rack. Cover and cook on HIGH 3½ to 4 hours. Turn out on cooling rack. Serve warm or cool.

# Date & Nut Loaf

*O*ur favorite bread. For added goodness, spread thinly sliced bread with butter, cream cheese or peanut butter. ■ MAKES 6 SERVINGS

1 cup boiling water
1 cup chopped dates
¾ cup sugar
1 egg, slightly beaten
1½ teaspoons baking soda
¼ teaspoon salt

1 teaspoon vanilla extract
1 tablespoon vegetable oil
1½ cups all-purpose flour
½ cup walnuts, chopped
2 cups hot water

Place a metal rack or trivet in a slow cooker. Grease a 6-cup mold. In a large bowl, pour boiling water over dates. Let stand 5 to 10 minutes. Stir in sugar, egg, baking soda, salt, vanilla, oil, flour and walnuts. Pour into prepared mold. Cover with foil. Pour 2 cups hot water into slow cooker. Place filled and covered mold on rack. Cover and cook on HIGH 2½ to 3 hours. Remove mold from slow cooker. Let stand 10 minutes in mold. Transfer to cooling rack.

# FRUITS & DESSERTS

✕✿✕✿✕✿✕✿✕✿✕✿✕✿✕✿✕✿✕✿✕✿✕✿✕✿✕✿✕✿✕✿

*Y*ou can make many delicious desserts in your slow cooker. Actually, several types of desserts are perfectly suited because the slow cooker brings out those good old-fashioned flavors. It's hard to beat the taste of a fruit compote prepared in a slow cooker. Long cooking at very low temperatures blends the fruit flavors with the spices, wines or liqueurs.

Fresh or dried fruits may be used in many combinations, depending on what's available in your market. Dried fruits are especially good when prepared in a slow cooker. Firm fruits like apples and pears are also well suited to slow cooking. Baked Apples and St. Helena Pears bring out their fall flavors.

If you have never tried real homemade mincemeat, try Gar's Famous Mincemeat recipe. It is a variation of an old Pennsylvania Dutch mince pie. Don't be frightened by the long list of ingredients. Cut the recipe in half if you want to start off on a smaller scale.

Traditional Apple Butter is so easy to make in a slow cooker. In the past you had to stir it almost constantly to keep it from sticking and scorching. That was before electric slow cookers with low and even temperatures.

And, you can "bake" custard in a slow cooker. With Grandma's Rice Pudding or Trade Winds Baked Custard, turn the control to HIGH. The custardy mixture must be cooked on a trivet in hot water, so the trick is to cook it on HIGH.

We've included more steamed recipes in this section, such as Kahlua Bread Pudding.

Before starting one of these, be sure you have a mold that will fit in your slow cooker. Or, you can cut some of the recipes down to fit your pot. To buy a mold to use in your slow cooker, measure the inside of your pot carefully, then take your tape measure with you when you shop.

# Apple Peanut Crumble

*T*opping with a slight peanut butter flavor provides an interesting contrast to the apples.

■ MAKES 5 TO 6 SERVINGS

5 cooking apples, peeled, cored and
   sliced
2/3 cup packed brown sugar
1/2 cup all-purpose flour
1/2 cup quick-cooking rolled oats

1/2 teaspoon ground cinnamon
1/2 teaspoon freshly grated nutmeg
1/3 cup margarine or butter, room
   temperature
2 tablespoons peanut butter

Place apple slices in a slow cooker. In a medium bowl, combine sugar, flour, oats, cinnamon and nutmeg. Mix in margarine or butter and peanut butter with a pastry blender or fork until crumbly. Sprinkle over apples. Cover and cook on LOW 5 to 6 hours. Serve warm, plain or with ice cream or whipped cream.

# Garden of Eden Apples

*B*efore starting to make this dish, be sure that the apples will fit into your slow cooker; four large apples will not work in smaller pots.  ■ MAKES 4 SERVINGS

¾ cup chopped dried figs
2 tablespoons chopped blanched almonds
⅓ cup boiling water
½ cup honey
1 teaspoon margarine or butter
4 medium to large baking apples

### ALMOND CREAM

½ cup nonfat sour cream
4 teaspoons powdered sugar
¼ teaspoon almond extract

In a small bowl, combine figs and almonds; set aside. In another bowl, stir together boiling water, honey and margarine or butter.

Starting at blossom end, peel apples about one-third of the way down; remove most of core and seeds, leaving a small amount of core at bottom. Spoon about 2 tablespoons fig and almond mixture into each apple. Place in a 4-quart or larger slow cooker. Pour honey mixture over apples. Cover and cook on LOW 3 to 4 hours or until apples are tender. Baste apples with cooking juices. While apples cook, prepare Almond Cream.

To serve, spoon a little of the honey syrup just off center on each dessert plate. Spoon about 2 tablespoons of Almond Cream next to it; place an apple on top in center. Repeat on 3 more dessert plates.

# Almond Cream

In a small bowl, mix together all ingredients. Refrigerate at least 1 hour for flavors to mingle. Makes ½ cup.

> Per serving: Cal 377 · Carb 87 gm · Prot 3 gm · Total fat 4 gm · Sat fat 0.5 gm · Cal from fat 36 · Chol 4 mg · Sodium 59 mg

# Slow-Cooker Baked Cranberry Apples

*B*e sure to check if all the apples will fit into your slow cooker before peeling them.

■ MAKES 5 SERVINGS

5 medium baking apples
⅓ cup fresh or frozen cranberries, chopped
¼ cup packed light brown sugar

¼ teaspoon ground cinnamon
⅛ teaspoon ground nutmeg
2 tablespoons chopped walnuts
Whipped or sour cream (optional)

Peel each apple about a fourth of the way down; remove core and seeds. In a small bowl, combine cranberries, sugar, cinnamon, nutmeg and walnuts. Spoon cranberry mixture into center of each apple. Place in a 4-quart or larger slow cooker. Cover and cook on LOW 4 to 5 hours or until apples are tender.

Serve warm or at room temperature. Top with whipped or sour cream, if desired.

> Per serving: Cal 132 · Carb 33 gm · Prot 0 gm · Total fat 1 gm · Sat fat 0 gm · Cal from fat 9 · Chol 0 mg · Sodium 4 mg

# Dried Cherry and Apple Snack

*D*ried tart cherries and oatmeal topping turn ordinary cooking apples into an extraordinary dessert. ■ MAKES 4 TO 6 SERVINGS

½ cup dried pitted tart cherries
½ cup apple juice
3 large tart green apples, peeled,
   cored, and sliced
¼ cup all-purpose flour
½ cup sugar

½ teaspoon ground cinnamon
½ cup old-fashioned rolled oats
2 tablespoons light brown sugar
2 tablespoons margarine or butter, at
   room temperature

Place a metal rack in a 4- to 5-quart or larger slow cooker. Grease a 5- or 6-cup mold or baking dish; set aside. In a medium bowl, combine cherries and apple juice; let stand about 1 hour or until reconstituted. Stir in apples.

In a small bowl, combine flour, sugar and cinnamon. Add flour mixture to cherry mixture and stir until combined. Spoon into greased mold or baking dish.

With a pastry blender, combine oats, brown sugar and margarine or butter until crumbly. Spoon on top of apple mixture in mold. Cover with foil. Place on rack in slow cooker. Cover and cook on HIGH 4 to 5 hours. Remove mold from slow cooker. Remove foil and let stand 5 minutes. Cut into slices or squares.

Per serving: Cal 389 · Carb 73 gm · Prot 5 gm · Total fat 10 gm · Sat fat 2 gm · Cal from fat 90 · Chol 0 mg · Sodium 104 mg

# Poached Apples 'n' Cranberries

A delicious way to satisfy one of your daily fruit requirements. ■ MAKES 6 TO 7 SERVINGS

- 1½ cups dry red wine
- 1 cup reduced-calorie cranberry juice
- ⅓ cup honey
- ¼ teaspoon Angostura aromatic bitters
- 5 cups peeled, thick slices cooking apples
- ¾ cup dried cranberries
- 5 whole allspice
- 5 whole cloves
- 1 (3-inch) cinnamon stick

ORANGE CREAM

- ¾ cup nonfat sour cream
- 1½ teaspoons grated orange peel
- 1½ teaspoons sugar

Combine red wine, cranberry juice, honey and bitters in a 3½-quart slow cooker. Stir until honey is dissolved. Add apples and cranberries; stir to mix. Tie allspice, cloves and cinnamon in a small piece of cheesecloth or place in a metal spice ball. Bury spices among apples and cranberries. Cover and cook on LOW 5 hours or until apples are tender. Let cool. While fruit cools, prepare Orange Cream.

Spoon Orange Cream over fruit and cooking juice.

## Orange Cream

Combine ingredients in a small bowl; cover and chill at least 1 hour.

Per serving: Cal 220 • Carb 49 gm • Prot 1 gm • Total fat 0 gm • Sat fat 0 gm • Cal from fat 0 • Chol 4 mg • Sodium 46 mg

# Apple Brown Betty

*F*or a special treat, top this dessert with light cream or a scoop of ice cream. ■ MAKES 4 TO 5 SERVINGS

5 slices bread, cut into ¹⁄₂-inch cubes
¹⁄₂ cup margarine or butter, melted
¹⁄₂ teaspoon ground cinnamon
¹⁄₄ teaspoon freshly grated nutmeg
¹⁄₈ teaspoon salt
³⁄₄ cup packed brown sugar
4 medium cooking apples, peeled, cored and chopped

In a medium bowl, mix bread cubes with margarine or butter, cinnamon, nutmeg, salt and brown sugar. Arrange in alternate layers with apples in a slow cooker. Cover and cook on HIGH 1¹⁄₂ to 2¹⁄₂ hours or until apples are tender. Serve warm.

# Baked Apples

*U*se fresh, crisp apples for this wintertime treat. ■ MAKES 5 TO 6 SERVINGS

5 or 6 baking apples, such as Rome Beauty or Granny Smith
¹⁄₂ cup raisins or chopped dates
1 cup packed brown sugar
1 cup boiling water
2 tablespoons margarine or butter
¹⁄₂ teaspoon ground cinnamon
¹⁄₄ teaspoon freshly grated nutmeg

Core apples and peel each about one-quarter of the way down. Arrange in a slow cooker. Fill centers with raisins or dates. In a small bowl, combine sugar, water, margarine or butter, cinnamon and nutmeg. Pour over apples. Cover and cook on LOW 2 to 4 hours (depending on size and variety of apples) or until apples are tender. Serve warm or cool.

# Stewed Pears with Ginger

*A* simple dessert that's not too sweet. Bosc or Anjou pears work best. ■ MAKES 4 TO 5 SERVINGS

| | |
|---|---|
| 1 cup vermouth | 4 or 5 firm pears |
| ½ cup orange juice | 1 (3-oz.) package cream cheese, room |
| 2 tablespoons fresh lemon juice | temperature |
| ½ cup plus 1 teaspoon sugar | 3 tablespoons chopped almonds or |
| 1 tablespoon minced crystallized | pecans |
| ginger | 2 to 3 tablespoons vermouth or milk |

In a slow cooker, combine vermouth, orange juice, lemon juice, ½ cup of the sugar and ginger. Peel, halve and core pears. Drop into vermouth mixture and stir. Be sure pears are covered with liquid. Cover and cook on LOW 2 to 3 hours or until pears are tender. In a small bowl, mix cream cheese, nuts, vermouth or milk and remaining 1 teaspoon sugar until well blended. Spoon pears and juice into bowls. Top with cream cheese mixture.

# Pear Streusel

✕◇✕◇✕◇✕◇✕◇✕◇✕◇✕◇✕◇✕◇✕◇✕◇✕◇✕◇✕◇✕◇✕◇✕◇✕◇✕◇✕◇✕◇✕◇✕◇✕◇✕◇✕◇✕

𝒩o need to heat up the kitchen for this lovely and luscious dessert.  ■ MAKES ABOUT 4 SERVINGS

| | |
|---|---|
| ⅓ cup crunchy nutlike cereal nuggets | ½ teaspoon ground ginger |
| 3 tablespoons all-purpose flour | 4 Bartlett pears, peeled, cored, and |
| 3 tablespoons light brown sugar | cut into ½-inch slices |
| 2 tablespoons soft reduced-fat | 3 tablespoons fresh lemon juice |
| margarine | ¼ cup granulated sugar |
| 1 teaspoon grated lemon peel | |

In a small bowl, combine cereal, flour, brown sugar, margarine, lemon peel and ginger. Mix with a fork until mixture is crumbly; set aside.

In a 1-quart casserole dish that fits into a 4- or 5-quart slow cooker, combine pears, lemon juice and granulated sugar. Sprinkle crumb mixture evenly over top. Place casserole in slow cooker. Cover and cook on HIGH 2 hours or until pears are fork tender. Serve warm.

Per serving: Cal 264 • Carb 60 gm • Prot 2 gm • Total fat 4 gm • Sat fat 0.5 gm • Cal from fat 36 • Chol 0 mg • Sodium 134 mg

# St. Helena Pears

※◇※◇※◇※◇※◇※◇※◇※◇※◇※◇※◇※◇※◇※◇※◇※◇※◇※◇※◇※◇※◇※◇※◇※◇※

*M*acaroon crumbs add a little crunch to this rich, fruity dessert. For an exciting taste contrast, top each serving with a dollop of sour cream. ■ MAKES 6 SERVINGS

6 pears
1/2 cup raisins
1/4 cup packed brown sugar
1 teaspoon grated lemon peel
1/4 cup brandy
1/2 cup Sauterne wine
1/2 cup macaroon crumbs

Peel, halve and core pears; cut into thin slices. Mix raisins with sugar and lemon peel. Arrange alternately with pear slices in a slow cooker. Pour brandy and wine over pears. Cover and cook on LOW 4 to 6 hours or until pears are tender. Spoon pears into serving dishes and allow to cool. Sprinkle with crumbs.

# Chocolate Fondue

When the slow cooker is turned on LOW, it keeps this chocolate mixture at just the right temperature for each person to dip his or her favorite treat. ■ MAKES 3 CUPS

6 (1-oz.) squares unsweetened
  chocolate
1½ cups sugar
1 cup half-and-half
½ cup margarine or butter
⅛ teaspoon salt

3 tablespoons crème de cacao or
  coffee-flavored liqueur
Angel cake cubes
Marshmallows
Fruits (strawberries, bananas, etc.)

Place chocolate in a slow cooker. Cover and heat on HIGH about 30 minutes or until chocolate melts. Stir in sugar, half-and-half, margarine or butter and salt. Cook on HIGH, stirring occasionally, 10 to 15 minutes. Whisk until smooth. Add liqueur. Turn control to LOW. Spear cake chunks, marshmallows or fruits with fondue forks. Dip into hot chocolate mixture.

# Chocolate Mint Dessert

Instead of whipped cream, top with vanilla ice cream and a fresh raspberry sauce. ■ MAKES 4 TO 6 SERVINGS

1 cup sugar
¼ cup margarine or butter, room
  temperature
1 egg
3 tablespoons all-purpose flour
1 cup fine dry bread crumbs
1½ teaspoons baking powder

¾ cup evaporated milk
2 oz. unsweetened chocolate, melted
1 teaspoon peppermint extract
¼ cup chopped walnuts
2 cups water
Whipped cream (optional)

Place a metal rack or trivet in a slow cooker. Grease a 1-quart mold or metal bowl. In a large bowl, cream sugar, margarine or butter and egg. Combine flour, bread crumbs and baking powder. Mix in flour mixture, alternating with milk. Stir in melted chocolate, peppermint extract and walnuts. Pour into prepared mold. Cover with foil; crimp edges to seal. Add water to slow cooker. Place mold on rack in slow cooker. Cover and cook on HIGH 2 to 3 hours. Serve warm or cold, topped with whipped cream, if desired.

# Home-Style Applesauce

*T*his applesauce will be slightly chunky. Put through a food processor or blender for a smoother texture. ■ MAKES 3½ TO 4 CUPS

    8 to 9 medium cooking apples, peeled, cored and finely chopped
    ½ cup water
    ¾ cup sugar
    Ground cinnamon

In a slow cooker, combine apples and water. Cover and cook on LOW about 6 hours or until apples are very soft. Add sugar and cook on LOW another 30 minutes. Sprinkle with cinnamon at serving time.

# Chunky Black Cherry Applesauce

*T*he combination of flavors in this sauce are so interesting that it can serve as an accompaniment to pork chops or roast as well as a satisfying dessert. ■ MAKES ABOUT 6½ CUPS

8 large apples
1 (16-oz.) package frozen unsweetened pitted dark sweet cherries
½ cup sugar
¼ teaspoon ground nutmeg
½ teaspoon ground cinnamon
¼ teaspoon almond extract

Peel and core apples. Cut apples into ½-inch pieces. Combine apples, frozen cherries, sugar, nutmeg, cinnamon and almond extract in a 3½-quart slow cooker. Cover and cook on LOW about 10 hours or until fruit is very soft. Transfer to a bowl and refrigerate until cold.

Per ½ cup: Cal 121 • Carb 31 gm • Prot 1 gm • Total fat 0 gm • Sat fat 0 gm • Cal from fat 0 • Chol 0 mg • Sodium 1 mg

# Rosy Cinnamon Applesauce

✶✶✶✶✶✶✶✶✶✶✶✶✶✶✶✶✶✶✶✶✶✶✶✶✶✶✶✶✶✶✶✶✶✶✶✶✶✶✶✶

*T*he candies provide color, flavor and sweetening—all so amazingly simple.  ▪ MAKES 2 CUPS

> ¼ cup hot water
> ½ cup red hot candies
> 4 to 5 large Granny Smith apples
> ¼ cup sugar

In a slow cooker, combine hot water and red hot candies. Let stand 10 minutes. Peel, core and finely chop apples. Stir apples and sugar into water and red hots until thoroughly combined. Cover and cook on HIGH 3 to 4 hours. If a smooth sauce is desired, process in a blender or food processor until pureed. Serve warm or cold.

# Down-Home Rhubarb

✶✶✶✶✶✶✶✶✶✶✶✶✶✶✶✶✶✶✶✶✶✶✶✶✶✶✶✶✶✶✶✶✶✶✶✶✶✶✶✶

*D*uring rhubarb season, double or triple this recipe and keep it in the refrigerator for snacking.  ▪ MAKES ABOUT 3½ CUPS

> 2 lb. fresh rhubarb
> 1½ cups sugar
> ½ cup water
> ½ teaspoon vanilla extract (optional)

Trim rhubarb and cut into 1-inch pieces; place in a slow cooker. Dissolve sugar in water; pour over rhubarb. Cover and cook on LOW about 3 hours or until tender. Add vanilla if desired. Chill before serving.

# Rhubarb-Apple Compote

Choose firm, bright red stalks of rhubarb for this fruit-filled treat. ■ MAKES 5 TO 6 SERVINGS

1 lb. fresh rhubarb, cut into 1-inch pieces
4 large cooking apples, peeled, cored, and cut into thin wedges
½ cup sugar
2 teaspoons minced candied ginger
1 teaspoon grated orange peel
¼ cup apple juice
Ground nutmeg

Combine rhubarb, apples, sugar, candied ginger, orange peel and apple juice in a 3½- or 4-quart slow cooker. Cover and cook on LOW about 5 hours or until rhubarb and apples are soft.

Spoon into dessert dishes. Sprinkle with nutmeg.

Per serving: Cal 178 · Carb 46 gm · Prot 1 gm · Total fat 1 gm · Sat fat 0 gm · Cal from fat 9 · Chol 0 mg · Sodium 5 mg

# Apple-Cranberry Compote

*F*resh crisp apples and tart cranberries in the market mean that fall has arrived and it's time for making fruit compotes. ■ MAKES 5 TO 6 SERVINGS

　　5 or 6 cooking apples, peeled, cored and sliced
　　1 cup fresh cranberries
　　1 cup sugar
　　1/2 teaspoon grated orange peel
　　1/2 cup cranberry-raspberry juice
　　1/4 cup port wine
　　Sour cream

Put apple slices and cranberries into a slow cooker. Sprinkle sugar over fruit. Add orange peel, juice and wine. Stir to mix ingredients. Cover and cook on LOW 4 to 6 hours or until apples are tender. Serve warm fruits with the juices, topped with a dab of sour cream.

# Holiday Fruit Compote

*I*f you wish this dessert to be nonalcoholic, substitute apple or cranberry juice for the wine. ■ MAKES 4 TO 6 SERVINGS

| | |
|---|---|
| ¼ cup port wine | 4 medium apples, peeled, cored and |
| 1 tablespoon margarine or butter | sliced |
| 1¼ cups sugar | 2 cups fresh cranberries |
| 1 tablespoon grated lemon peel | ½ cup chopped pitted dates |
| ⅛ teaspoon ground cinnamon | ⅓ cup chopped walnuts |
| ⅛ teaspoon freshly grated nutmeg | Sour cream or ice cream |

In a slow cooker, combine wine, margarine or butter, sugar, lemon peel and spices. Add apples and cranberries. Cover and cook on LOW 4 to 6 hours. Stir in dates and walnuts. Serve warm or cold with a dollop of sour cream or use as a sauce for ice cream.

# Orange-Prune Compote

*S*erve this at your next brunch. Your guests will appreciate a change from the usual fare.
■ MAKES 8 TO 10 SERVINGS

| | |
|---|---|
| 1 lb. pitted dried prunes | ⅓ cup sugar |
| 3 cups water | ¼ cup Cointreau or Curaçao |
| 2 (11-oz.) cans mandarin oranges, | ½ cup orange juice |
| drained | 2 bananas, sliced |

Combine prunes with water in a slow cooker. Cover and cook on LOW 2 to 2½ hours. Cool and drain. Combine with mandarin oranges, sugar, Cointreau and orange juice. Cover and refrigerate several hours before serving. Just before serving, stir in bananas.

# Fruit Medley

✳✳✳✳✳✳✳✳✳✳✳✳✳✳✳✳✳✳✳✳✳✳✳✳✳✳✳✳✳✳✳✳

*F*or a different final touch, whip sour cream with sugar to taste and a sprinkle of nutmeg.
■ MAKES 5 TO 6 SERVINGS

| | |
|---|---|
| 1½ lb. mixed dried fruits | ⅛ teaspoon freshly grated nutmeg |
| 2½ cups water | 1 cinnamon stick |
| 1 cup sugar | Water |
| 1 tablespoon honey | 3 tablespoons cornstarch |
| Peel of ½ lemon, cut into thin strips | ¼ cup Cointreau |

Put dried fruit into a slow cooker. Pour in water. Stir in sugar, honey, lemon peel and spices. Cover and cook on LOW 2 to 3 hours. Turn control to HIGH. In small amount of water, mix cornstarch; stir into fruit mixture. Cover and cook on HIGH 10 minutes or until thickened. Add Cointreau. Serve warm or chilled. May be served as fruit compote or as topping for ice cream.

# Brandied Fruit Compote

✳✳✳✳✳✳✳✳✳✳✳✳✳✳✳✳✳✳✳✳✳✳✳✳✳✳✳✳✳✳✳✳

*T*his is a colorful and glistening medley of flavorful fruits; serve as a wholesome dessert or accompaniment to pork or chicken dishes. ■ MAKES 12 TO 14 SERVINGS

| | |
|---|---|
| 2 (8-oz.) packages dried mixed fruit | ½ cup honey |
| 1 cup diced dried pineapple | 2 cups hot water |
| ⅔ cup dried cranberries | ¾ teaspoon ground allspice |
| ½ cup golden raisins | ½ cup brandy |
| 1 medium orange | Frozen yogurt or ice cream (optional) |

Combine mixed fruit, pineapple, cranberries and raisins in a 3½-quart slow cooker. Remove a thin layer of orange part of peel from orange; cut into very thin strips. Squeeze juice from orange. Add peel, juice, honey, water and allspice to slow cooker, stirring until honey is dissolved.

Cover and cook on LOW 5 to 6 hours or until fruit is plump and tender. Stir in brandy; cool. Serve in a compote or over frozen yogurt or ice cream.

Per serving: Cal 185 · Carb 43 gm · Prot 1 gm · Total fat 0 gm · Sat fat 0 gm · Cal from fat 0 · Chol 0 mg · Sodium 20 mg

# Trade Winds Baked Custard

*T*raditional baked custard becomes exotic when it is adorned with a tropical topping.

■ MAKES 5 TO 6 SERVINGS

3 eggs, beaten slightly
1/3 cup sugar
1 teaspoon vanilla extract
2 cups milk

1/8 teaspoon freshly grated nutmeg
2 cups hot water
Toasted coconut (see Note, page 134)

### TRADE WINDS TOPPING

1 large mango, peeled and chopped
1/2 teaspoon minced crystallized
   ginger

1/4 teaspoon Chinese five-spice
   powder

Place a metal rack or trivet in a slow cooker. Grease a 1-quart baking dish. In a medium bowl, combine eggs, sugar and vanilla. Stir in milk. Pour into prepared dish. Sprinkle with nutmeg. Cover dish with foil. Add 2 cups hot water to slow cooker. Place filled dish on rack. Cover and cook on HIGH 2½ to 3 hours or until firm. Refrigerate until cool. Prepare Trade Winds Topping and spoon over custard; sprinkle with coconut.

# Trade Winds Topping

Combine ingredients in a small bowl.

# Traditional Apple Butter

*W*hen apples are in season, buy or, better yet, pick a large amount of fruit and make your own butter. ▪ MAKES ABOUT 8 CUPS

12 to 14 cooking apples (about 16 cups chopped)
2 cups apple cider
2 cups sugar
1 teaspoon ground cinnamon
¼ teaspoon ground cloves

Core and chop apples. (Do not peel.) Combine apples and cider in a slow cooker. Cover and cook on LOW 10 to 12 hours or until apples are mushy. Puree in a food mill or sieve. Return pureed mixture to slow cooker. Add sugar, cinnamon and cloves. Cover and cook on LOW 1 hour.

NOTE: Apple butter will keep several weeks in the refrigerator. For longer storage, can in sterilized jars following proper canning procedures or pour into freezer containers and freeze.

# Gar's Famous Mincemeat

※※※※※※※※※※※※※※※※※※※※※※※※※※※※※※※※※※※※※※※※

*M*y husband, Gar, worked diligently to produce this family favorite. All early mincemeat recipes contained meat, as this one does. ■ MAKES 3 QTS. MINCEMEAT OR ENOUGH FOR FOUR 9-INCH PIES

2½ lb. beef shanks
4 cups water
½ lb. beef suet
2 lb. tart apples, peeled and diced
1 (15-oz.) package raisins
1 (11-oz.) package currants
1 tablespoon grated lemon peel
1 tablespoon fresh lemon juice
1 tablespoon grated orange peel

¼ cup orange juice
1 teaspoon cinnamon
½ teaspoon ground cloves
½ teaspoon freshly grated nutmeg
1 teaspoon salt
2 cups molasses
½ cup packed brown sugar
1½ cups apple cider

Combine beef and water in a slow cooker. Cover and cook on LOW 8 to 10 hours. Save all the broth; remove beef from bones. In food chopper, grind beef and suet together. Combine beef with ½ cup of reserved broth and remaining ingredients in slow cooker. Cover and cook on LOW 8 to 10 hours.

When making pies, 2 or 3 tablespoons brandy or bourbon may be added to filling for each pie. Filling can be kept in refrigerator for several days or frozen for about 6 months. Extra broth can be used for a soup base.

# Nectarine Chutney

✕◇✕◇✕◇✕◇✕◇✕◇✕◇✕◇✕◇✕◇✕◇✕◇✕◇✕◇✕◇✕◇✕◇✕◇✕◇✕◇✕◇✕◇✕◇✕◇✕◇✕◇✕◇✕◇✕

*S*erve warm or cold, and create a spicy accent for broiled chicken or fish. ■ MAKES ABOUT 5 CUPS

2 cups chopped fresh nectarines or peeled peaches
2 cups chopped peeled apples
1 small onion, chopped
½ cup dried cherries
½ cup golden raisins
1 tablespoon honey
½ cup cider vinegar
¾ cup packed brown sugar
¼ teaspoon ground cinnamon
¼ teaspoon red (cayenne) pepper
¼ teaspoon ground cloves
1 teaspoon ground ginger
1 teaspoon mustard seeds

Combine all ingredients in a slow cooker. Cover and cook on LOW 4 to 6 hours. Serve warm or cold. To keep chutney, place in a covered container and refrigerate. It will keep for weeks.

# Fresh Mango Chutney

*S*erve this savory condiment with your favorite chicken recipe, or as an accompaniment to curry. ■ MAKES 2 CUPS

½ cup cider vinegar
¾ cup packed brown sugar
1 tablespoon finely chopped
  gingerroot
½ teaspoon ground allspice
¼ teaspoon freshly grated nutmeg

½ teaspoon dried red pepper flakes
1 onion, finely chopped
½ teaspoon grated lemon peel
½ cup golden raisins
2 mangoes, peeled and coarsely
  chopped

Combine all ingredients in a slow cooker. Cover and cook on HIGH 2 hours, then simmer uncovered on HIGH an additional 2 hours or until mixture becomes syrupy. Cool to room temperature or refrigerate before serving. To keep chutney, place in a covered container and refrigerate. It will keep for weeks.

# Polynesian Pineapple-Mango Relish

*T*his exotic South Seas combo is guaranteed to perk up your next tropical dinner party. Serve it with poultry or pork. ■ MAKES ABOUT 4 CUPS

1 small fresh pineapple
1 mango
¾ cup sugar
2 tablespoons chopped gingerroot
½ cup golden raisins
1 jalapeño chile, seeded and chopped

1 onion, coarsely chopped
1 small red or green bell pepper,
  diced
1 clove garlic, finely chopped
¼ cup white vinegar
⅛ teaspoon ground turmeric

Peel, core and dice pineapple. Peel, pit and dice mango. Combine pineapple and mango in a 3½-quart slow cooker. Stir in sugar, ginger, raisins, jalapeño chile, onion, bell pepper, garlic, vinegar and turmeric. Cover and cook on LOW about 5 hours or until onion is tender.

> Per ¼ cup: Cal 74 • Carb 19 gm • Prot 0 gm • Total fat 0 gm • Sat fat 0 gm • Cal from fat 0 • Chol 0 mg • Sodium 1 mg

# Autumn Surprise Relish

*P*acked with the flavor of fruit and spices, this is an interesting accompaniment to baked ham or pork roast. ■ MAKES ABOUT 3 CUPS

1 cooking apple, peeled, cored and diced
1 acorn squash, seeded, peeled and diced
1 orange, peeled, seeded and diced
½ cup dried currants
¼ teaspoon ground cinnamon
2 tablespoons chopped candied ginger
¼ cup white vinegar
½ cup packed light brown sugar
⅛ teaspoon ground red pepper

Combine apple, squash, orange and currants in a 3½-quart slow cooker. Stir in cinnamon, ginger, vinegar, brown sugar and red pepper. Cover and cook on LOW about 8 hours. Turn control to HIGH and cook, uncovered, 2 hours.

> Per ¼ cup: Cal 78 • Carb 20 gm • Prot 1 gm • Total fat 0 gm • Sat fat 0 gm • Cal from fat 0 • Chol 0 mg • Sodium 4 mg

# METRIC CONVERSION CHARTS

## COMPARISON TO METRIC MEASURE

| When You Know | Symbol | Multiply By | To Find | Symbol |
|---|---|---|---|---|
| teaspoons | tsp. | 5.0 | milliliters | ml |
| tablespoons | tbsp. | 15.0 | milliliters | ml |
| fluid ounces | fl. oz. | 30.0 | milliliters | ml |
| cups | c | 0.24 | liters | l |
| pints | pt. | 0.47 | liters | l |
| quarts | qt. | 0.95 | liters | l |
| ounces | oz. | 28.0 | grams | g |
| pounds | lb. | 0.45 | kilograms | kg |
| Fahrenheit | F | 5/9 (after subtracting 32) | Celsius | C |

## FAHRENHEIT TO CELSIUS

| F | C |
|---|---|
| 200–205 | 95 |
| 220–225 | 105 |
| 245–250 | 120 |
| 275 | 135 |
| 300–305 | 150 |
| 325–330 | 165 |
| 345–350 | 175 |
| 370–375 | 190 |
| 400–405 | 205 |
| 425–430 | 220 |
| 445–450 | 230 |
| 470–475 | 245 |
| 500 | 260 |

## LIQUID MEASURE TO MILLILITERS

| 1/4 | teaspoon | = | 1.25 | milliliters |
|---|---|---|---|---|
| 1/2 | teaspoon | = | 2.5 | milliliters |
| 3/4 | teaspoon | = | 3.75 | milliliters |
| 1 | teaspoon | = | 5.0 | milliliters |
| 1-1/4 | teaspoons | = | 6.25 | milliliters |
| 1-1/2 | teaspoons | = | 7.5 | milliliters |
| 1-3/4 | teaspoons | = | 8.75 | milliliters |
| 2 | teaspoons | = | 10.0 | milliliters |
| 1 | tablespoon | = | 15.0 | milliliters |
| 2 | tablespoons | = | 30.0 | milliliters |

## LIQUID MEASURE TO LITERS

| 1/4 | cup | = | 0.06 | liters |
|---|---|---|---|---|
| 1/2 | cup | = | 0.12 | liters |
| 3/4 | cup | = | 0.18 | liters |
| 1 | cup | = | 0.24 | liters |
| 1-1/4 | cups | = | 0.3 | liters |
| 1-1/2 | cups | = | 0.36 | liters |
| 2 | cups | = | 0.48 | liters |
| 2-1/2 | cups | = | 0.6 | liters |
| 3 | cups | = | 0.72 | liters |
| 3-1/2 | cups | = | 0.84 | liters |
| 4 | cups | = | 0.96 | liters |
| 4-1/2 | cups | = | 1.08 | liters |
| 5 | cups | = | 1.2 | liters |
| 5-1/2 | cups | = | 1.32 | liters |

# INDEX

# Mable Hoffman

$\mathcal{M}$able Hoffman is a professional home economist and director of Hoffman Food Consultants. She concentrates her efforts on food consulting, food styling, recipe development and writing.

Included in Mable's writings are *Mable Hoffman's Crockery Cookery, Healthy Crockery Cookery, Appetizers and Small Meals,* and *Mable and Gar Hoffman's California Flavors.* Her books have won four R. T. French Tastemaker Awards, the "Oscar" for cookbooks, as Best Soft-Cover Cookbook of the year. Both *Crockery Cookery* and *Crepe Cookery* became #1 *New York Times* bestsellers.

Slow cooking is different and requires special recipes. Mable developed every recipe specifically for slow cookers. Mable's recipes invite culinary creativity. Just add a pinch of your own ingenuity to the pot. You'll find slow cooking makes good eating!